FINAL

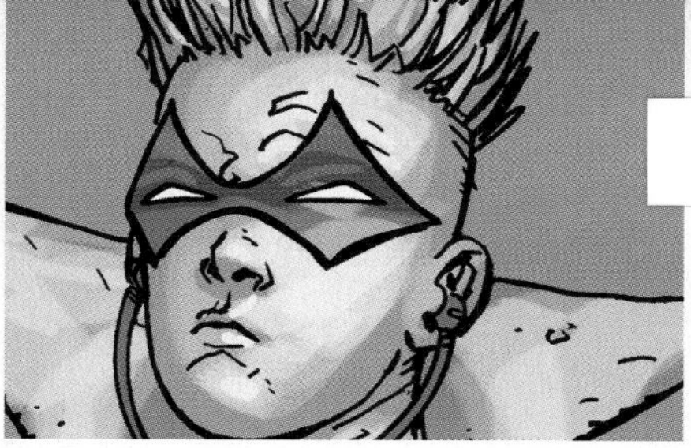

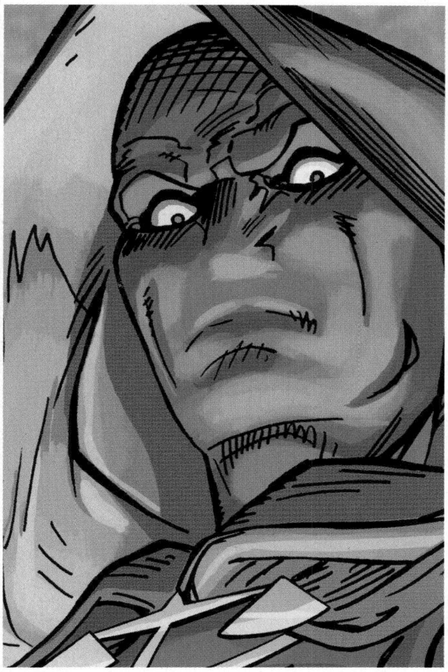

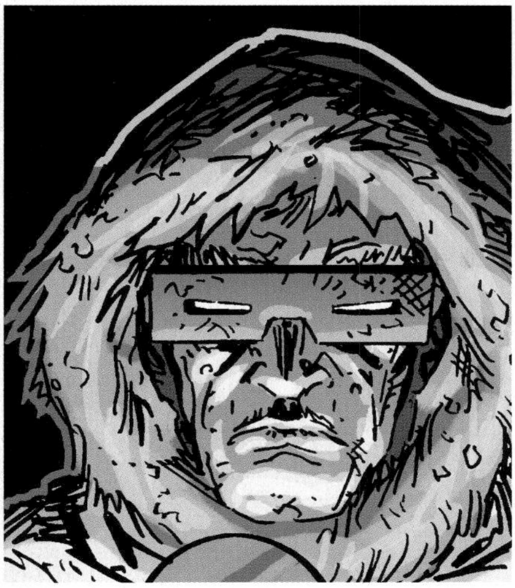

CRISIS

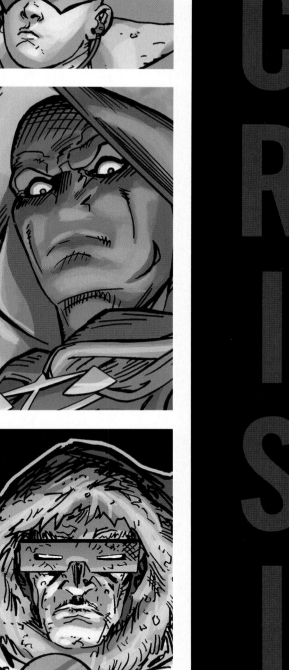

FINAL CRISIS ROGUES' REVENGE

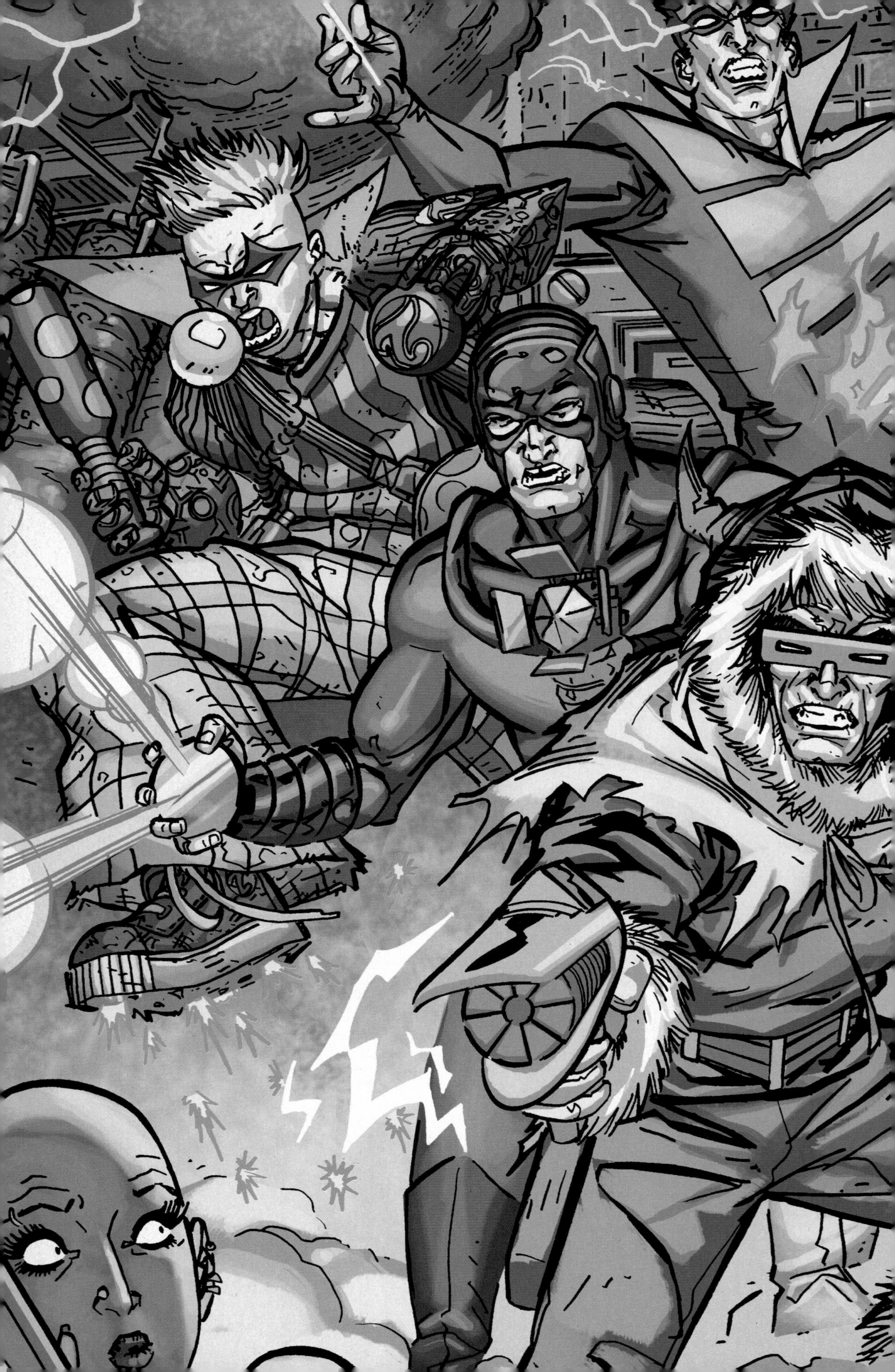

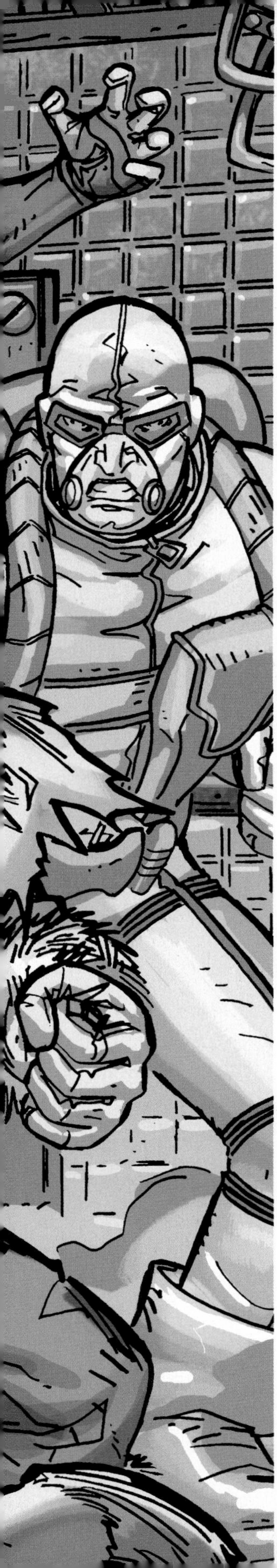

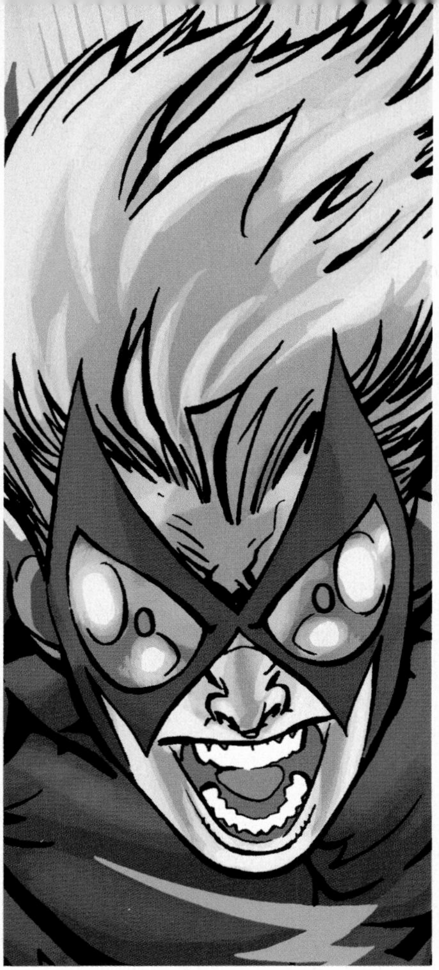

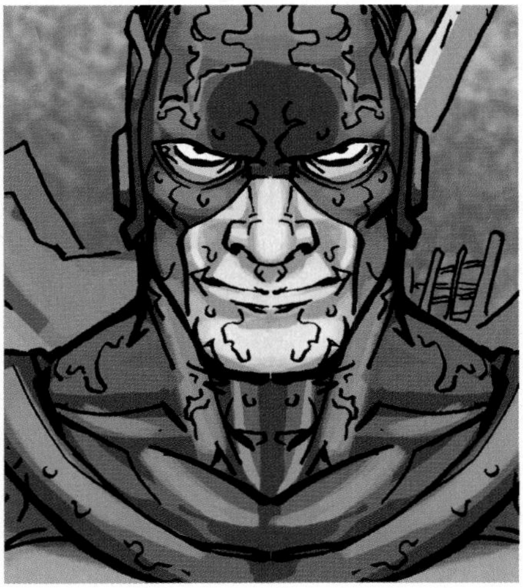

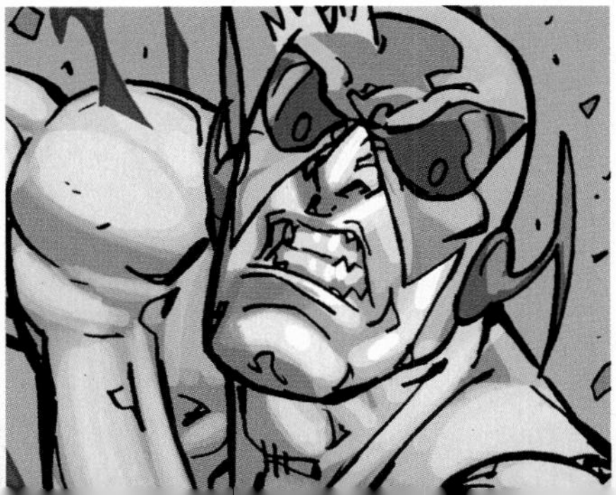

FINAL CRISIS ROGUES' REVENGE

Geoff Johns
Writer

ROGUES' REVENGE
Scott Kolins
Artist and Covers

Dave McCaig
Colorist

Nick J. Napolitano
Letterer

ABSOLUTE ZERO
Scott Kolins
Penciller

Dan Panosian
Inker

James Sinclair
Colorist

Digtal Chameleon
Separator

Gaspar
Letterer

ROGUE PROFILE: ZOOM
Scott Kolins
Penciller

Doug Hazlewood
Inker

James Sinclair
Colorist & Separator

Kurt Hathaway
Letterer

Dan DiDio   Senior VP-Executive Editor

Joey Cavalieri   Editor-original series

Chris Conroy   Assistant Editor-original series

Sean Mackiewicz   Editor-collected edition

Robbin Brosterman   Senior Art Director

Paul Levitz   President & Publisher

Georg Brewer   VP-Design & DC Direct Creative

Richard Bruning   Senior VP-Creative Director

Patrick Caldon   Executive VP-Finance & Operations

Chris Caramalis   VP-Finance

John Cunningham   VP-Marketing

Terri Cunningham   VP-Managing Editor

Amy Genkins   Senior VP-Business & Legal Affairs

Alison Gill   VP-Manufacturing

David Hyde   VP-Publicity

Hank Kanalz   VP-General Manager, WildStorm

Jim Lee   Editorial Director-WildStorm

Gregory Noveck   Senior VP-Creative Affairs

Sue Pohja   VP-Book Trade Sales

Steve Rotterdam   Senior VP-Sales & Marketing

Cheryl Rubin   Senior VP-Brand Management

Alysse Soll   VP-Advertising & Custom Publishing

Jeff Trojan   VP-Business Development, DC Direct

Bob Wayne   VP-Sales

Cover by Scott Kolins

FINAL CRISIS: ROGUES' REVENGE

DC Comics, 1700 Broadway, New York, NY 10019
A Warner Bros. Entertainment Company
Printed in the USA. First Printing.

ISBN: 978-1-4012-2333-5
SC ISBN: 978-1-4012-2334-2

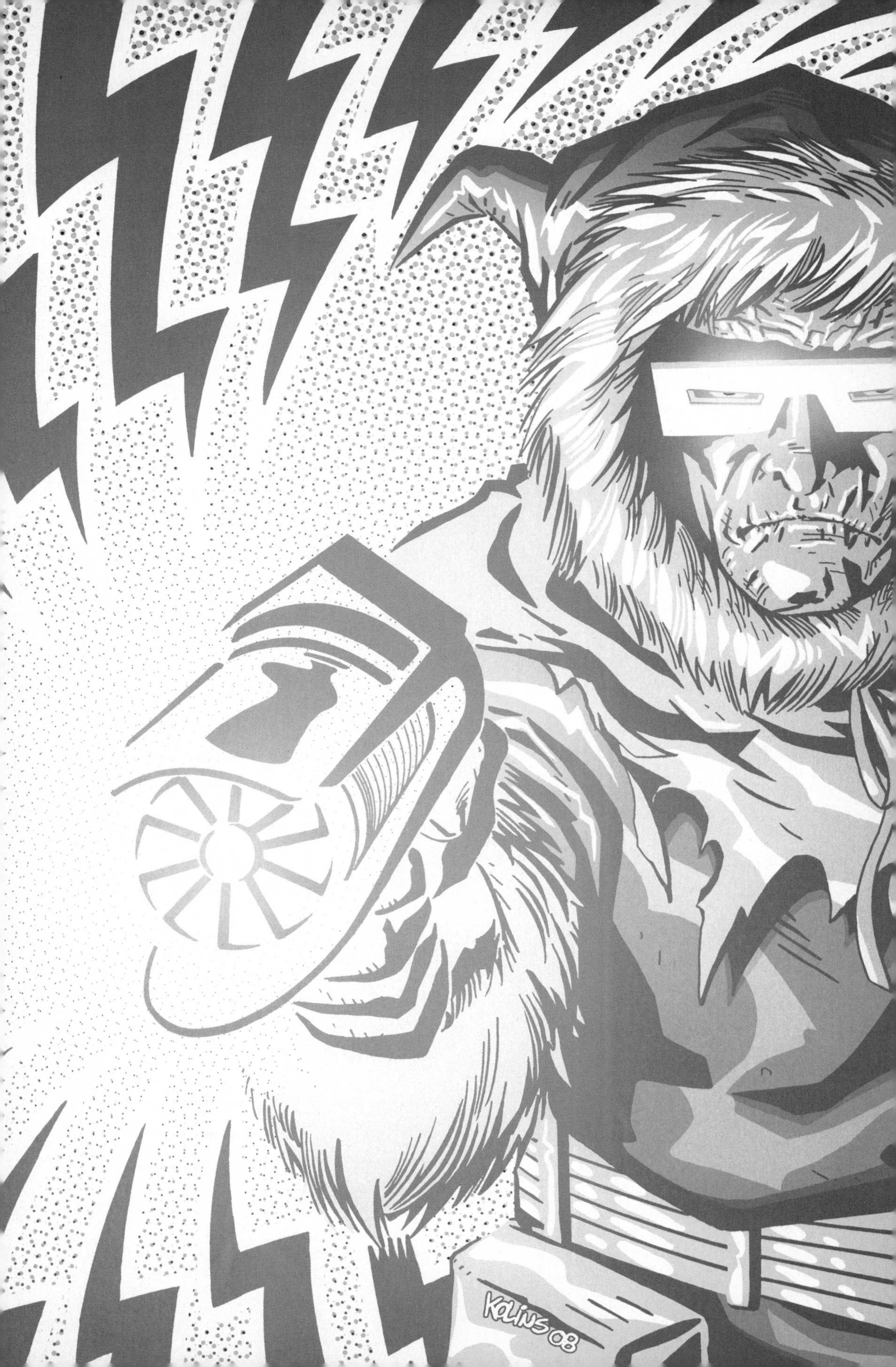
KOLINS 08

KOLINS

Sliver cover to FINAL CRISIS: ROGUES' REVENGE #1

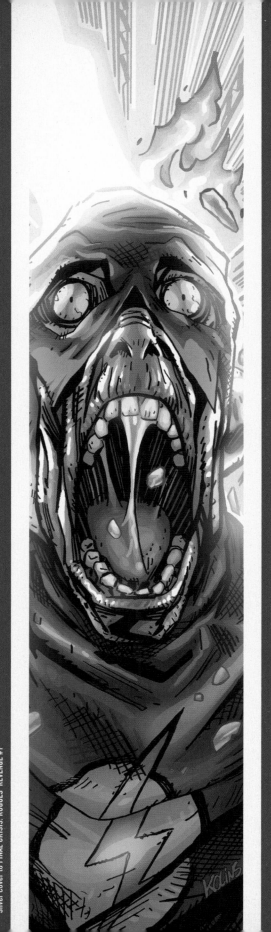

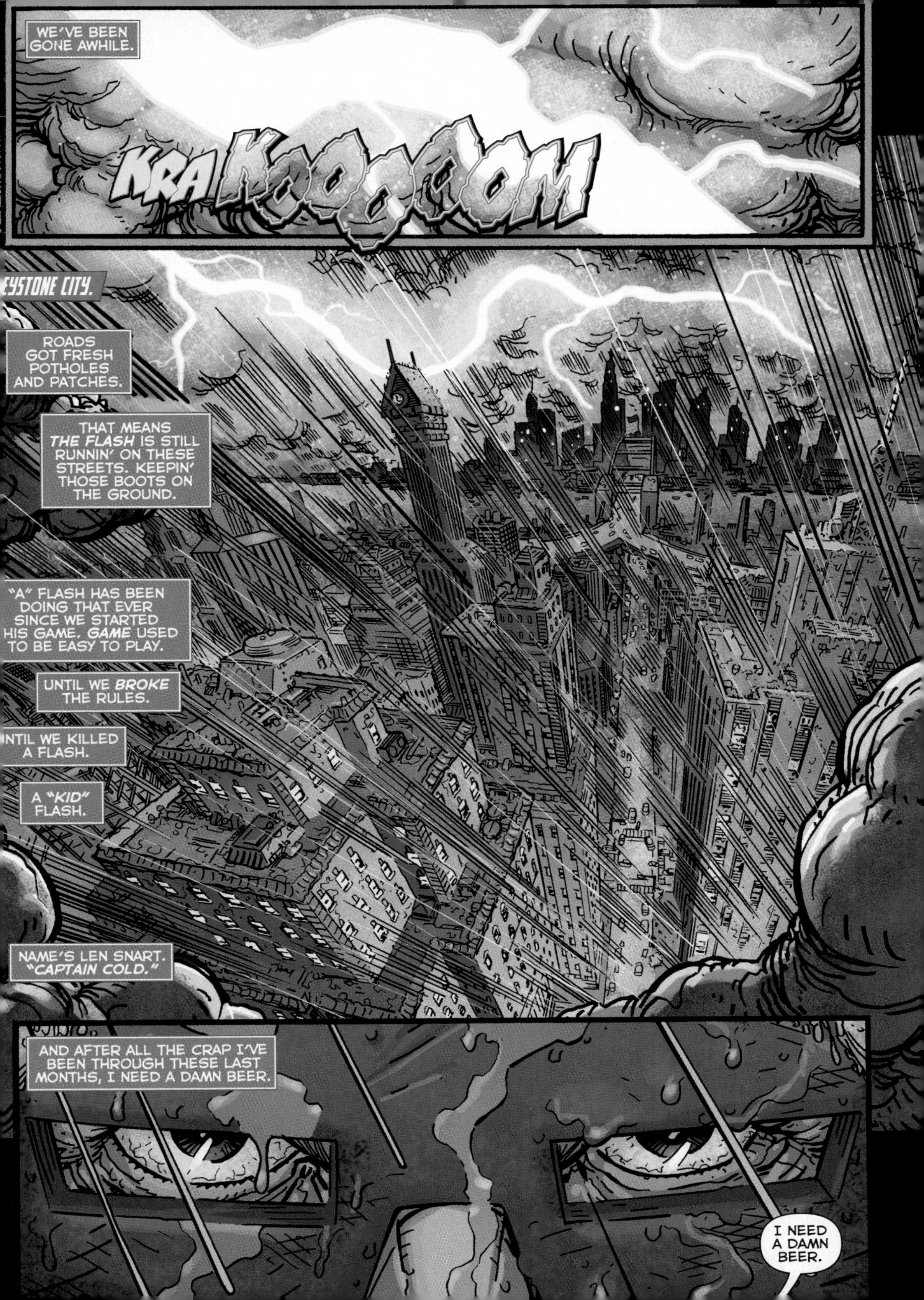

WE'VE BEEN GONE AWHILE.
KRA KOOOOOM
EYSTONE CITY.
ROADS GOT FRESH POTHOLES AND PATCHES.
THAT MEANS *THE FLASH* IS STILL RUNNIN' ON THESE STREETS. KEEPIN' THOSE BOOTS ON THE GROUND.
"A" FLASH HAS BEEN DOING THAT EVER SINCE WE STARTED HIS GAME. *GAME* USED TO BE EASY TO PLAY.
UNTIL WE *BROKE* THE RULES.
NTIL WE KILLED A FLASH.
A *"KID"* FLASH.
NAME'S LEN SNART. *"CAPTAIN COLD."*
AND AFTER ALL THE CRAP I'VE BEEN THROUGH THESE LAST MONTHS, I NEED A DAMN BEER.
I NEED A DAMN BEER.

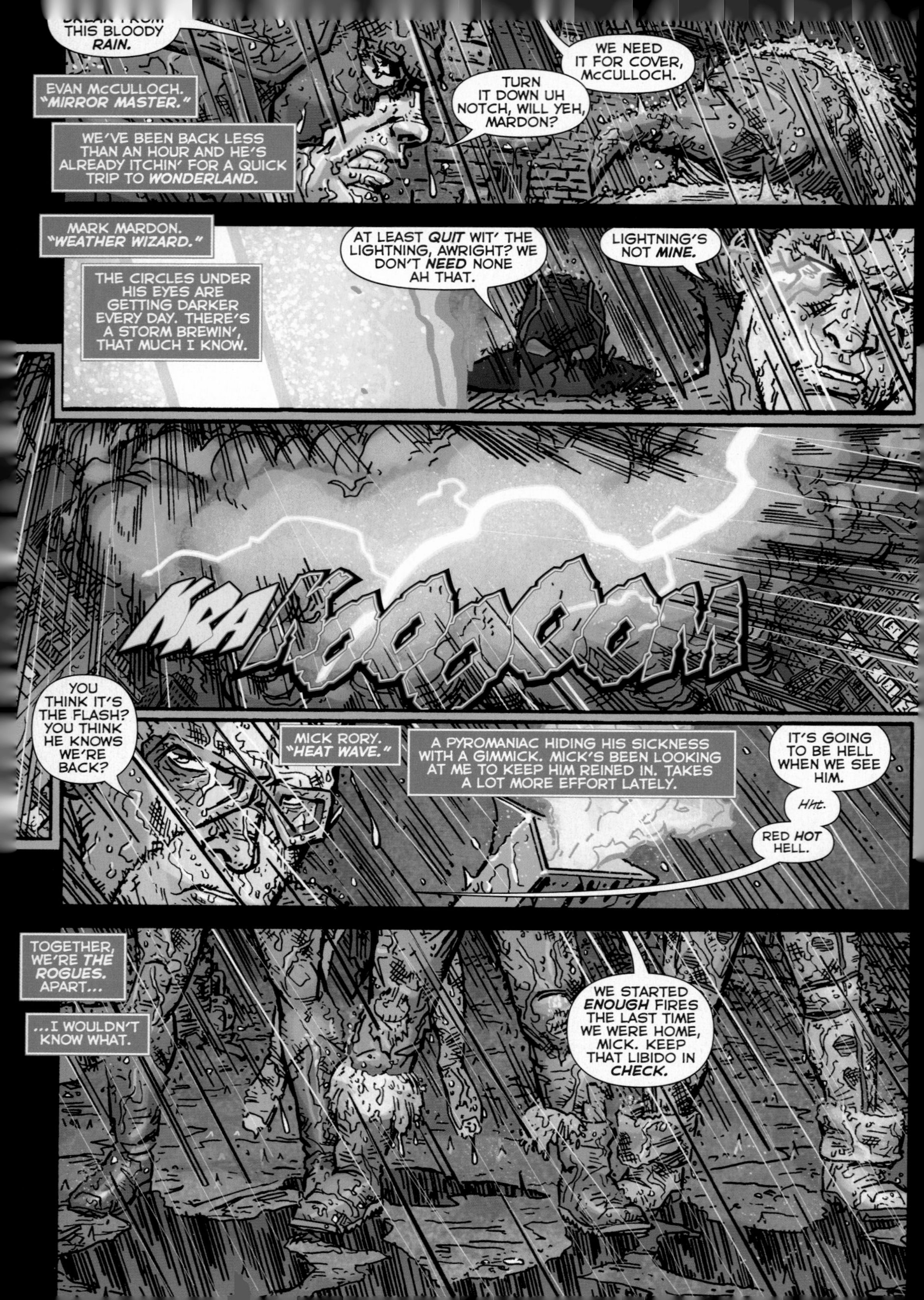
THIS BLOODY RAIN.
EVAN McCULLOCH. "MIRROR MASTER."
WE'VE BEEN BACK LESS THAN AN HOUR AND HE'S ALREADY ITCHIN' FOR A QUICK TRIP TO WONDERLAND.
TURN IT DOWN UH NOTCH, WILL YEH, MARDON?
WE NEED IT FOR COVER, McCULLOCH.
MARK MARDON. "WEATHER WIZARD."
THE CIRCLES UNDER HIS EYES ARE GETTING DARKER EVERY DAY. THERE'S A STORM BREWIN', THAT MUCH I KNOW.
AT LEAST QUIT WIT' THE LIGHTNING, AWRIGHT? WE DON'T NEED NONE AH THAT.
LIGHTNING'S NOT MINE.
KRA KOOOOOM
YOU THINK IT'S THE FLASH? YOU THINK HE KNOWS WE'RE BACK?
MICK RORY. "HEAT WAVE."
A PYROMANIAC HIDING HIS SICKNESS WITH A GIMMICK. MICK'S BEEN LOOKING AT ME TO KEEP HIM REINED IN. TAKES A LOT MORE EFFORT LATELY.
IT'S GOING TO BE HELL WHEN WE SEE HIM.
Hht.
RED HOT HELL.
TOGETHER, WE'RE THE ROGUES. APART...
...I WOULDN'T KNOW WHAT.
WE STARTED ENOUGH FIRES THE LAST TIME WE WERE HOME, MICK. KEEP THAT LIBIDO IN CHECK.

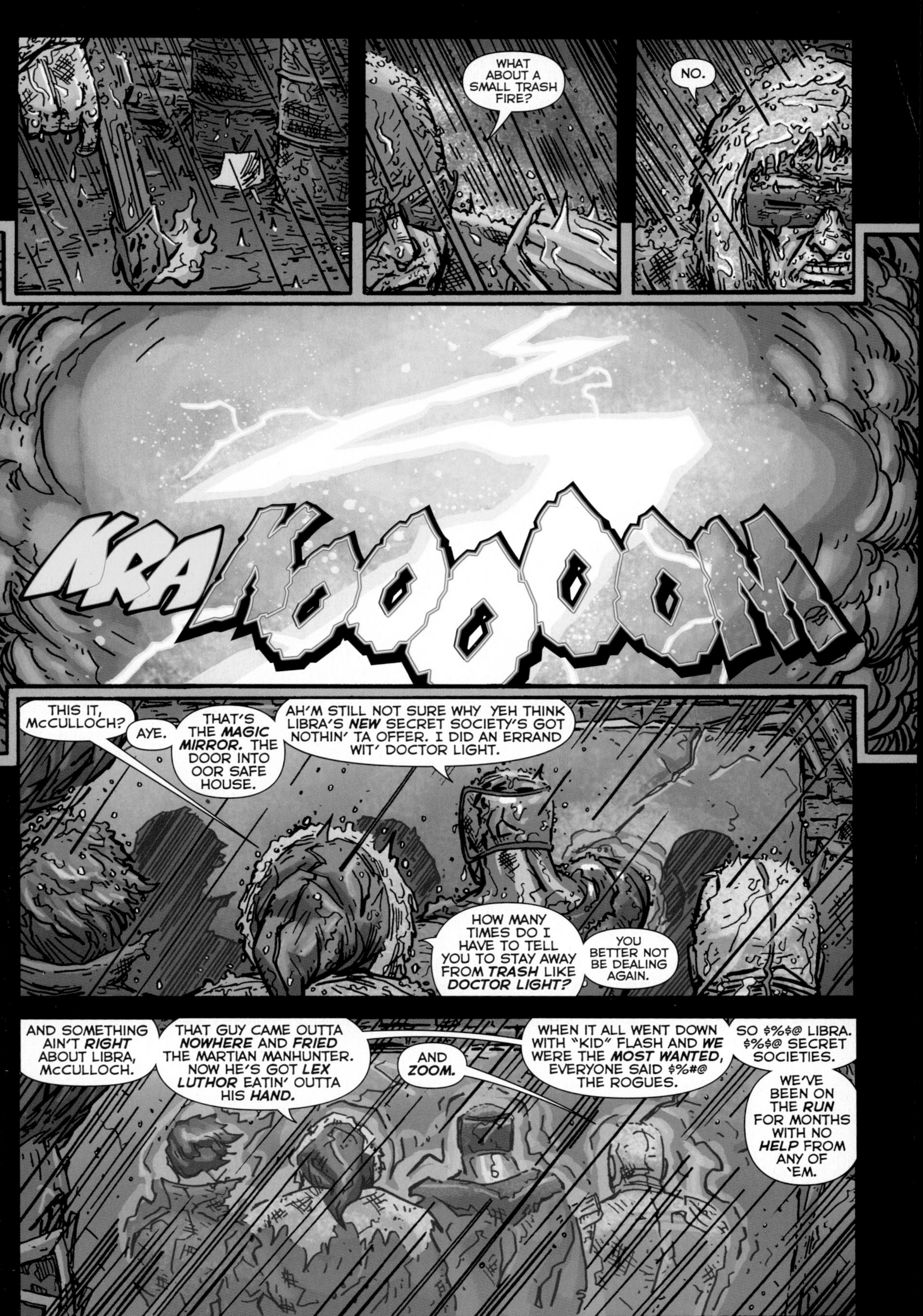

WHAT ABOUT A SMALL TRASH FIRE?
NO.
KRAKOOOOOM
THIS IT, McCULLOCH?
AYE.
THAT'S THE *MAGIC MIRROR.* THE DOOR INTO OOR SAFE HOUSE.
AH'M STILL NOT SURE WHY YEH THINK LIBRA'S *NEW* SECRET SOCIETY'S GOT NOTHIN' TA OFFER. I DID AN ERRAND WIT' DOCTOR LIGHT.
HOW MANY TIMES DO I HAVE TO TELL YOU TO STAY AWAY FROM *TRASH* LIKE *DOCTOR LIGHT?*
YOU BETTER NOT BE DEALING AGAIN.
AND SOMETHING AIN'T *RIGHT* ABOUT LIBRA, McCULLOCH.
THAT GUY CAME OUTTA *NOWHERE* AND *FRIED* THE MARTIAN MANHUNTER. NOW HE'S GOT *LEX LUTHOR* EATIN' OUTTA HIS *HAND.*
AND *ZOOM.*
WHEN IT ALL WENT DOWN WITH "KID" FLASH AND *WE* WERE THE *MOST WANTED*, EVERYONE SAID $%#@ THE ROGUES.
SO $%$@ LIBRA. $%$@ SECRET SOCIETIES.
WE'VE BEEN ON THE *RUN* FOR MONTHS WITH NO *HELP* FROM ANY OF 'EM.

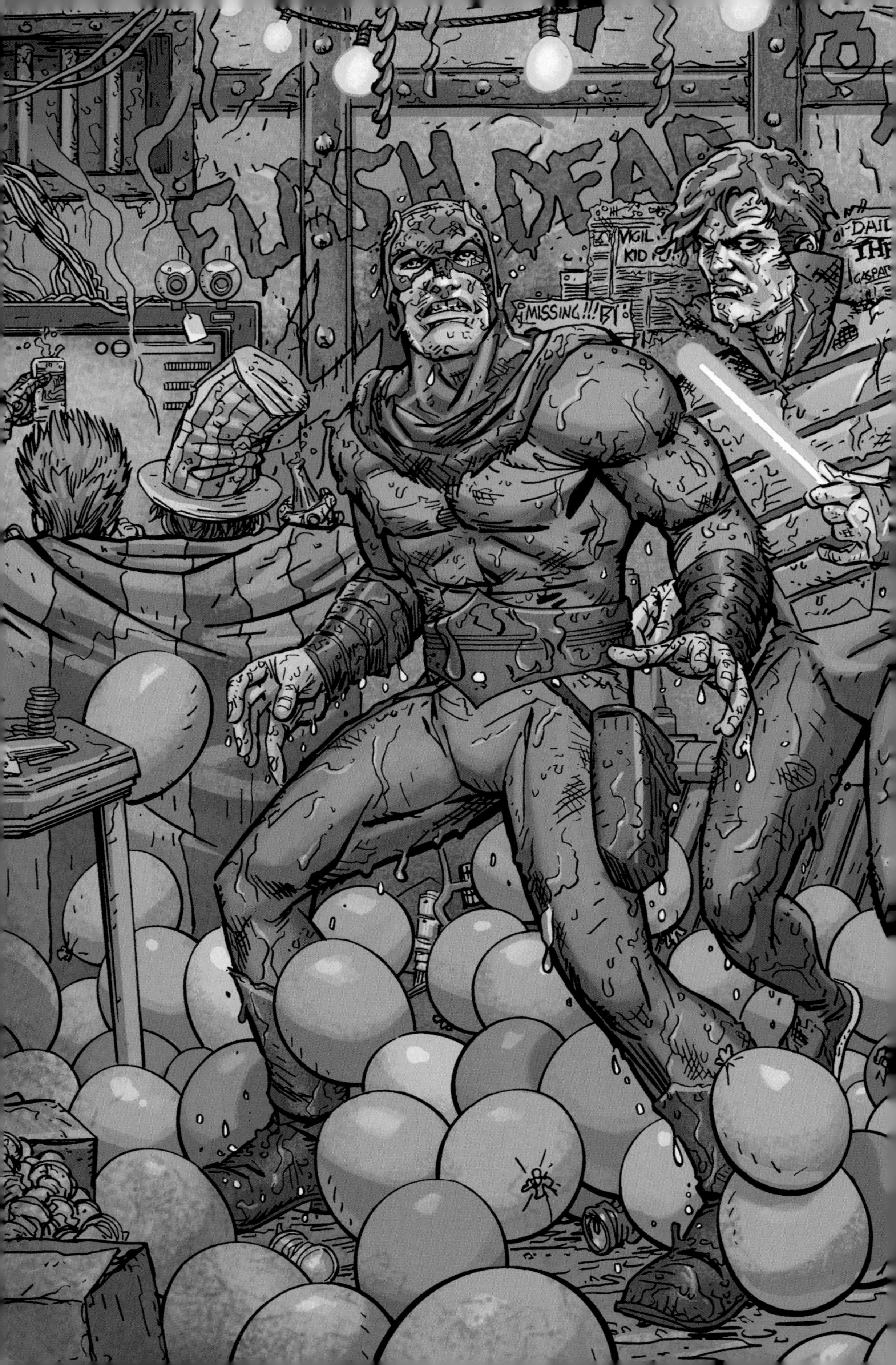

FLASH DEAD
VIGIL KID
MISSING!!! BY
GASPAR

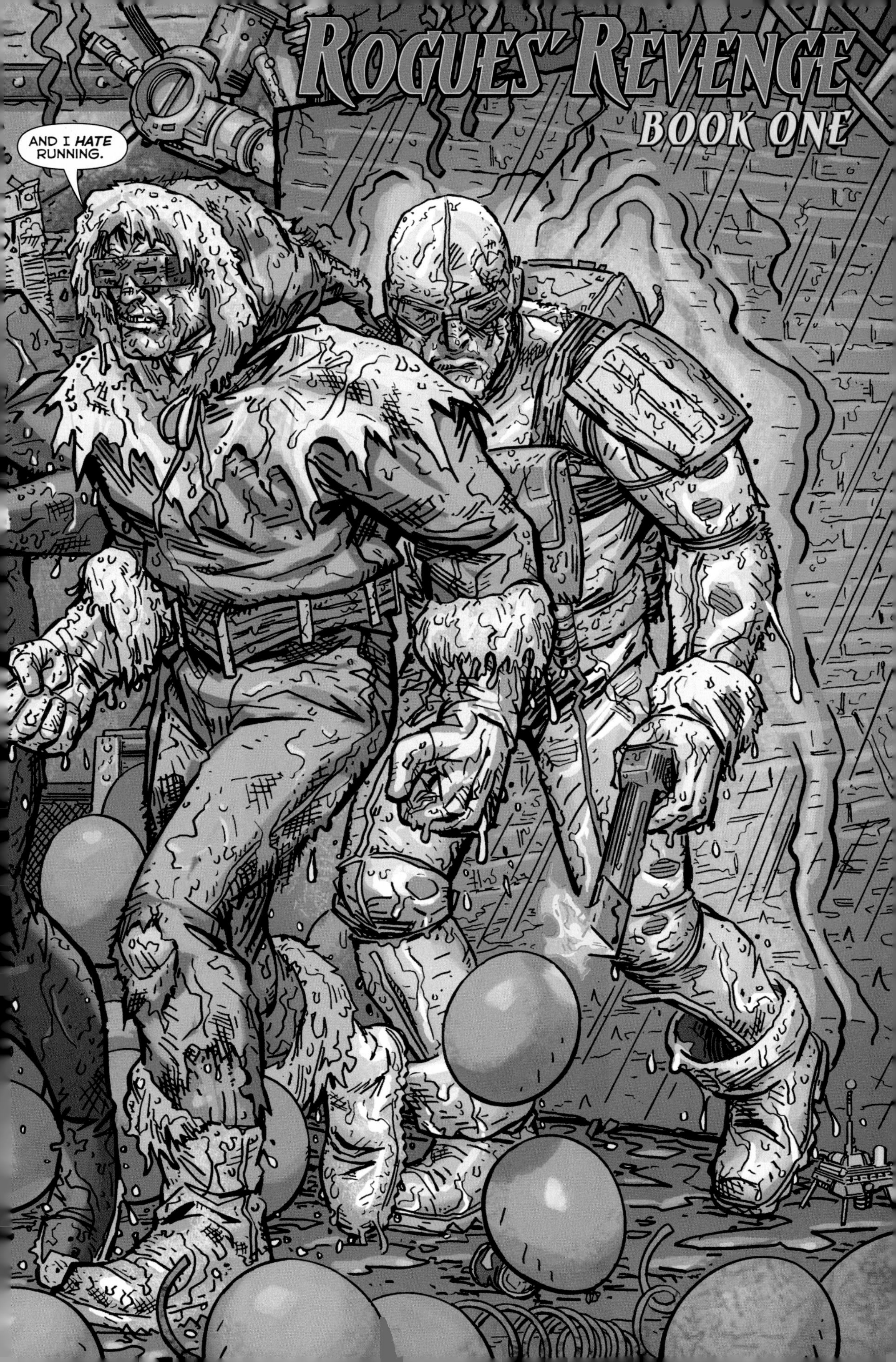
ROGUES' REVENGE
BOOK ONE
AND I *HATE* RUNNING.

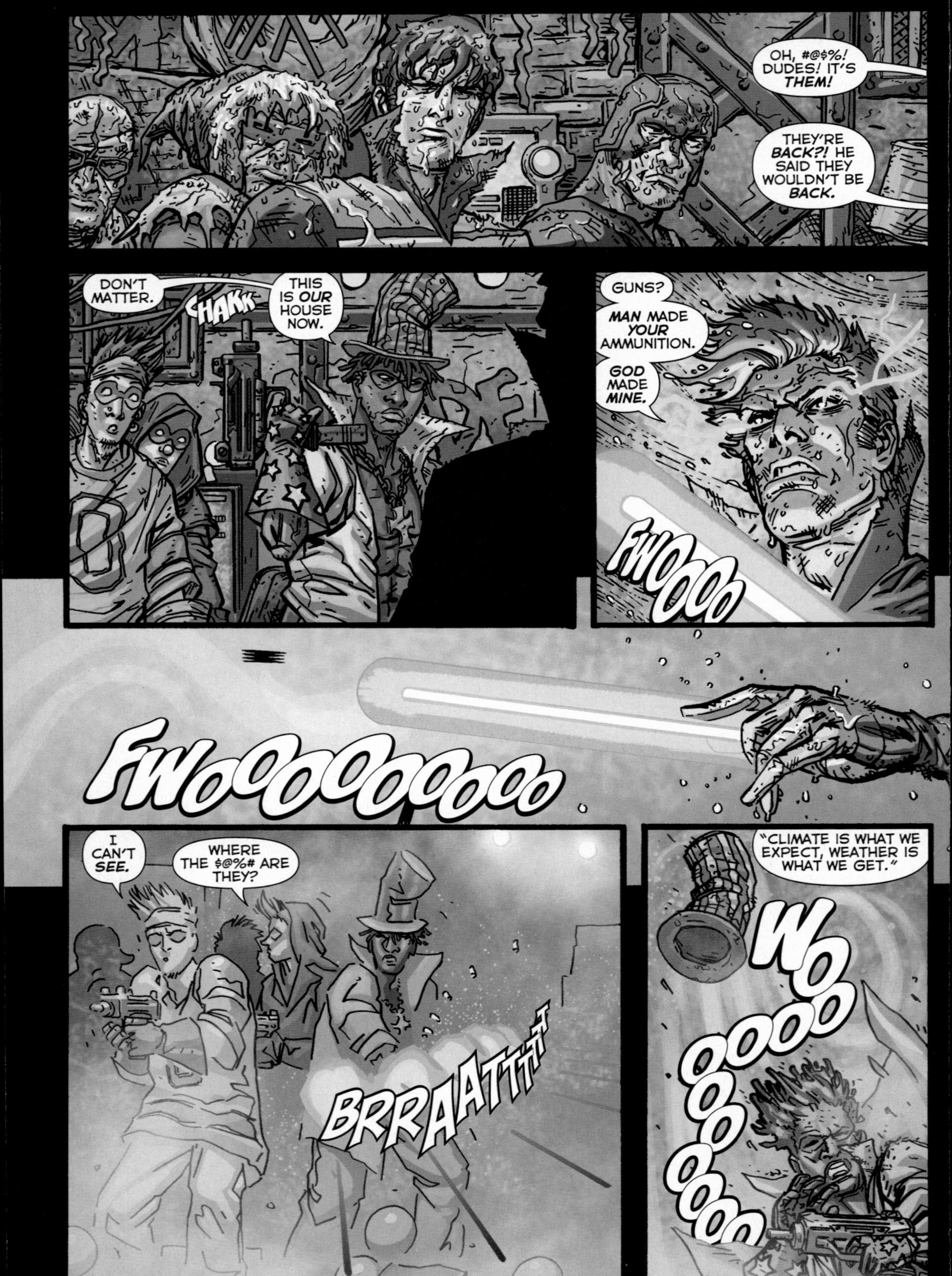

OH, #@$%! DUDES! IT'S THEM!
THEY'RE BACK?! HE SAID THEY WOULDN'T BE BACK.
DON'T MATTER.
CHAKK
THIS IS OUR HOUSE NOW.
GUNS?
MAN MADE YOUR AMMUNITION.
GOD MADE MINE.
FWOOOOO
FWOOOOOOOOOO
I CAN'T SEE.
WHERE THE $@%# ARE THEY?
BRRAATTTTT
"CLIMATE IS WHAT WE EXPECT, WEATHER IS WHAT WE GET."
WOOOOOOOOOOOO

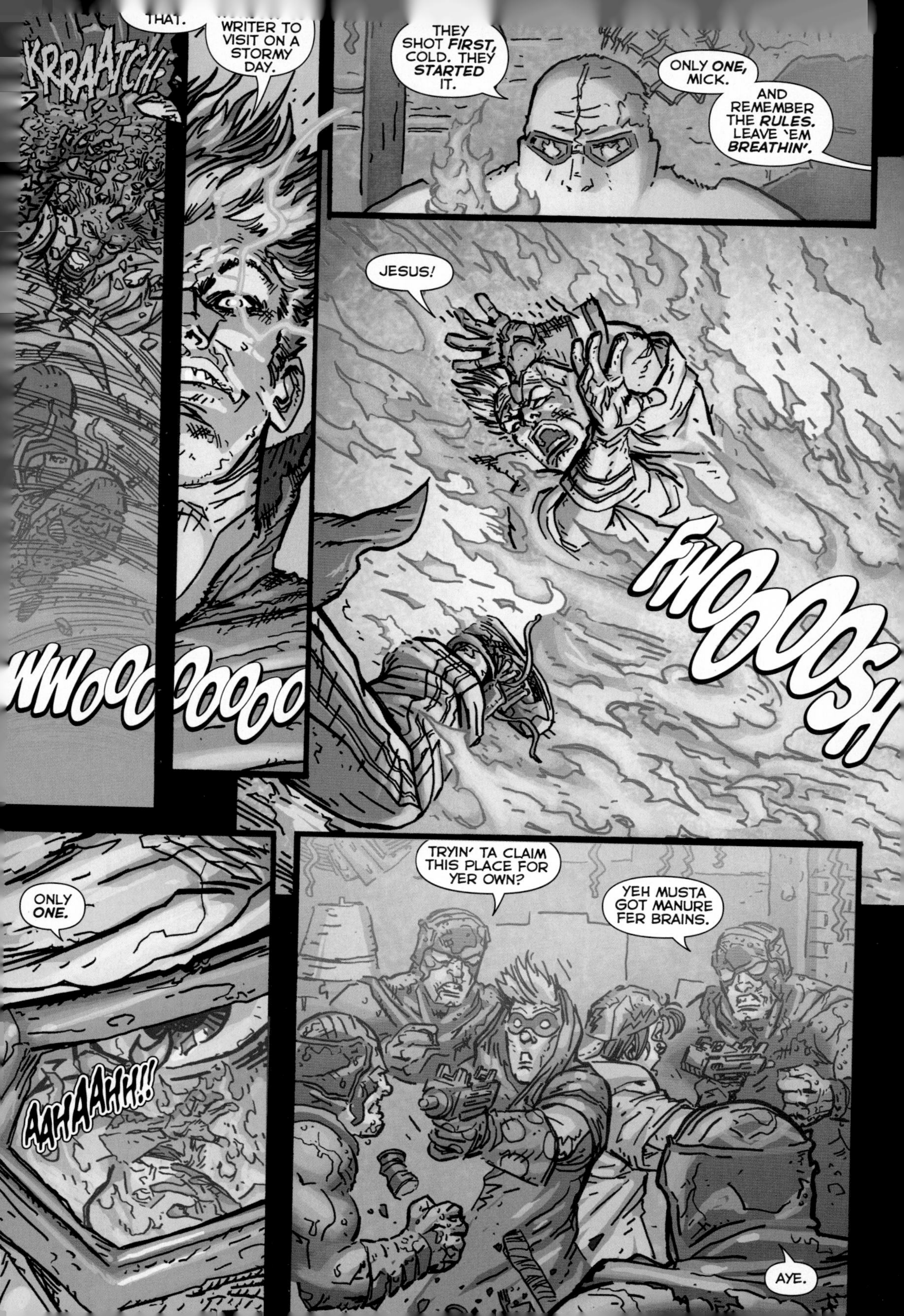
THAT.
WRITER TO VISIT ON A STORMY DAY.
KRRAATCH
THEY SHOT FIRST, COLD. THEY STARTED IT.
ONLY ONE, MICK.
AND REMEMBER THE RULES. LEAVE 'EM BREATHIN'.
JESUS!
FWOOOOSH
WWOOOOOOOOO
ONLY ONE.
AAHAAHH!!
TRYIN' TA CLAIM THIS PLACE FOR YER OWN?
YEH MUSTA GOT MANURE FER BRAINS.
AYE.

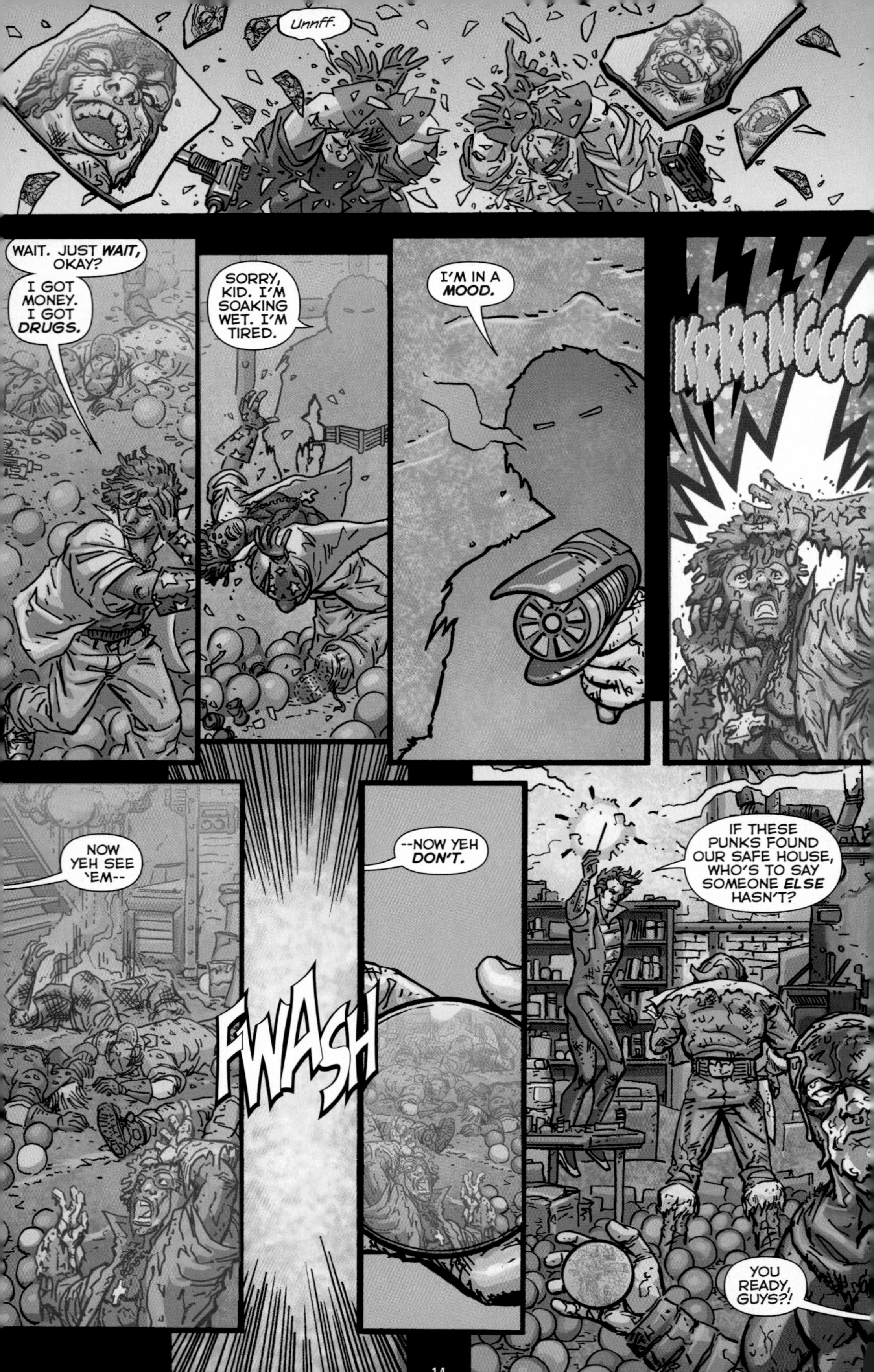
Unnff.
WAIT. JUST WAIT, OKAY?
I GOT MONEY. I GOT DRUGS.
SORRY, KID. I'M SOAKING WET. I'M TIRED.
I'M IN A MOOD.
KRRRNGGG
NOW YEH SEE 'EM--
FWASH
--NOW YEH DON'T.
IF THESE PUNKS FOUND OUR SAFE HOUSE, WHO'S TO SAY SOMEONE ELSE HASN'T?
YOU READY, GUYS?!

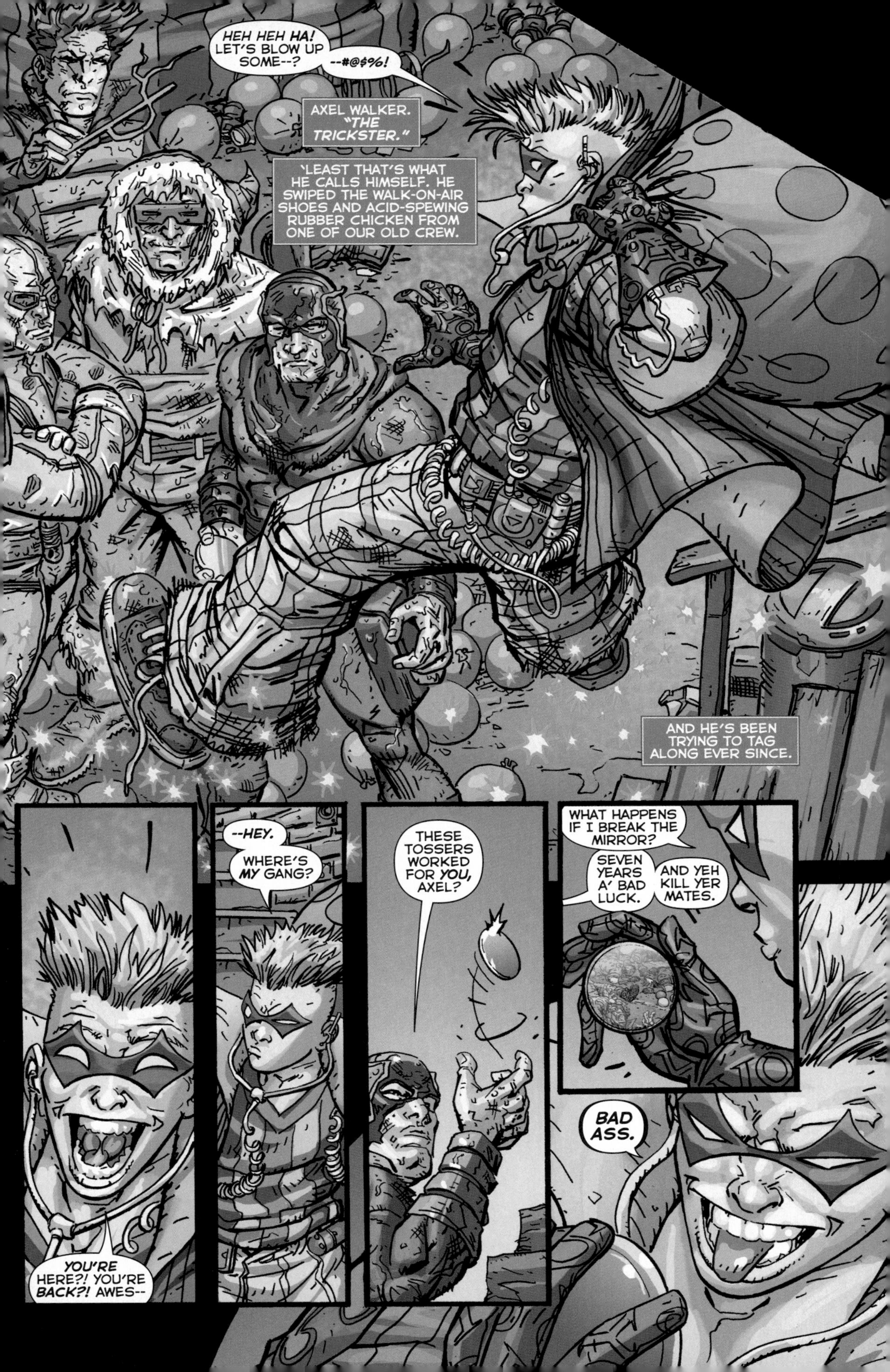

HEH HEH HA! LET'S BLOW UP SOME--?
--#@$%!
AXEL WALKER. "THE TRICKSTER."
'LEAST THAT'S WHAT HE CALLS HIMSELF. HE SWIPED THE WALK-ON-AIR SHOES AND ACID-SPEWING RUBBER CHICKEN FROM ONE OF OUR OLD CREW.
AND HE'S BEEN TRYING TO TAG ALONG EVER SINCE.
YOU'RE HERE?! YOU'RE BACK?! AWES--
--HEY.
WHERE'S MY GANG?
THESE TOSSERS WORKED FOR YOU, AXEL?
WHAT HAPPENS IF I BREAK THE MIRROR?
SEVEN YEARS A' BAD LUCK.
AND YEH KILL YER MATES.
BAD ASS.

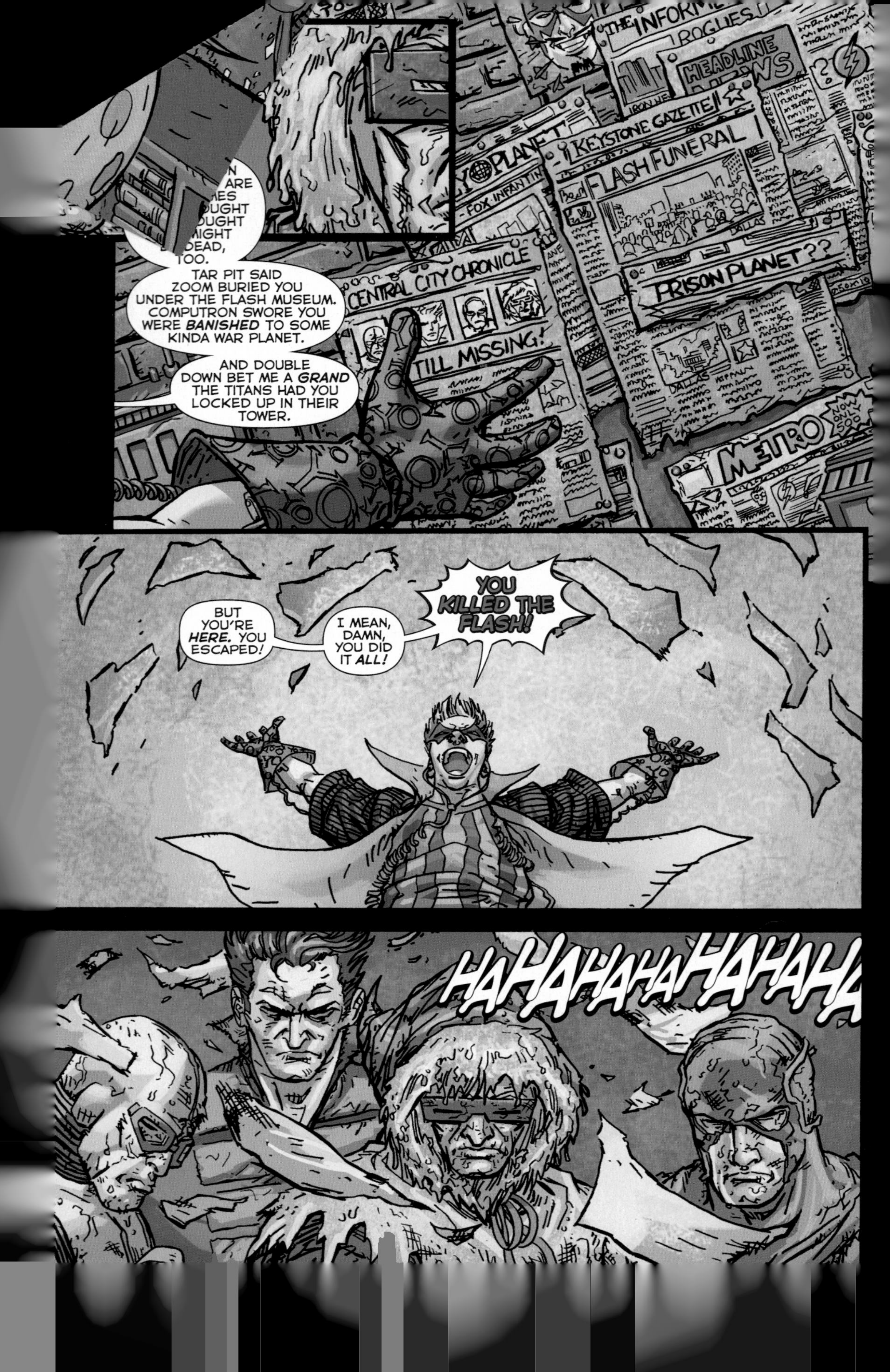

ARE
DEAD, TOO.
TAR PIT SAID ZOOM BURIED YOU UNDER THE FLASH MUSEUM. COMPUTRON SWORE YOU WERE BANISHED TO SOME KINDA WAR PLANET.
AND DOUBLE DOWN BET ME A GRAND THE TITANS HAD YOU LOCKED UP IN THEIR TOWER.
ROGUES
KEYSTONE GAZETTE
FLASH FUNERAL
CENTRAL CITY CHRONICLE
PRISON PLANET??
METRO
NOW ONLY 50¢
BUT YOU'RE HERE. YOU ESCAPED!
I MEAN, DAMN, YOU DID IT ALL!
YOU KILLED THE FLASH!
HAHAHAHAHAHAHAHA

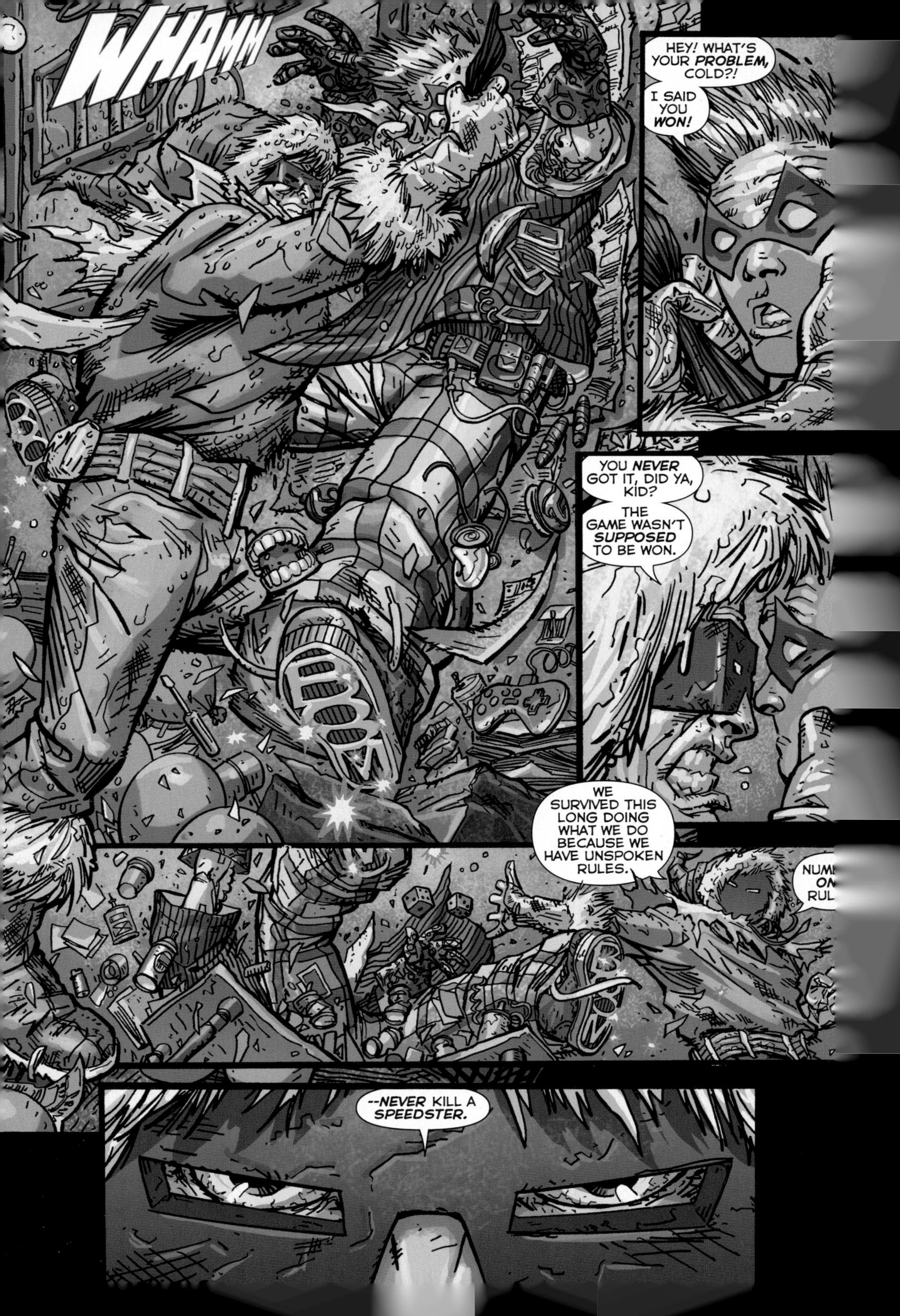
WHAMM
HEY! WHAT'S YOUR PROBLEM, COLD?!
I SAID YOU WON!
YOU NEVER GOT IT, DID YA, KID?
THE GAME WASN'T SUPPOSED TO BE WON.
WE SURVIVED THIS LONG DOING WHAT WE DO BECAUSE WE HAVE UNSPOKEN RULES.
--NEVER KILL A SPEEDSTER.

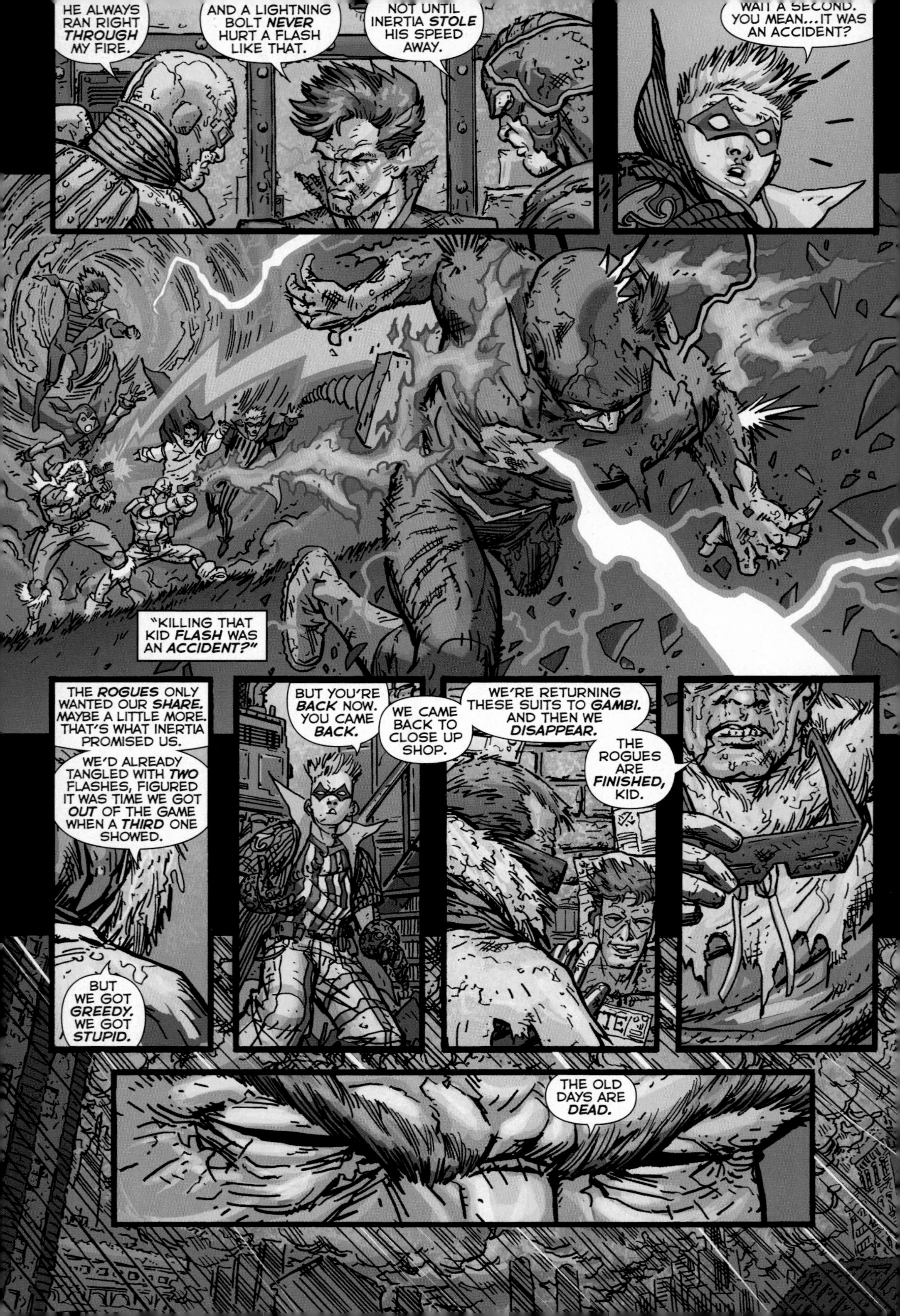
HE ALWAYS RAN RIGHT THROUGH MY FIRE.
AND A LIGHTNING BOLT NEVER HURT A FLASH LIKE THAT.
NOT UNTIL INERTIA STOLE HIS SPEED AWAY.
WAIT A SECOND. YOU MEAN...IT WAS AN ACCIDENT?
"KILLING THAT KID FLASH WAS AN ACCIDENT?"
THE ROGUES ONLY WANTED OUR SHARE. MAYBE A LITTLE MORE. THAT'S WHAT INERTIA PROMISED US.
WE'D ALREADY TANGLED WITH TWO FLASHES, FIGURED IT WAS TIME WE GOT OUT OF THE GAME WHEN A THIRD ONE SHOWED.
BUT WE GOT GREEDY. WE GOT STUPID.
BUT YOU'RE BACK NOW. YOU CAME BACK.
WE CAME BACK TO CLOSE UP SHOP.
WE'RE RETURNING THESE SUITS TO GAMBI. AND THEN WE DISAPPEAR.
THE ROGUES ARE FINISHED, KID.
THE OLD DAYS ARE DEAD.

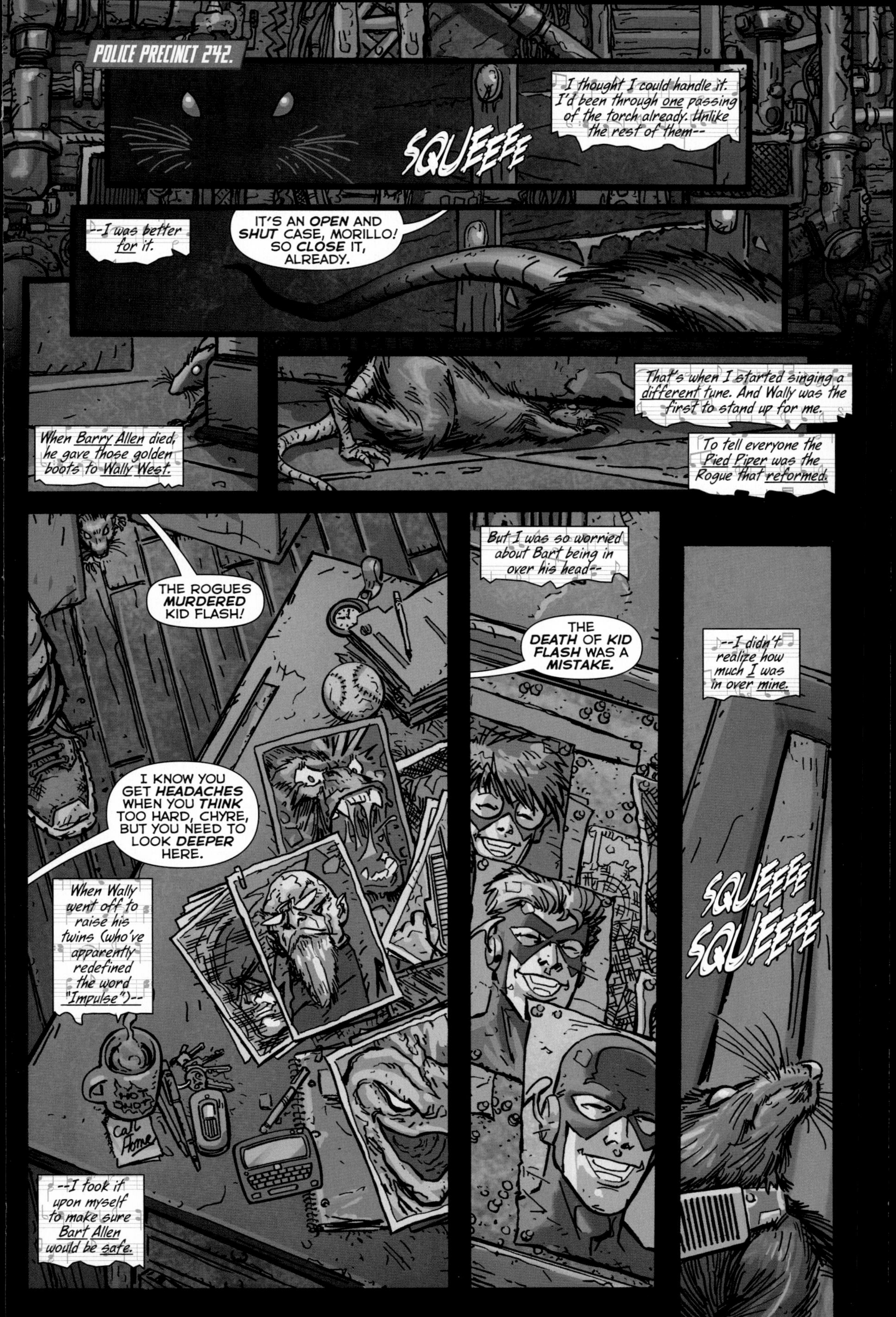
POLICE PRECINCT 242.
SQUEEEE
I thought I could handle it. I'd been through one passing of the torch already. Unlike the rest of them--
--I was better for it.
IT'S AN OPEN AND SHUT CASE, MORILLO! SO CLOSE IT, ALREADY.
When Barry Allen died, he gave those golden boots to Wally West.
That's when I started singing a different tune. And Wally was the first to stand up for me.
To tell everyone the Pied Piper was the Rogue that reformed.
THE ROGUES MURDERED KID FLASH!
I KNOW YOU GET HEADACHES WHEN YOU THINK TOO HARD, CHYRE, BUT YOU NEED TO LOOK DEEPER HERE.
When Wally went off to raise his twins (who've apparently redefined the word "Impulse")--
--I took it upon myself to make sure Bart Allen would be safe.
But I was so worried about Bart being in over his head--
THE DEATH OF KID FLASH WAS A MISTAKE.
--I didn't realize how much I was in over mine.
SQUEEEE SQUEEEE

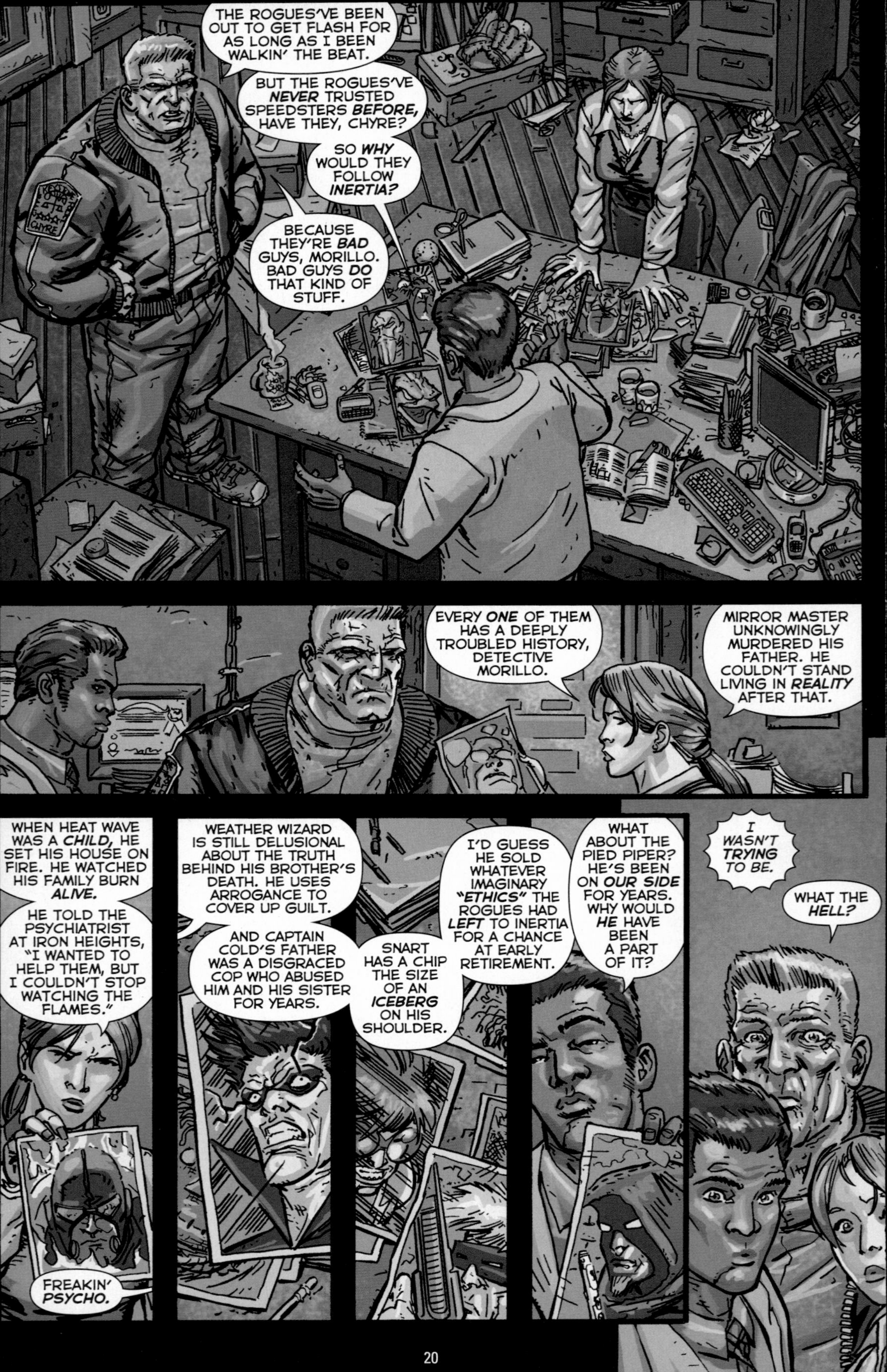
THE ROGUES'VE BEEN OUT TO GET FLASH FOR AS LONG AS I BEEN WALKIN' THE BEAT.
BUT THE ROGUES'VE NEVER TRUSTED SPEEDSTERS BEFORE, HAVE THEY, CHYRE?
SO WHY WOULD THEY FOLLOW INERTIA?
BECAUSE THEY'RE BAD GUYS, MORILLO. BAD GUYS DO THAT KIND OF STUFF.
EVERY ONE OF THEM HAS A DEEPLY TROUBLED HISTORY, DETECTIVE MORILLO.
MIRROR MASTER UNKNOWINGLY MURDERED HIS FATHER. HE COULDN'T STAND LIVING IN REALITY AFTER THAT.
WHEN HEAT WAVE WAS A CHILD, HE SET HIS HOUSE ON FIRE. HE WATCHED HIS FAMILY BURN ALIVE.
HE TOLD THE PSYCHIATRIST AT IRON HEIGHTS, "I WANTED TO HELP THEM, BUT I COULDN'T STOP WATCHING THE FLAMES."
FREAKIN' PSYCHO.
WEATHER WIZARD IS STILL DELUSIONAL ABOUT THE TRUTH BEHIND HIS BROTHER'S DEATH. HE USES ARROGANCE TO COVER UP GUILT.
AND CAPTAIN COLD'S FATHER WAS A DISGRACED COP WHO ABUSED HIM AND HIS SISTER FOR YEARS.
SNART HAS A CHIP THE SIZE OF AN ICEBERG ON HIS SHOULDER.
I'D GUESS HE SOLD WHATEVER IMAGINARY "ETHICS" THE ROGUES HAD LEFT TO INERTIA FOR A CHANCE AT EARLY RETIREMENT.
WHAT ABOUT THE PIED PIPER? HE'S BEEN ON OUR SIDE FOR YEARS. WHY WOULD HE HAVE BEEN A PART OF IT?
I WASN'T TRYING TO BE.
WHAT THE HELL?

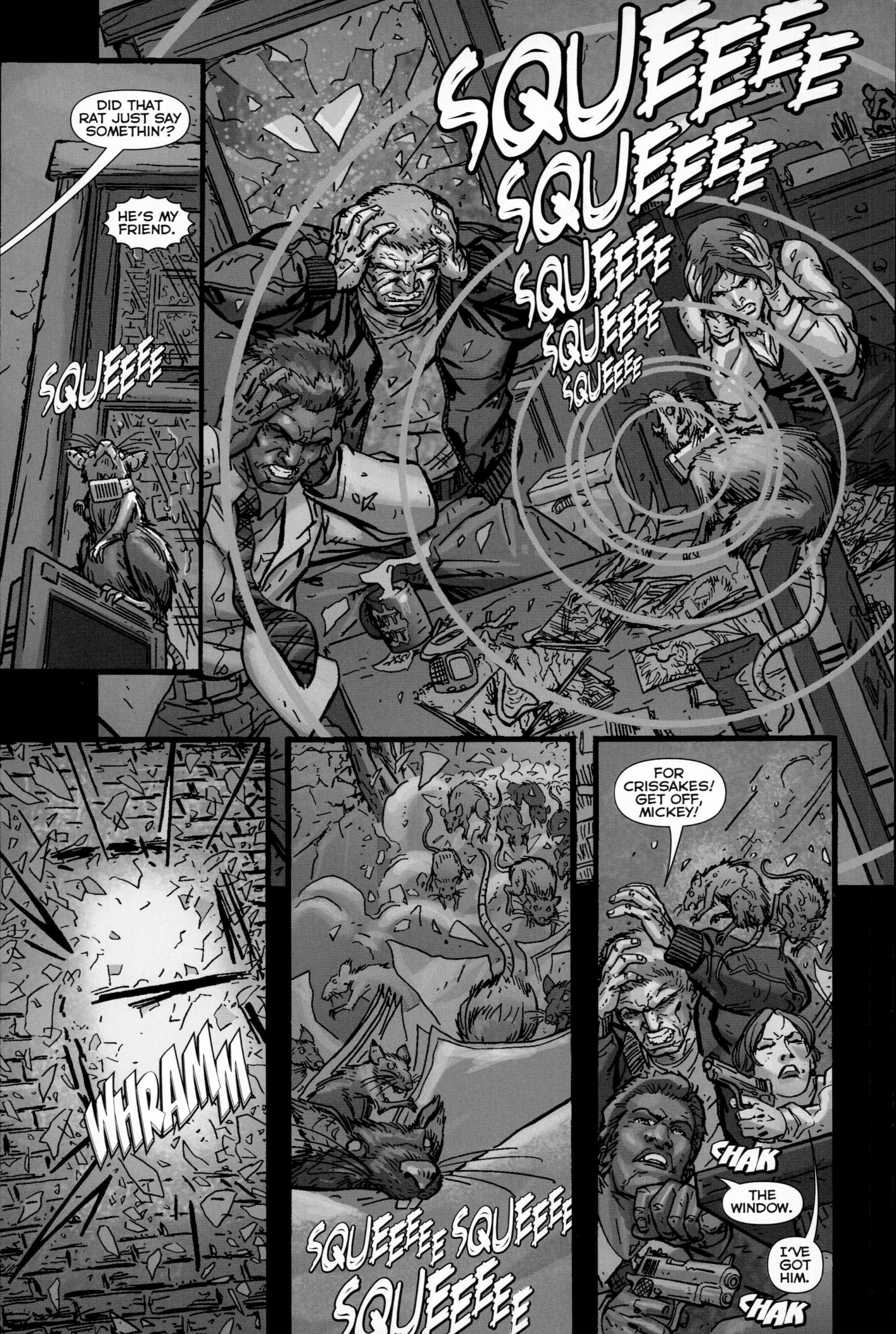

DID THAT RAT JUST SAY SOMETHIN'?
HE'S MY FRIEND.
SQUEEEEE
SQUEEEEE
SQUEEEEE
SQUEEEEE
SQUEEEEE
SQUEEEEE
WHRAMM
SQUEEEEE SQUEEEEE
SQUEEEEE
FOR CRISSAKES! GET OFF, MICKEY!
CHAK
THE WINDOW.
I'VE GOT HIM.
CHAK

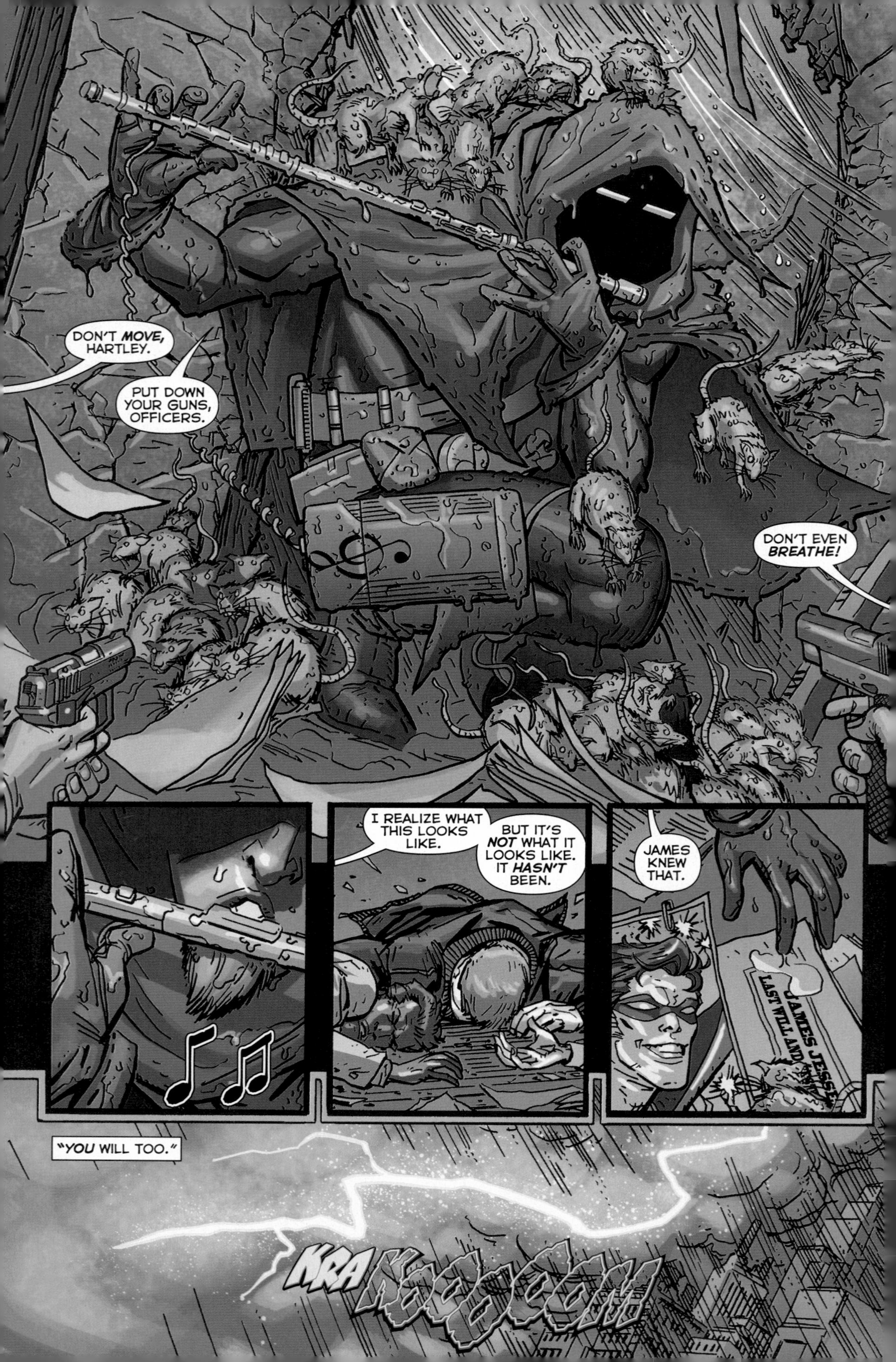

DON'T MOVE, HARTLEY.
PUT DOWN YOUR GUNS, OFFICERS.
DON'T EVEN BREATHE!
I REALIZE WHAT THIS LOOKS LIKE.
BUT IT'S NOT WHAT IT LOOKS LIKE. IT HASN'T BEEN.
JAMES KNEW THAT.
JAMES JESSE
LAST WILL AND
"YOU WILL TOO."
KRA KABOOM

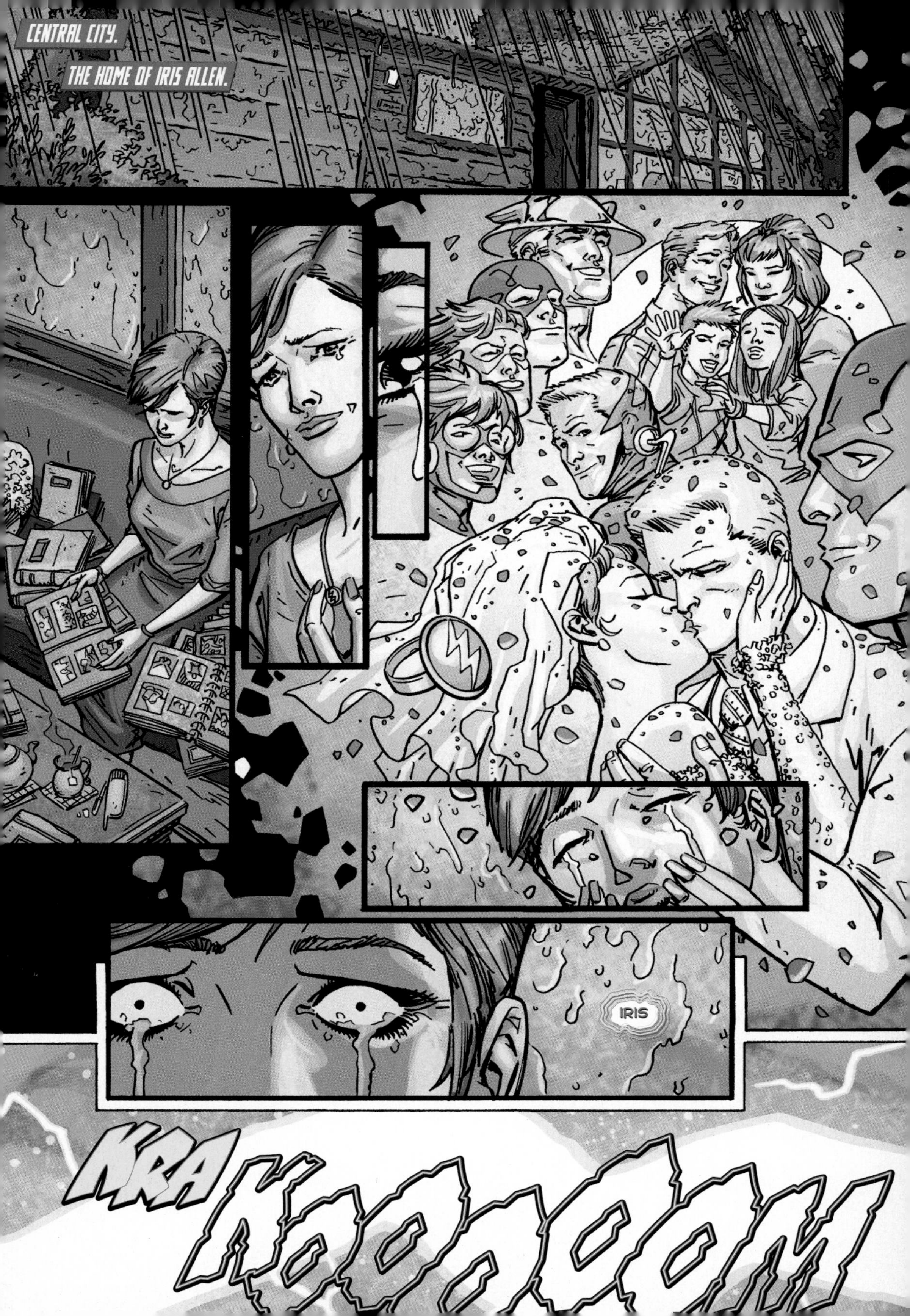
CENTRAL CITY.
THE HOME OF IRIS ALLEN.
IRIS
KRA
KOOOOOM

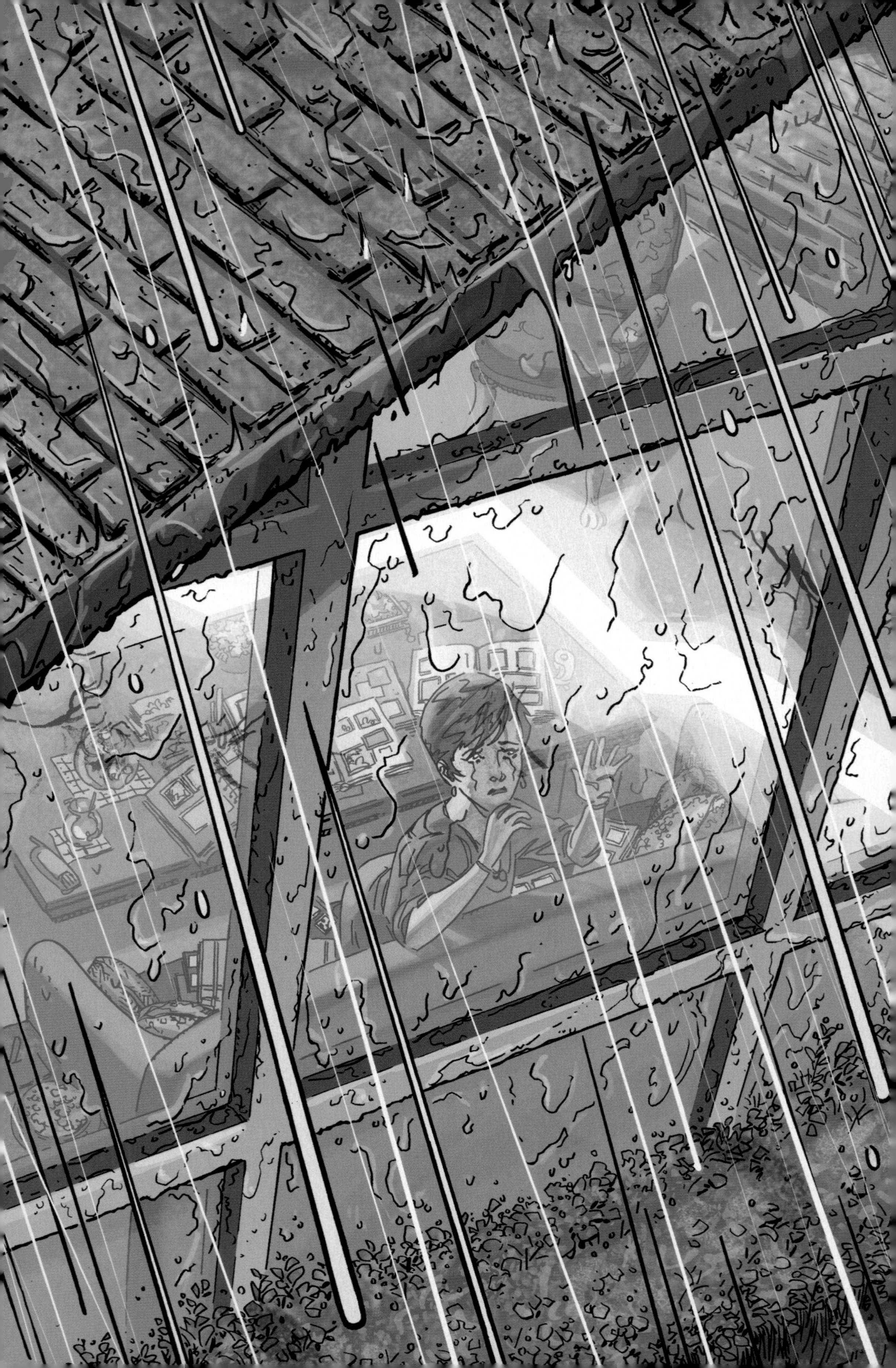

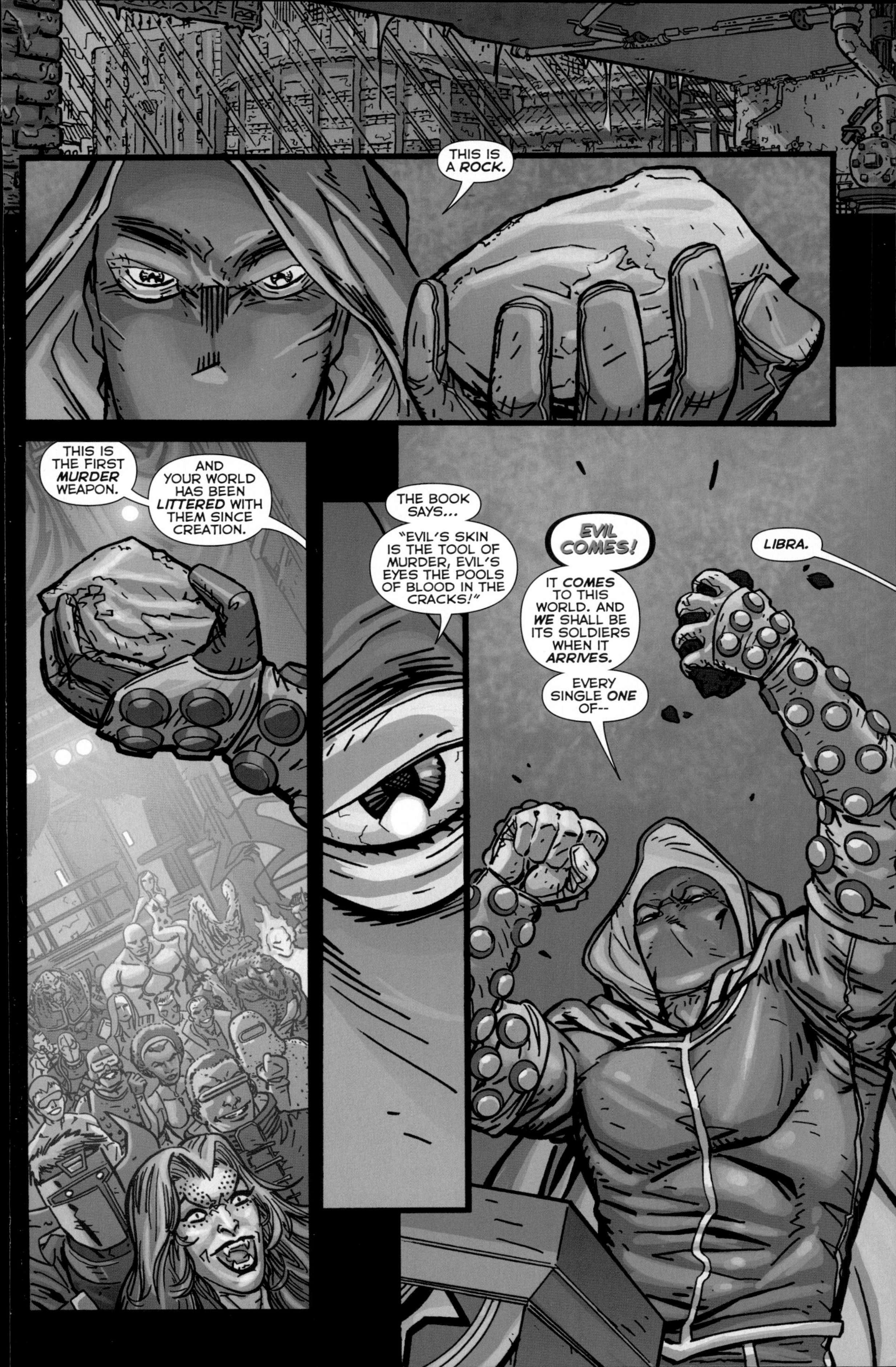
THIS IS A ROCK.
THIS IS THE FIRST MURDER WEAPON.
AND YOUR WORLD HAS BEEN LITTERED WITH THEM SINCE CREATION.
THE BOOK SAYS...
"EVIL'S SKIN IS THE TOOL OF MURDER, EVIL'S EYES THE POOLS OF BLOOD IN THE CRACKS!"
EVIL COMES!
IT COMES TO THIS WORLD. AND WE SHALL BE ITS SOLDIERS WHEN IT ARRIVES.
EVERY SINGLE ONE OF--
LIBRA.

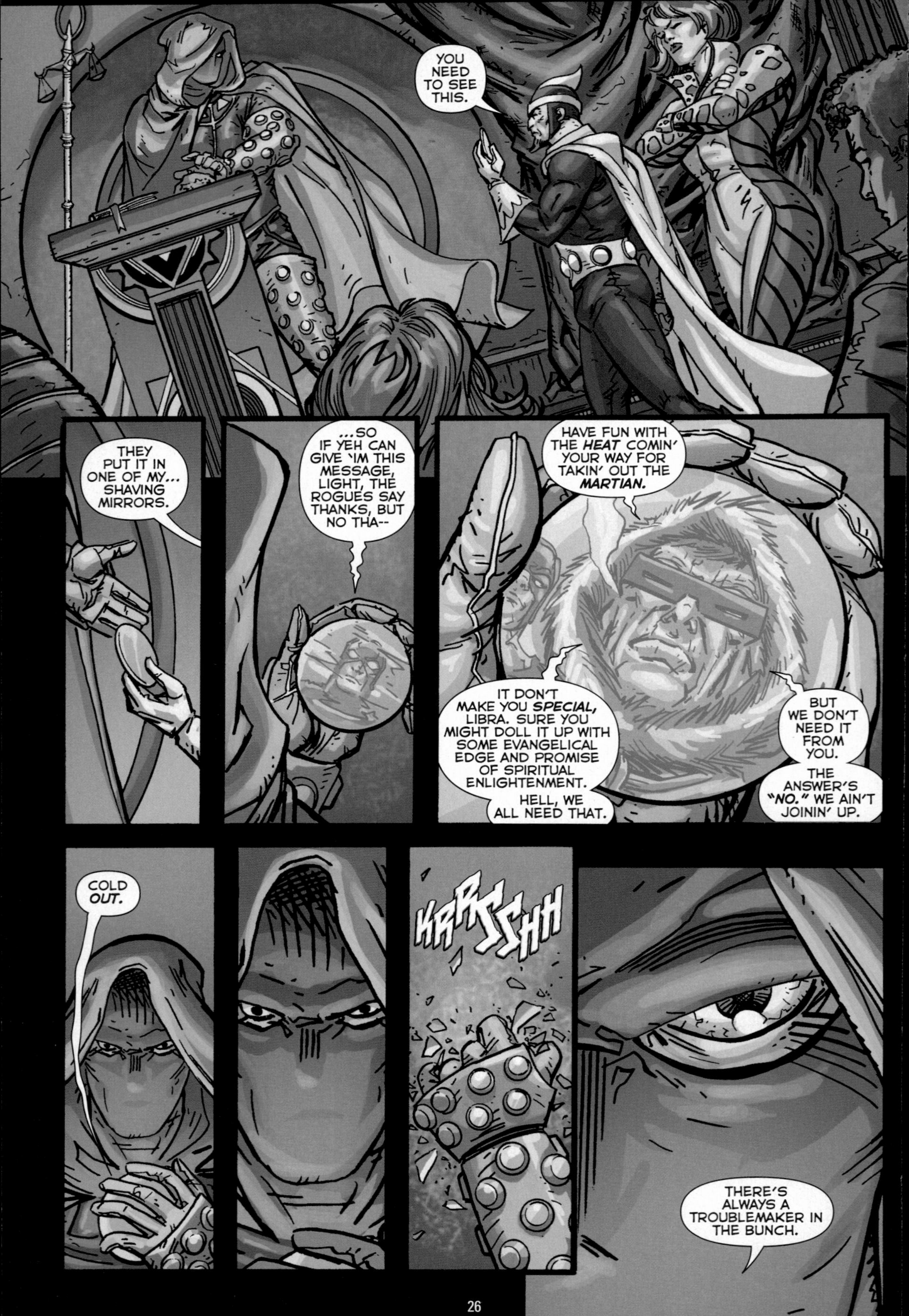
YOU NEED TO SEE THIS.
THEY PUT IT IN ONE OF MY... SHAVING MIRRORS.
...SO IF YEH CAN GIVE 'IM THIS MESSAGE, LIGHT, THE ROGUES SAY THANKS, BUT NO THA--
HAVE FUN WITH THE HEAT COMIN' YOUR WAY FOR TAKIN' OUT THE MARTIAN.
IT DON'T MAKE YOU SPECIAL, LIBRA. SURE YOU MIGHT DOLL IT UP WITH SOME EVANGELICAL EDGE AND PROMISE OF SPIRITUAL ENLIGHTENMENT.
HELL, WE ALL NEED THAT.
BUT WE DON'T NEED IT FROM YOU.
THE ANSWER'S "NO." WE AIN'T JOININ' UP.
COLD OUT.
KRRSSHH
THERE'S ALWAYS A TROUBLEMAKER IN THE BUNCH.

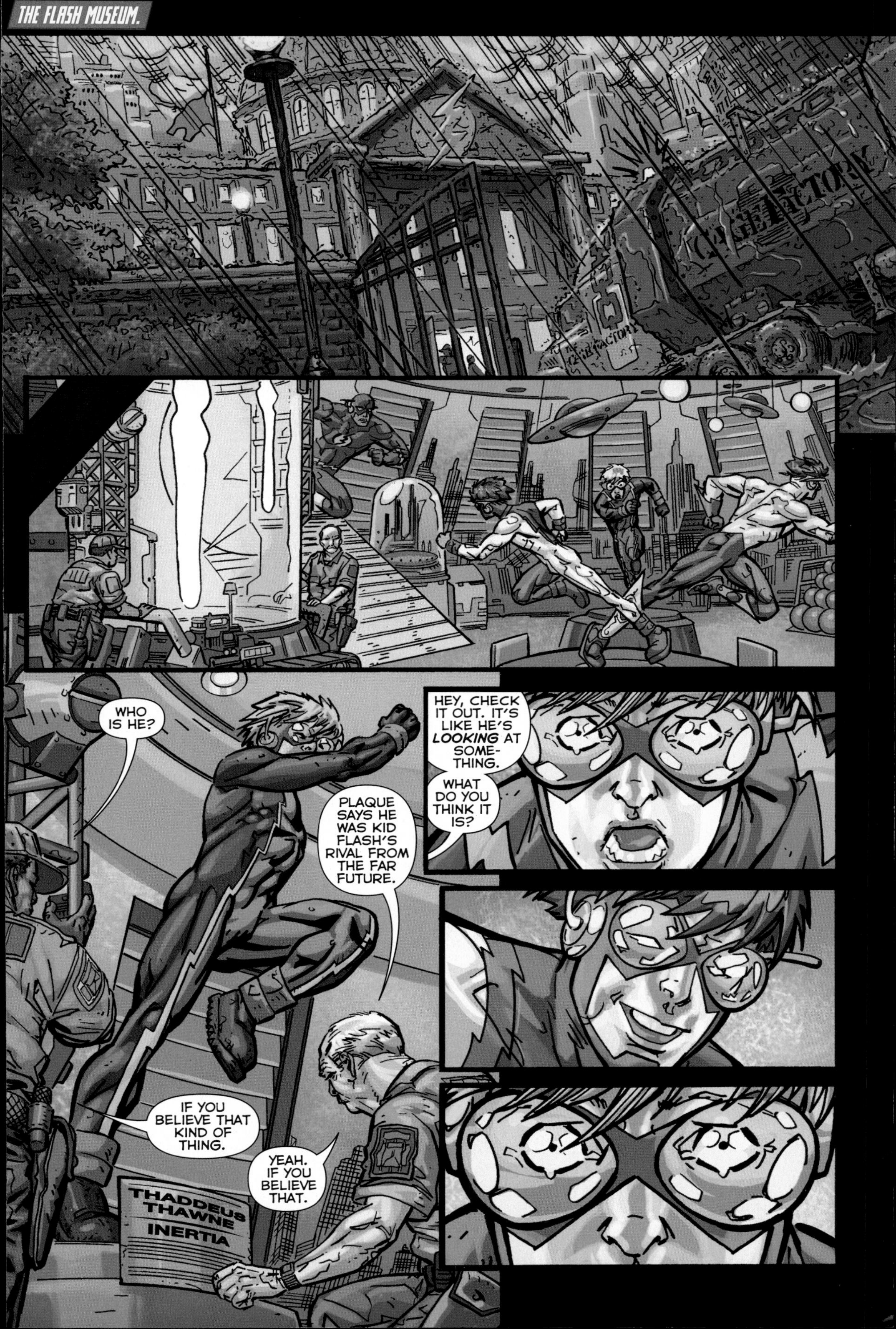
THE FLASH MUSEUM.
WHO IS HE?
PLAQUE SAYS HE WAS KID FLASH'S RIVAL FROM THE FAR FUTURE.
IF YOU BELIEVE THAT KIND OF THING.
YEAH. IF YOU BELIEVE THAT.
THADDEUS THAWNE
INERTIA
HEY, CHECK IT OUT. IT'S LIKE HE'S *LOOKING* AT SOME-THING.
WHAT DO YOU THINK IT IS?

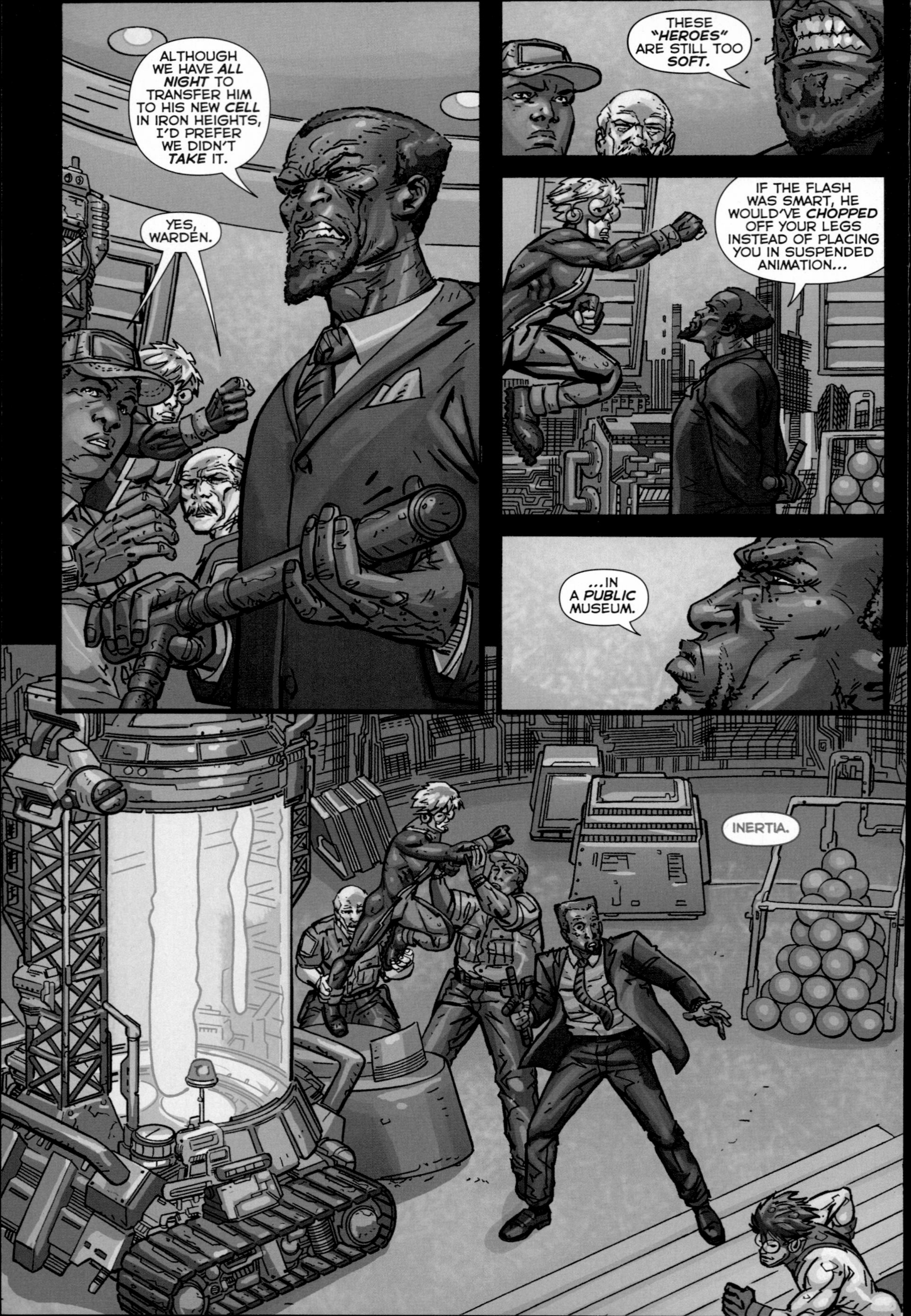
ALTHOUGH WE HAVE ALL NIGHT TO TRANSFER HIM TO HIS NEW CELL IN IRON HEIGHTS, I'D PREFER WE DIDN'T TAKE IT.
YES, WARDEN.
THESE "HEROES" ARE STILL TOO SOFT.
IF THE FLASH WAS SMART, HE WOULD'VE CHOPPED OFF YOUR LEGS INSTEAD OF PLACING YOU IN SUSPENDED ANIMATION...
...IN A PUBLIC MUSEUM.
INERTIA.

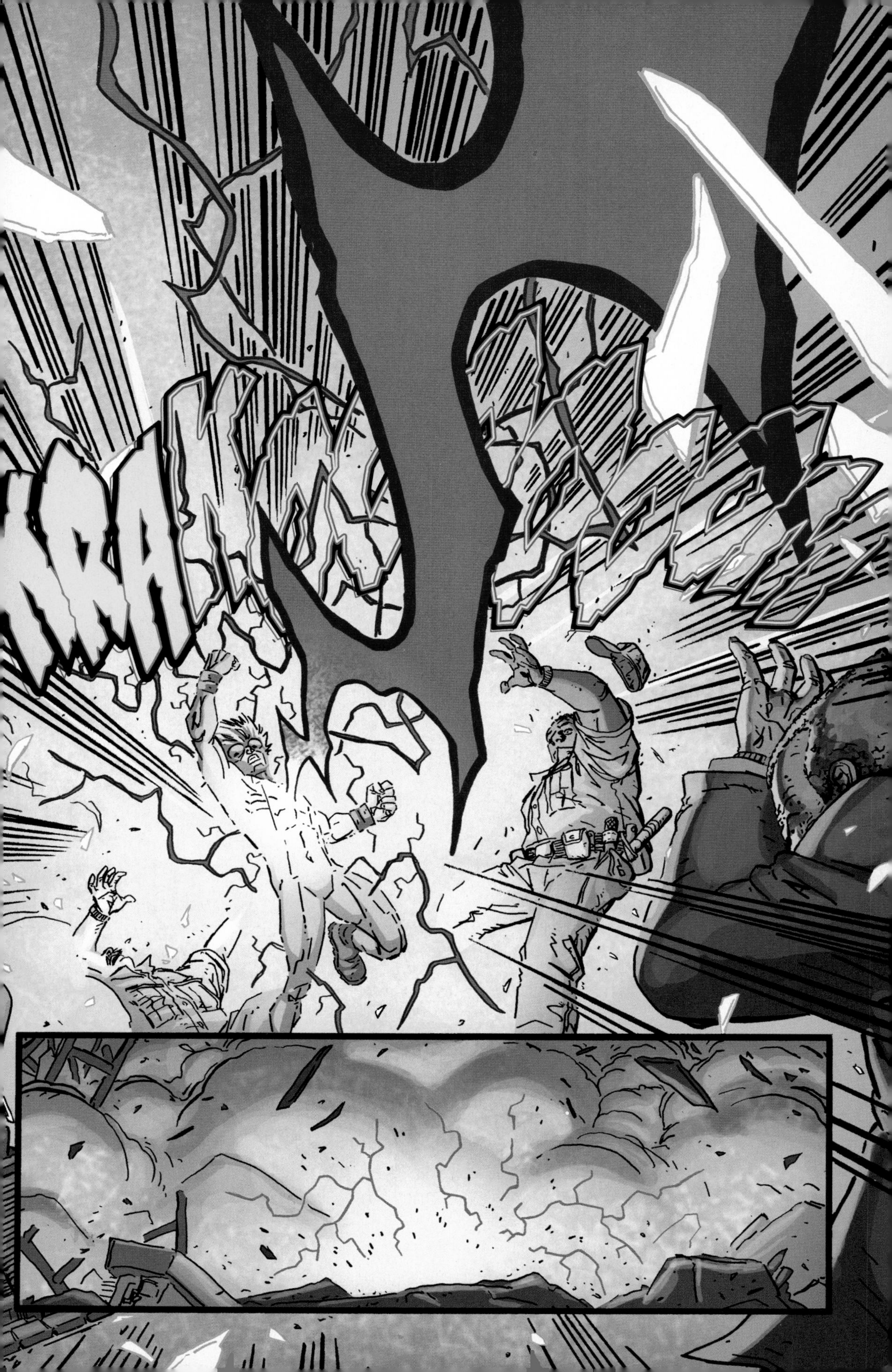

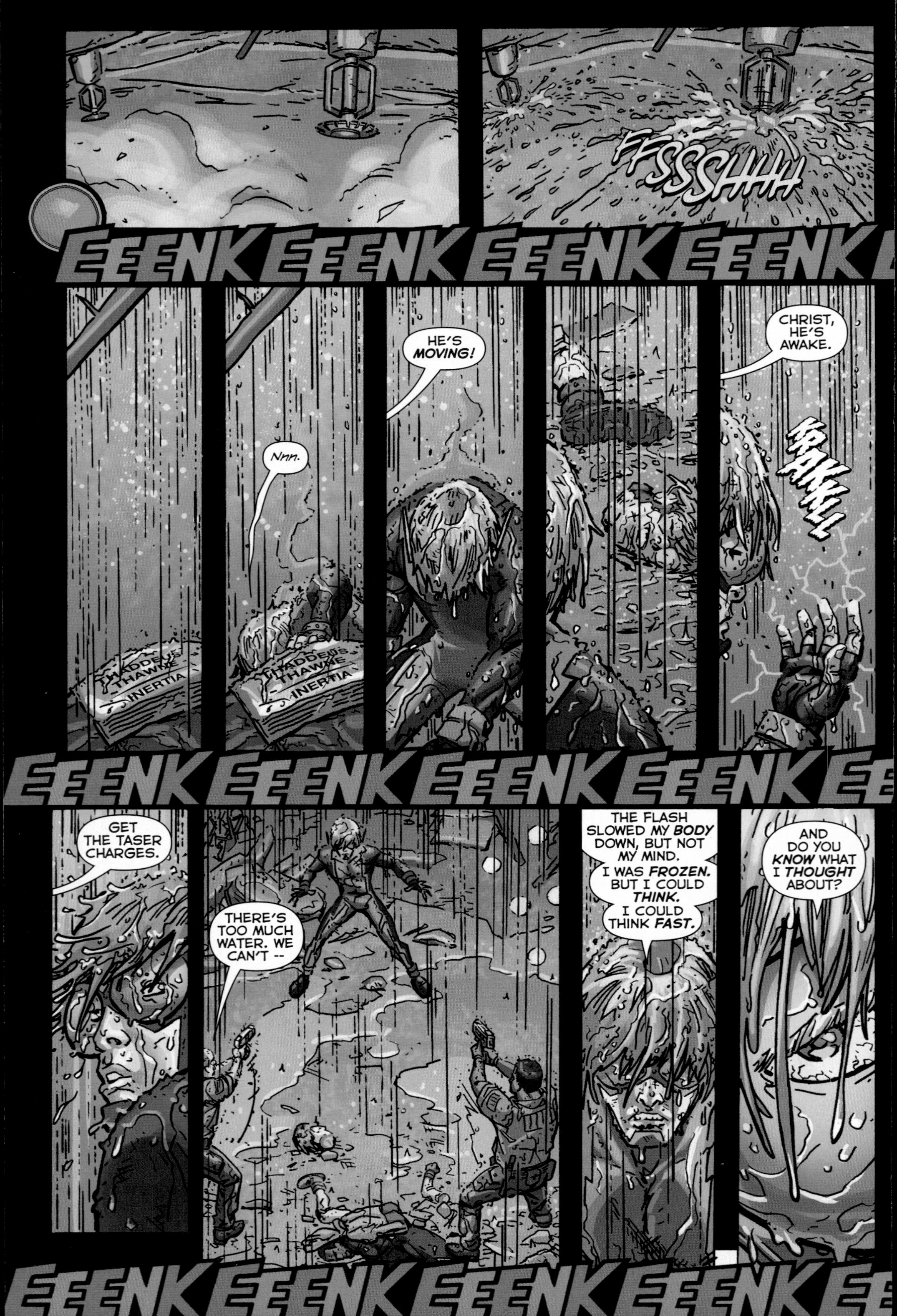
FFSSSHHH
EEENK EEENK EEENK EEENK
Nnn.
HE'S MOVING!
CHRIST, HE'S AWAKE.
KRAKK!
EEENK EEENK EEENK EEENK
GET THE TASER CHARGES.
THERE'S TOO MUCH WATER. WE CAN'T --
THE FLASH SLOWED MY BODY DOWN, BUT NOT MY MIND.
I WAS FROZEN. BUT I COULD THINK.
I COULD THINK FAST.
AND DO YOU KNOW WHAT I THOUGHT ABOUT?
EEENK EEENK EEENK EEENK

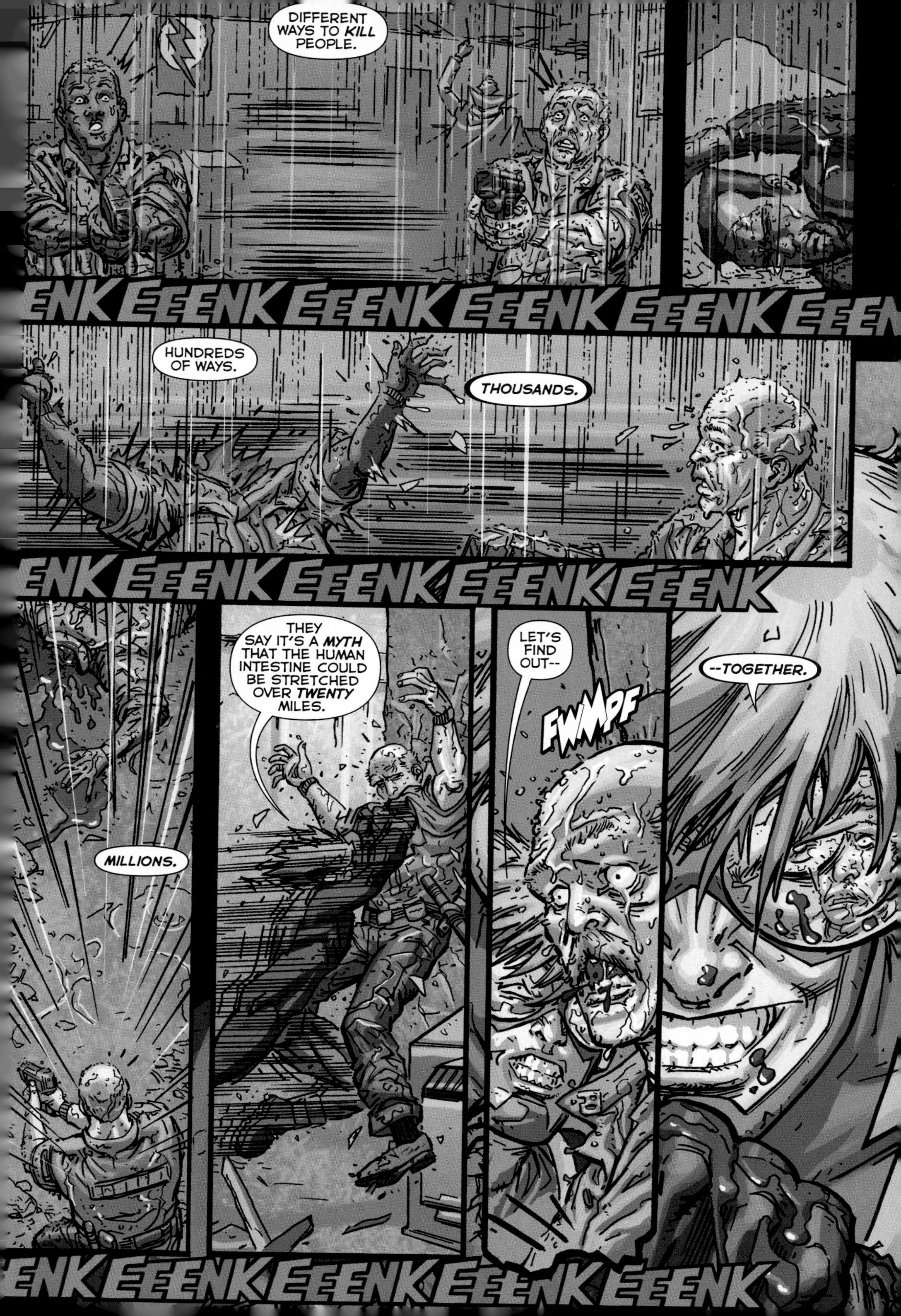

DIFFERENT WAYS TO KILL PEOPLE.
ENK EEEENK EEEENK EEEENK EEEENK EEEEN
HUNDREDS OF WAYS.
THOUSANDS.
ENK EEEENK EEEENK EEEENK EEEENK
MILLIONS.
THEY SAY IT'S A MYTH THAT THE HUMAN INTESTINE COULD BE STRETCHED OVER TWENTY MILES.
LET'S FIND OUT--
FWMPF
--TOGETHER.
ENK EEEENK EEEENK EEEENK EEEENK

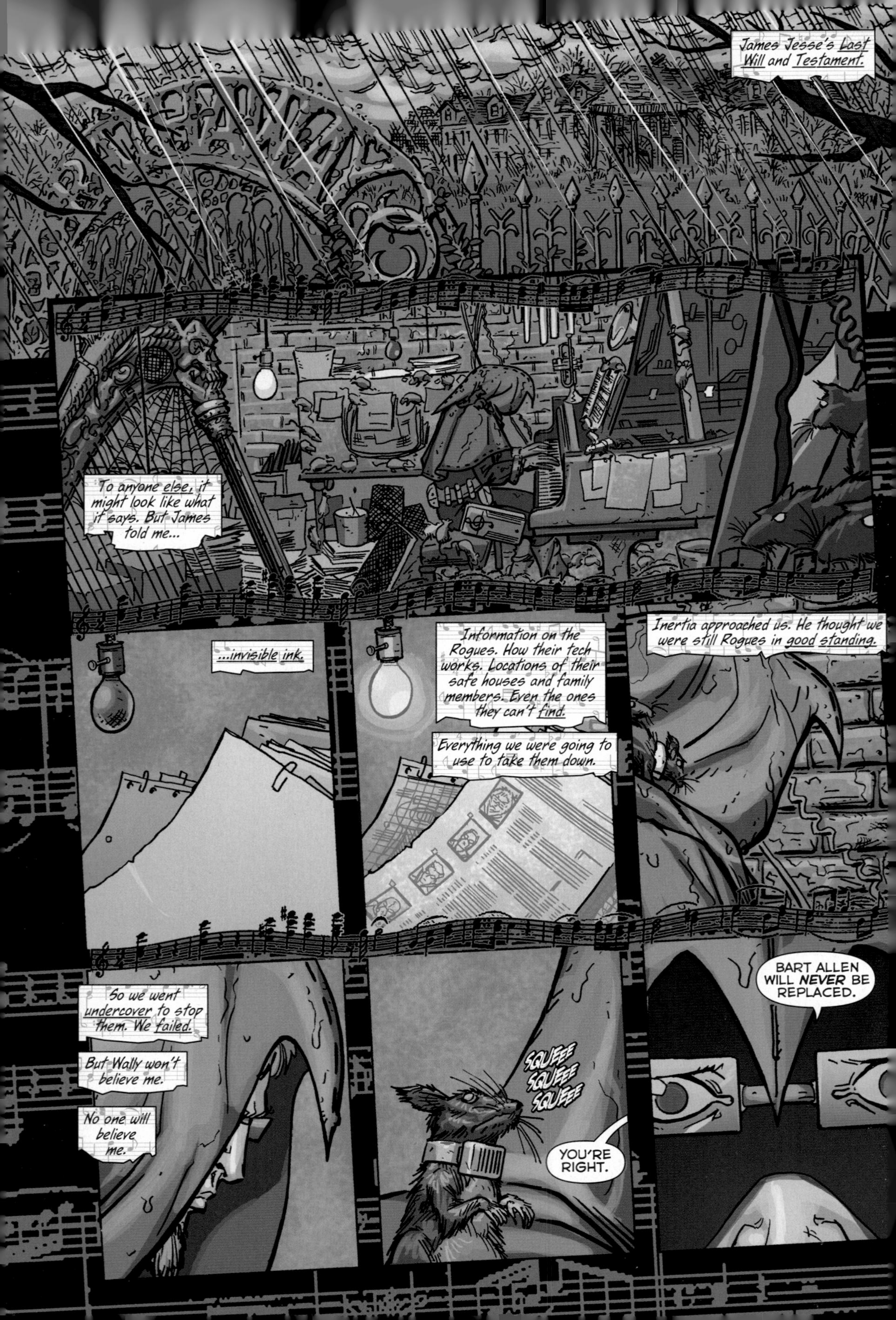

James Jesse's Last Will and Testament.
To anyone else, it might look like what it says. But James told me...
...invisible ink.
Information on the Rogues. How their tech works. Locations of their safe houses and family members. Even the ones they can't find.
Everything we were going to use to take them down.
Inertia approached us. He thought we were still Rogues in good standing.
So we went undercover to stop them. We failed.
But Wally won't believe me.
No one will believe me.
SQUEEE SQUEEE SQUEEE
YOU'RE RIGHT.
BART ALLEN WILL NEVER BE REPLACED.

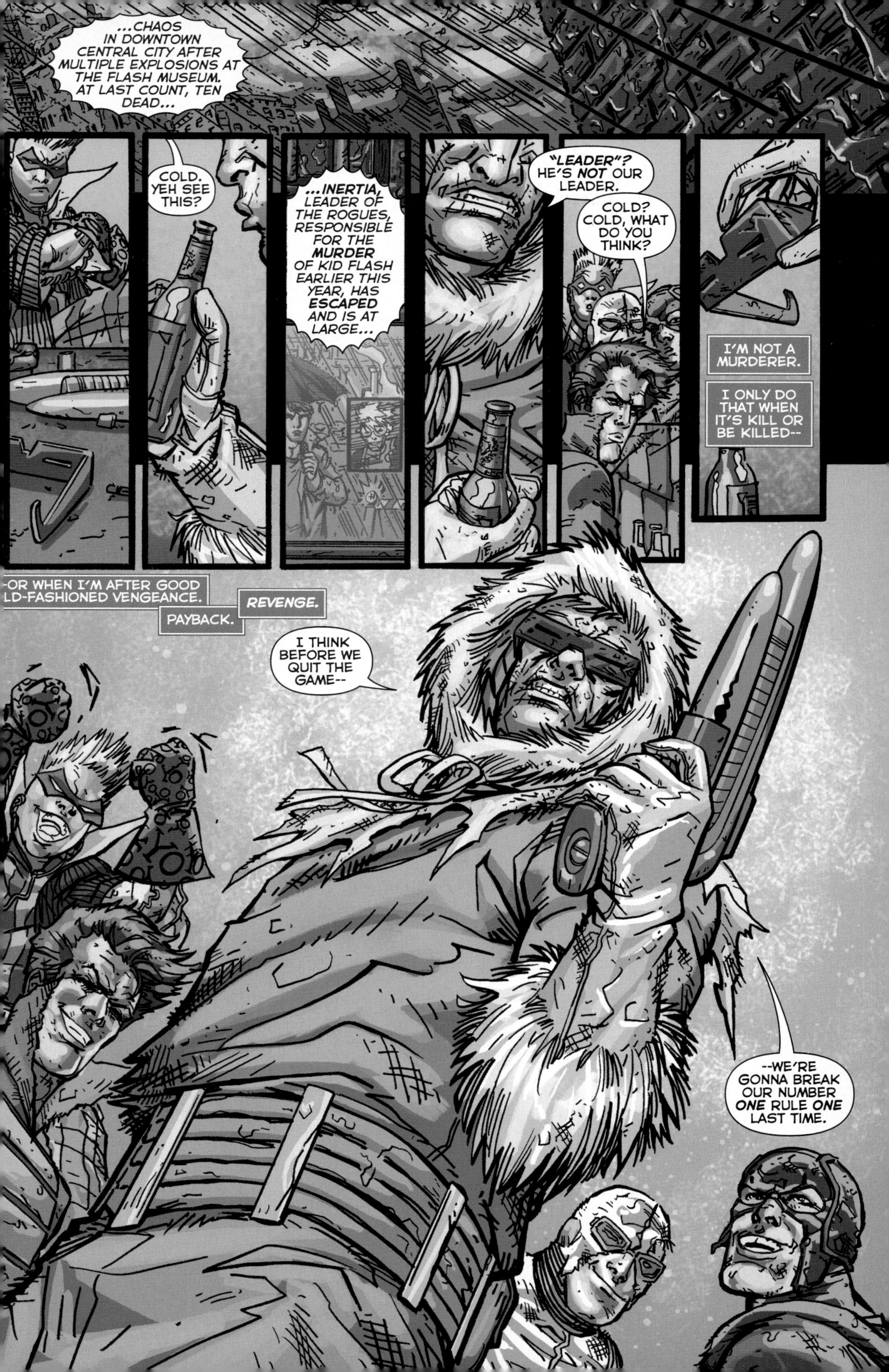
...CHAOS IN DOWNTOWN CENTRAL CITY AFTER MULTIPLE EXPLOSIONS AT THE FLASH MUSEUM. AT LAST COUNT, TEN DEAD...
COLD. YEH SEE THIS?
...INERTIA, LEADER OF THE ROGUES, RESPONSIBLE FOR THE MURDER OF KID FLASH EARLIER THIS YEAR, HAS ESCAPED AND IS AT LARGE...
"LEADER"? HE'S NOT OUR LEADER.
COLD? COLD, WHAT DO YOU THINK?
I'M NOT A MURDERER.
I ONLY DO THAT WHEN IT'S KILL OR BE KILLED--
-OR WHEN I'M AFTER GOOD
LD-FASHIONED VENGEANCE.
PAYBACK.
REVENGE.
I THINK BEFORE WE QUIT THE GAME--
--WE'RE GONNA BREAK OUR NUMBER ONE RULE ONE LAST TIME.

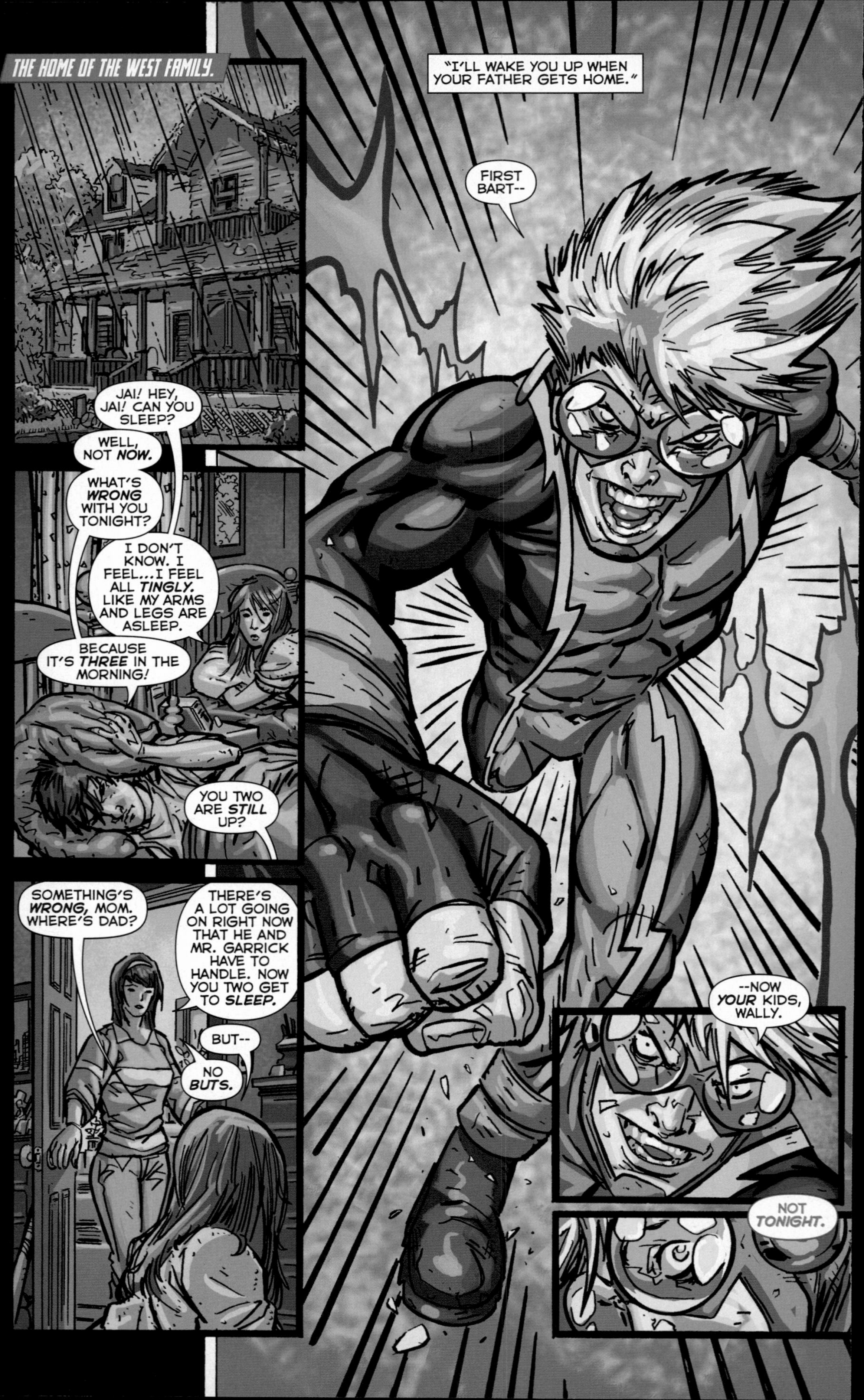
THE HOME OF THE WEST FAMILY.
JAI! HEY, JAI! CAN YOU SLEEP?
WELL, NOT NOW.
WHAT'S WRONG WITH YOU TONIGHT?
I DON'T KNOW. I FEEL...I FEEL ALL TINGLY. LIKE MY ARMS AND LEGS ARE ASLEEP.
BECAUSE IT'S THREE IN THE MORNING!
YOU TWO ARE STILL UP?
SOMETHING'S WRONG, MOM. WHERE'S DAD?
THERE'S A LOT GOING ON RIGHT NOW THAT HE AND MR. GARRICK HAVE TO HANDLE. NOW YOU TWO GET TO SLEEP.
BUT--
NO BUTS.
"I'LL WAKE YOU UP WHEN YOUR FATHER GETS HOME."
FIRST BART--
--NOW YOUR KIDS, WALLY.
NOT TONIGHT.

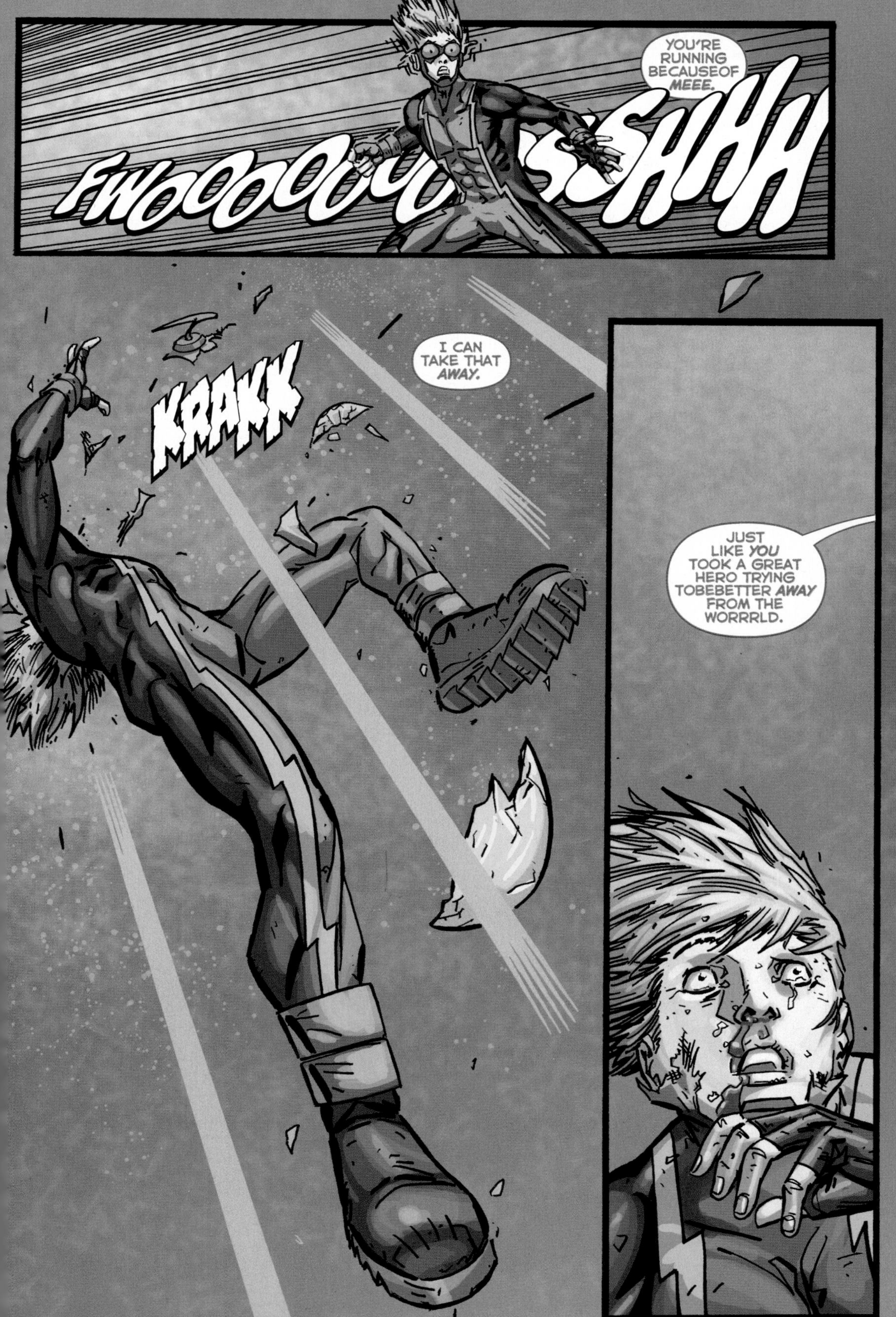
YOU'RE RUNNING BECAUSEOF *MEEE.*
FWOOOOOOOOSSHHH
I CAN TAKE THAT *AWAY.*
KRAKK
JUST LIKE *YOU* TOOK A GREAT HERO TRYING TOBEBETTER *AWAY* FROM THE WORRRLD.

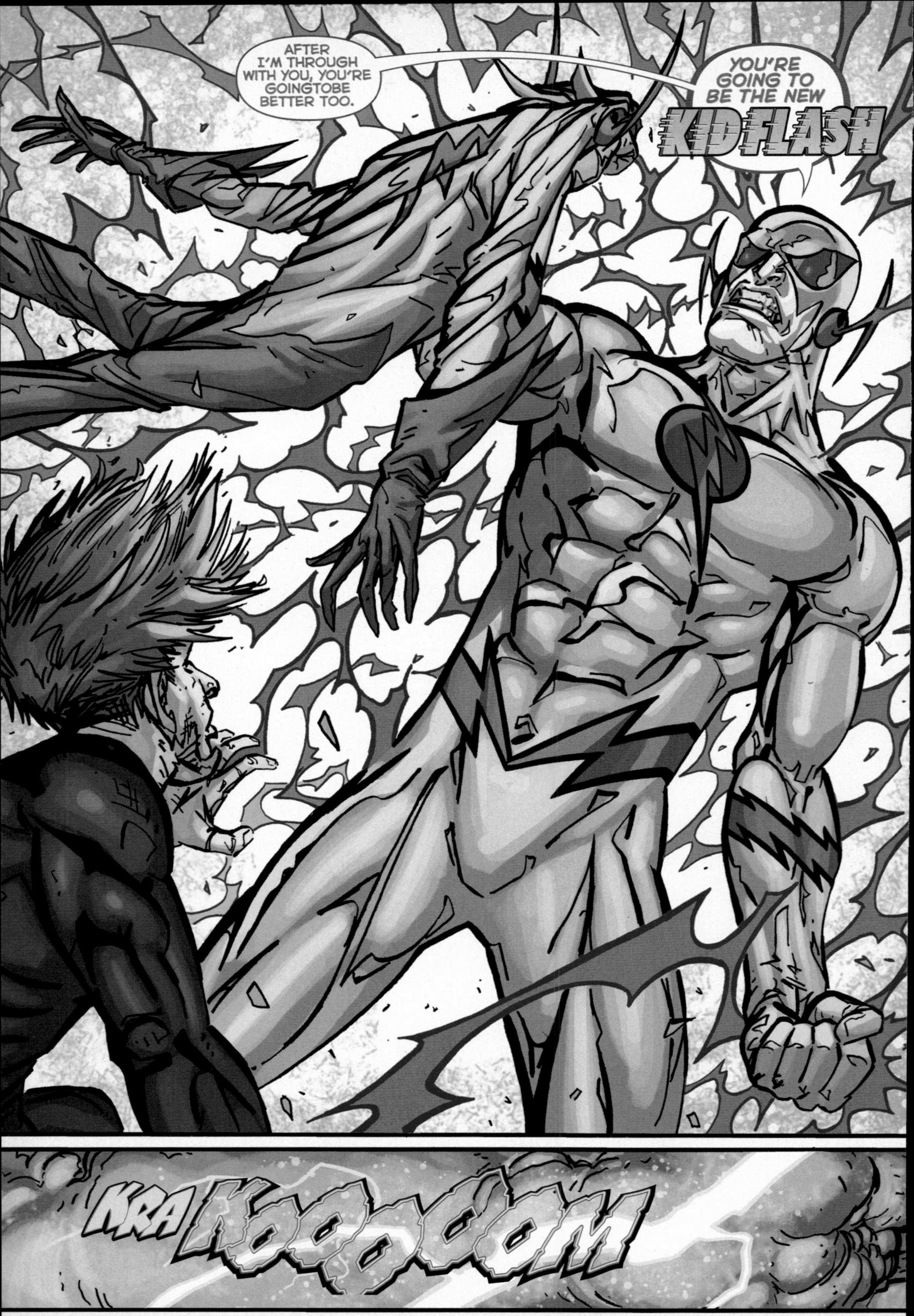
AFTER I'M THROUGH WITH YOU, YOU'RE GOINGTOBE BETTER TOO.
YOU'RE GOING TO BE THE NEW
KID FLASH
KRA KOOOOOM

over to FINAL CRISIS: ROGUES' REVENGE #2

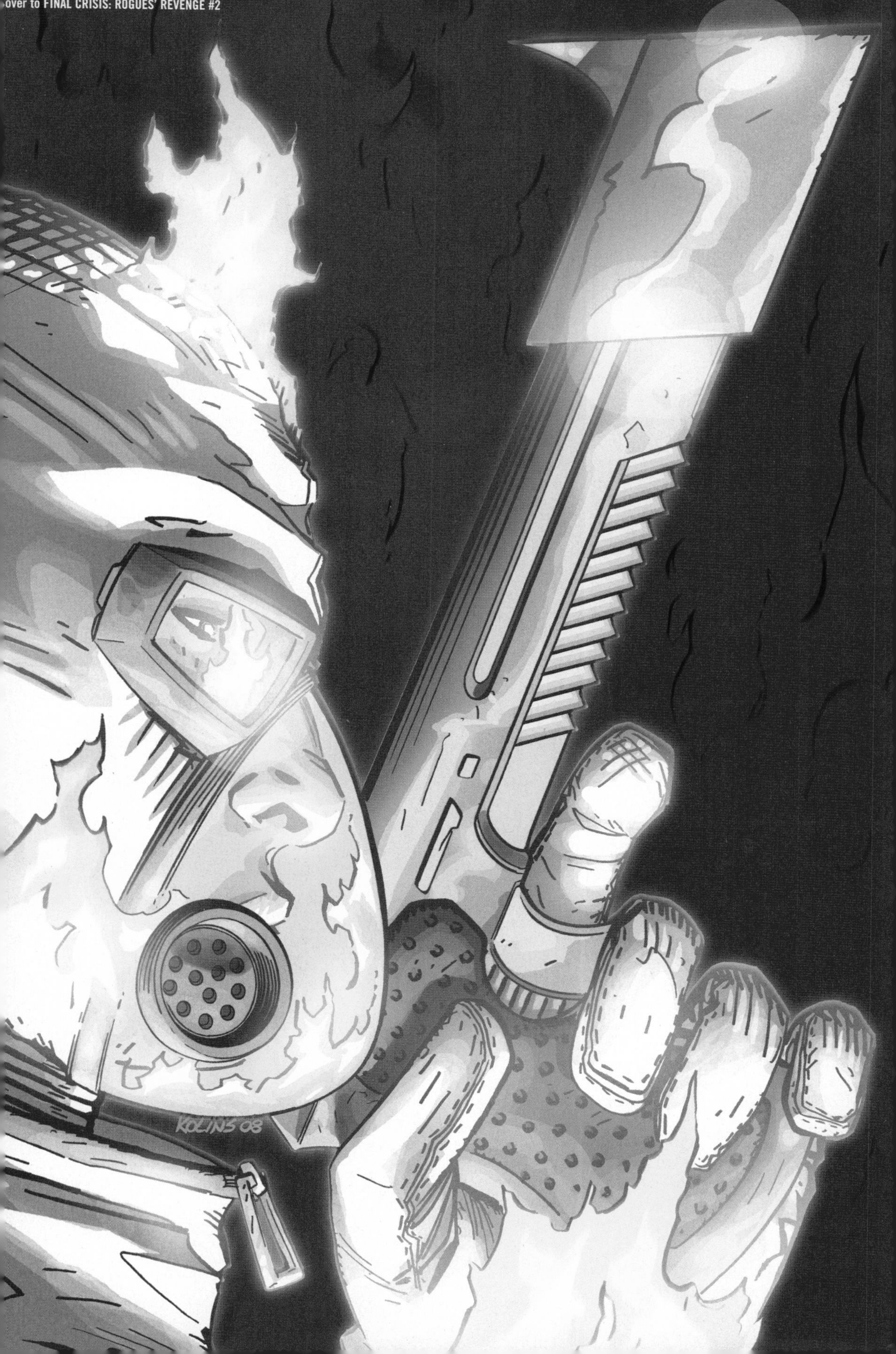
KOLINS 08

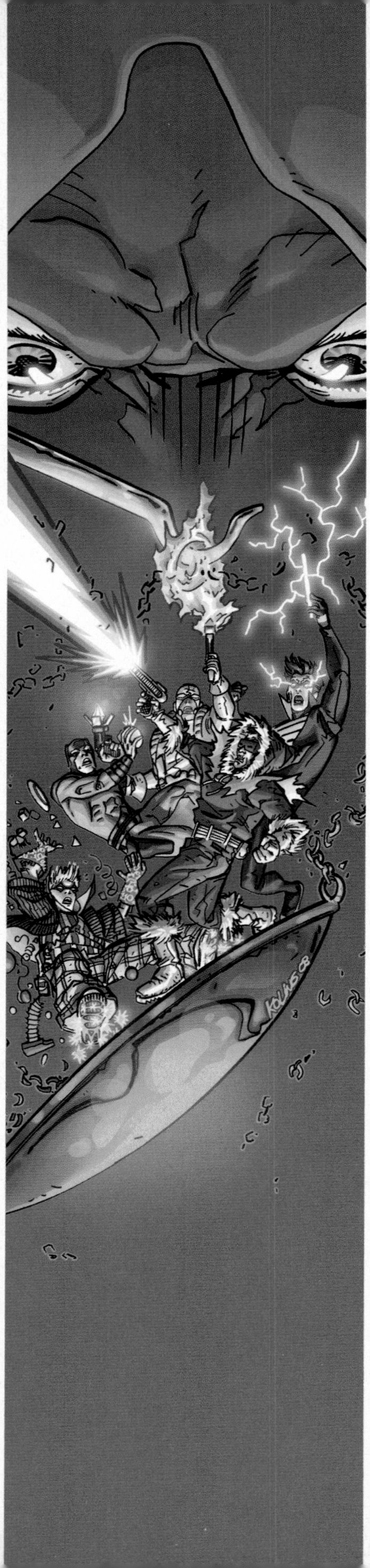

Sliver cover to FINAL CRISIS: ROGUES' REVENGE #2

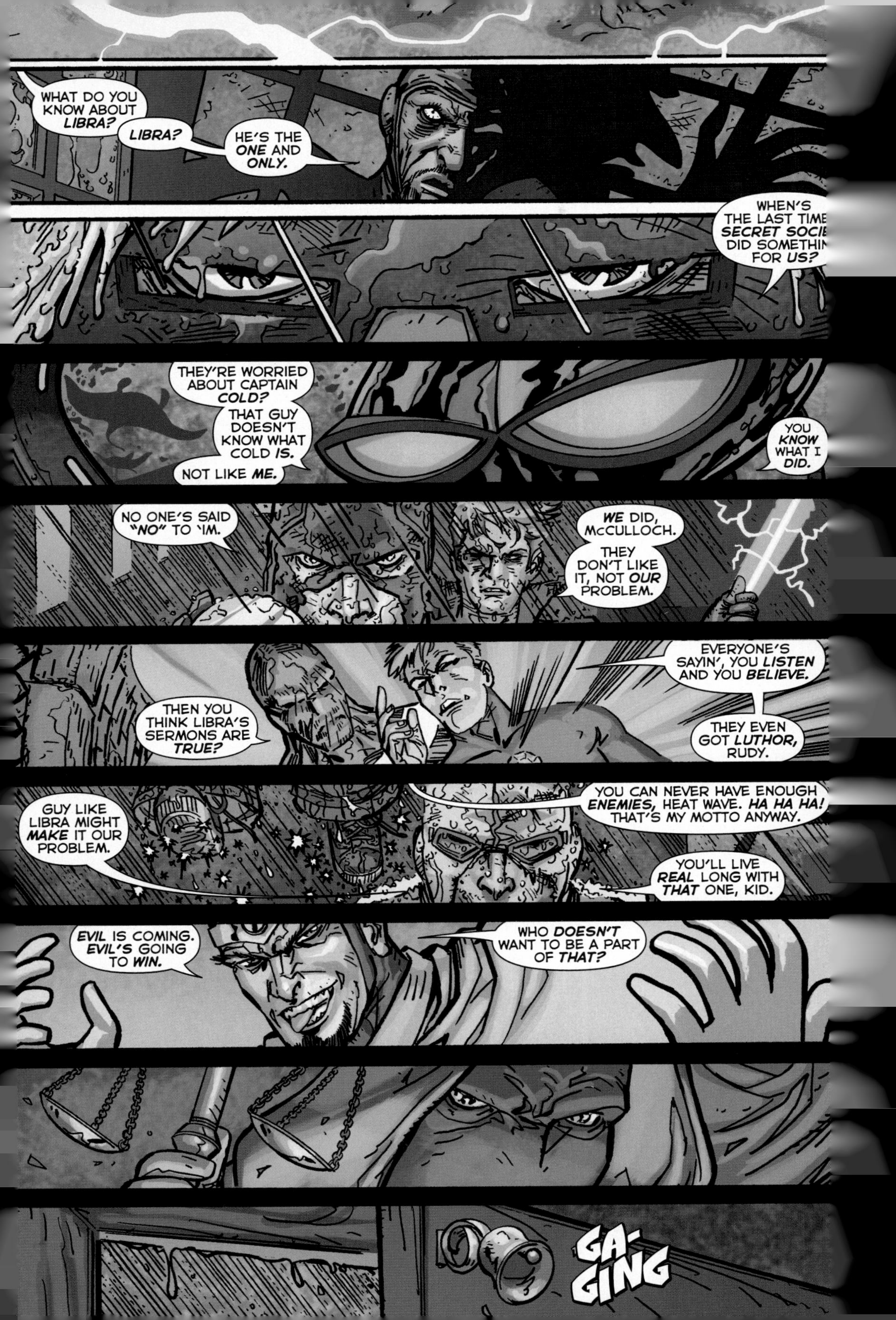
WHAT DO YOU KNOW ABOUT LIBRA?
LIBRA?
HE'S THE ONE AND ONLY.
WHEN'S THE LAST TIME SECRET SOCI DID SOMETHIN FOR US?
THEY'RE WORRIED ABOUT CAPTAIN COLD?
THAT GUY DOESN'T KNOW WHAT COLD IS.
NOT LIKE ME.
YOU KNOW WHAT I DID.
NO ONE'S SAID "NO" TO 'IM.
WE DID, McCULLOCH.
THEY DON'T LIKE IT, NOT OUR PROBLEM.
EVERYONE'S SAYIN', YOU LISTEN AND YOU BELIEVE.
THEN YOU THINK LIBRA'S SERMONS ARE TRUE?
THEY EVEN GOT LUTHOR, RUDY.
GUY LIKE LIBRA MIGHT MAKE IT OUR PROBLEM.
YOU CAN NEVER HAVE ENOUGH ENEMIES, HEAT WAVE. HA HA HA! THAT'S MY MOTTO ANYWAY.
YOU'LL LIVE REAL LONG WITH THAT ONE, KID.
EVIL IS COMING. EVIL'S GOING TO WIN.
WHO DOESN'T WANT TO BE A PART OF THAT?
GA-GING

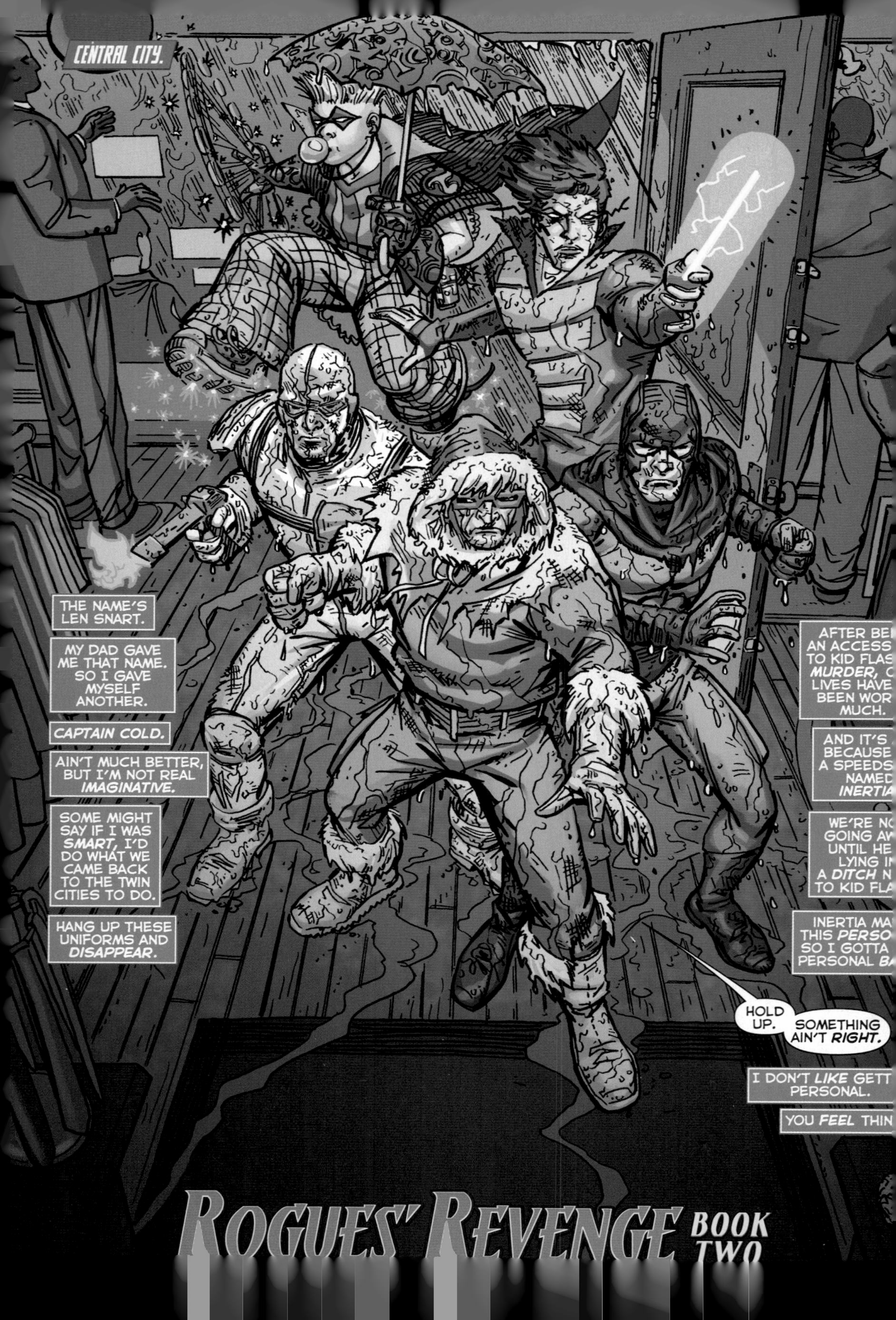
CENTRAL CITY.
THE NAME'S LEN SNART.
MY DAD GAVE ME THAT NAME. SO I GAVE MYSELF ANOTHER.
CAPTAIN COLD.
AIN'T MUCH BETTER, BUT I'M NOT REAL *IMAGINATIVE.*
SOME MIGHT SAY IF I WAS *SMART,* I'D DO WHAT WE CAME BACK TO THE TWIN CITIES TO DO.
HANG UP THESE UNIFORMS AND *DISAPPEAR.*
AFTER BE AN ACCESS TO KID FLAS *MURDER,* LIVES HAVE BEEN WOR MUCH.
AND IT'S BECAUSE A SPEEDS NAMED *INERTIA*
WE'RE N GOING A UNTIL HE LYING I A *DITCH* N TO KID FLA
INERTIA MA THIS *PERSO* SO I GOTTA PERSONAL
HOLD UP. SOMETHING AIN'T *RIGHT.*
I DON'T *LIKE* GETT PERSONAL.
YOU *FEEL* THIN
ROGUES' REVENGE BOOK TWO

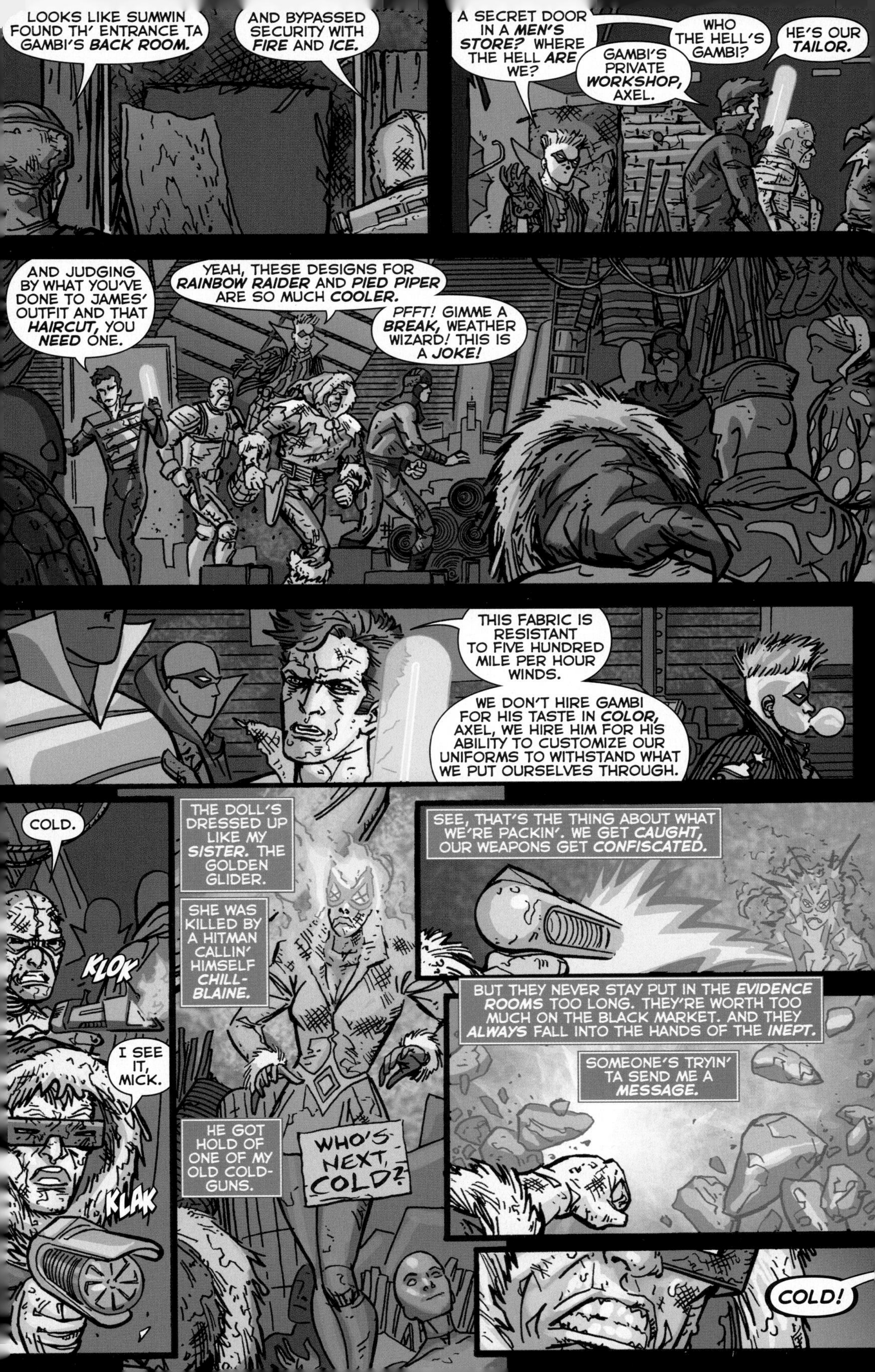
LOOKS LIKE SUMWIN FOUND TH' ENTRANCE TA GAMBI'S BACK ROOM.
AND BYPASSED SECURITY WITH FIRE AND ICE.
A SECRET DOOR IN A MEN'S STORE? WHERE THE HELL ARE WE?
GAMBI'S PRIVATE WORKSHOP, AXEL.
WHO THE HELL'S GAMBI?
HE'S OUR TAILOR.
AND JUDGING BY WHAT YOU'VE DONE TO JAMES' OUTFIT AND THAT HAIRCUT, YOU NEED ONE.
YEAH, THESE DESIGNS FOR RAINBOW RAIDER AND PIED PIPER ARE SO MUCH COOLER.
PFFT! GIMME A BREAK, WEATHER WIZARD! THIS IS A JOKE!
THIS FABRIC IS RESISTANT TO FIVE HUNDRED MILE PER HOUR WINDS.
WE DON'T HIRE GAMBI FOR HIS TASTE IN COLOR, AXEL, WE HIRE HIM FOR HIS ABILITY TO CUSTOMIZE OUR UNIFORMS TO WITHSTAND WHAT WE PUT OURSELVES THROUGH.
COLD.
KLOK
I SEE IT, MICK.
KLAK
THE DOLL'S DRESSED UP LIKE MY SISTER. THE GOLDEN GLIDER.
SHE WAS KILLED BY A HITMAN CALLIN' HIMSELF CHILL-BLAINE.
HE GOT HOLD OF ONE OF MY OLD COLD-GUNS.
WHO'S NEXT, COLD?
SEE, THAT'S THE THING ABOUT WHAT WE'RE PACKIN'. WE GET CAUGHT, OUR WEAPONS GET CONFISCATED.
BUT THEY NEVER STAY PUT IN THE EVIDENCE ROOMS TOO LONG. THEY'RE WORTH TOO MUCH ON THE BLACK MARKET. AND THEY ALWAYS FALL INTO THE HANDS OF THE INEPT.
SOMEONE'S TRYIN' TA SEND ME A MESSAGE.
COLD!

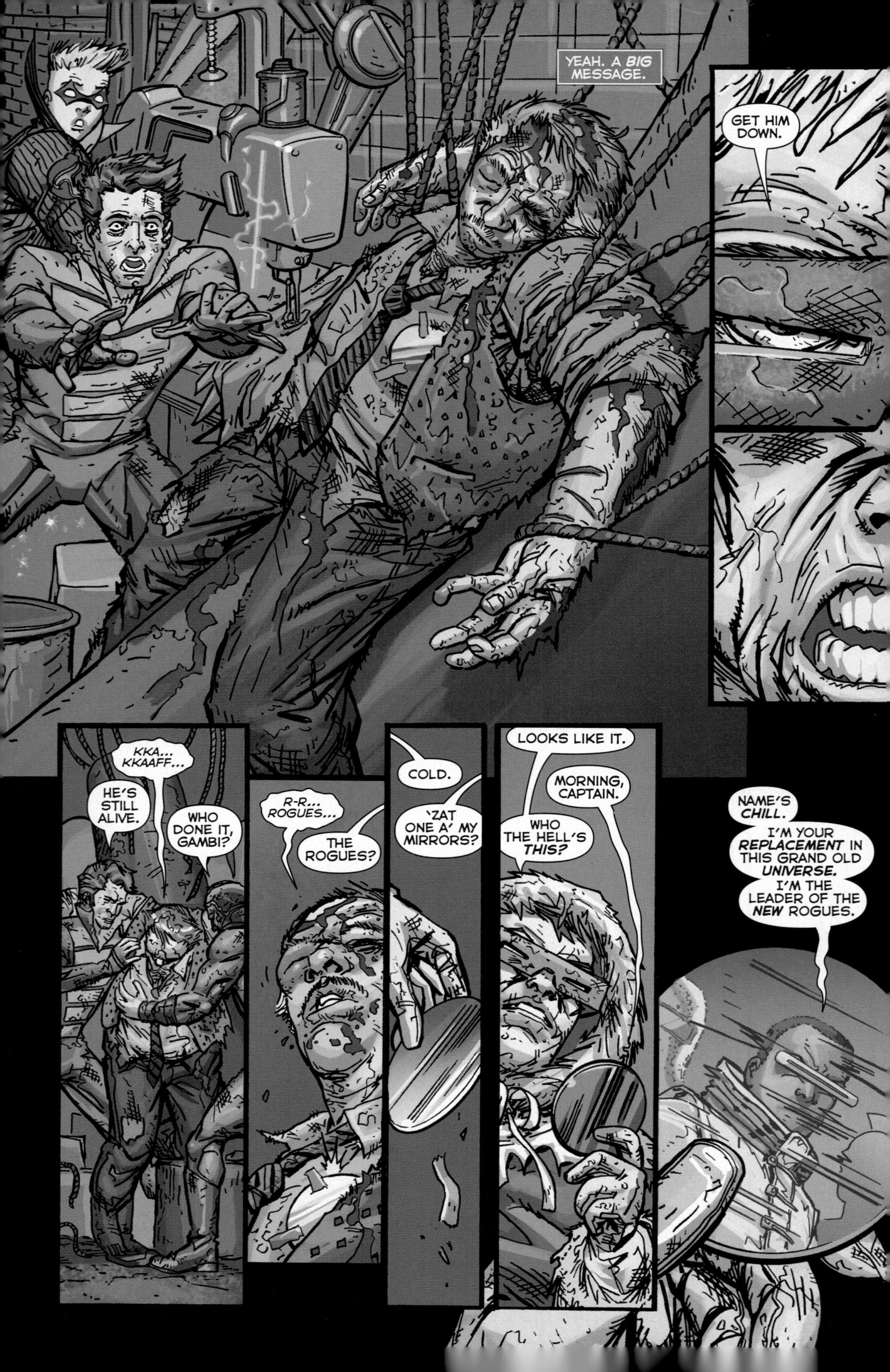
YEAH. A *BIG* MESSAGE.
GET HIM DOWN.
KKA... KKAAFF...
HE'S STILL ALIVE.
WHO DONE IT, GAMBI?
R-R... ROGUES...
THE ROGUES?
COLD.
'ZAT ONE A' MY MIRRORS?
LOOKS LIKE IT.
MORNING, CAPTAIN.
WHO THE HELL'S *THIS?*
NAME'S *CHILL.*
I'M YOUR *REPLACEMENT* IN THIS GRAND OLD *UNIVERSE.*
I'M THE LEADER OF THE *NEW* ROGUES.

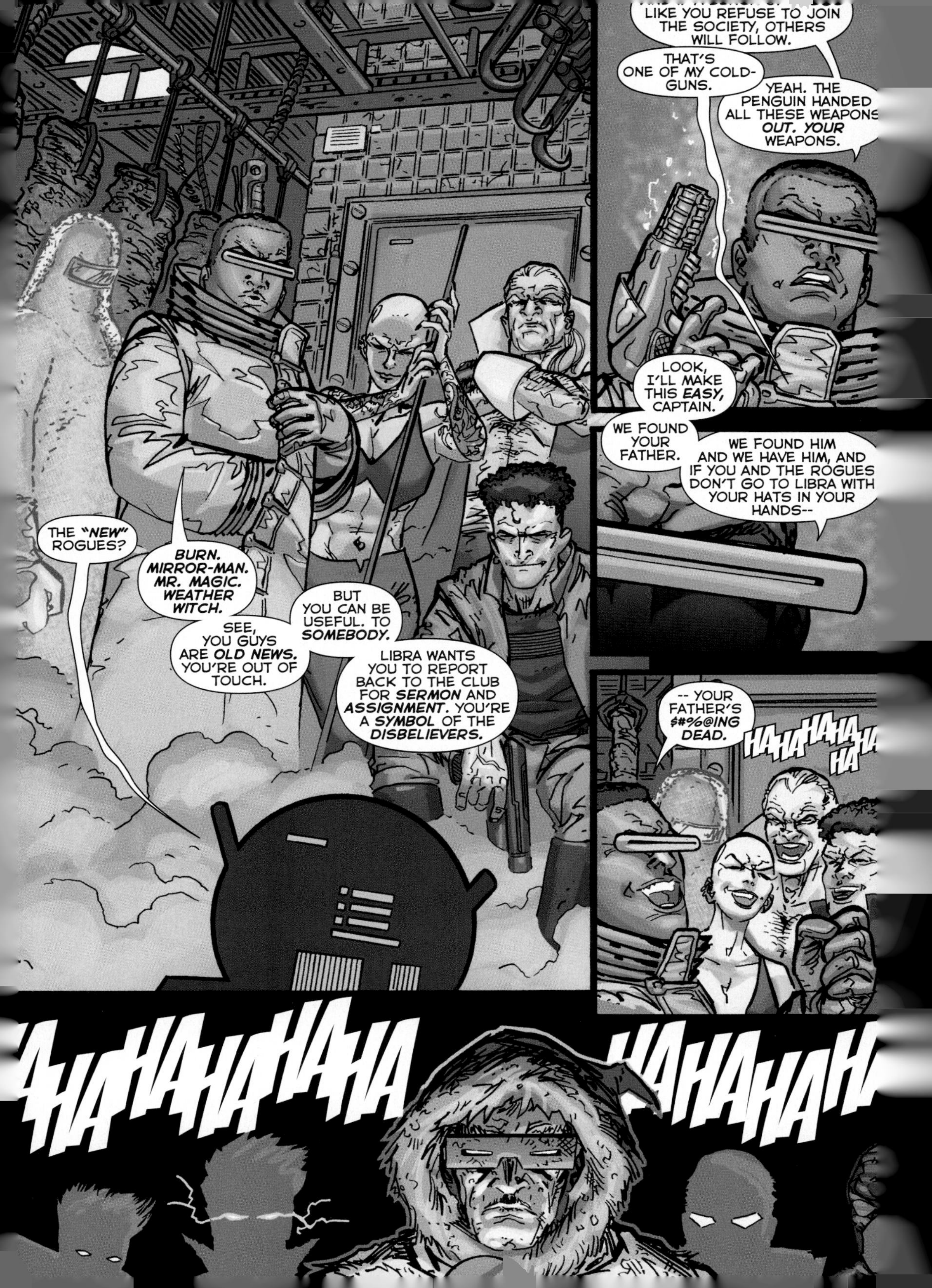
THE "NEW" ROGUES?
BURN. MIRROR-MAN. MR. MAGIC. WEATHER WITCH.
SEE, YOU GUYS ARE OLD NEWS. YOU'RE OUT OF TOUCH.
BUT YOU CAN BE USEFUL. TO SOMEBODY.
LIBRA WANTS YOU TO REPORT BACK TO THE CLUB FOR SERMON AND ASSIGNMENT. YOU'RE A SYMBOL OF THE DISBELIEVERS.
LIKE YOU REFUSE TO JOIN THE SOCIETY, OTHERS WILL FOLLOW.
THAT'S ONE OF MY COLD-GUNS.
YEAH. THE PENGUIN HANDED ALL THESE WEAPONS OUT. YOUR WEAPONS.
LOOK, I'LL MAKE THIS EASY, CAPTAIN.
WE FOUND YOUR FATHER.
WE FOUND HIM AND WE HAVE HIM, AND IF YOU AND THE ROGUES DON'T GO TO LIBRA WITH YOUR HATS IN YOUR HANDS--
-- YOUR FATHER'S $#%@ING DEAD.
HAHAHAHAHA
HAHAHAHAHAHAHAHA
HAHAHAHAH

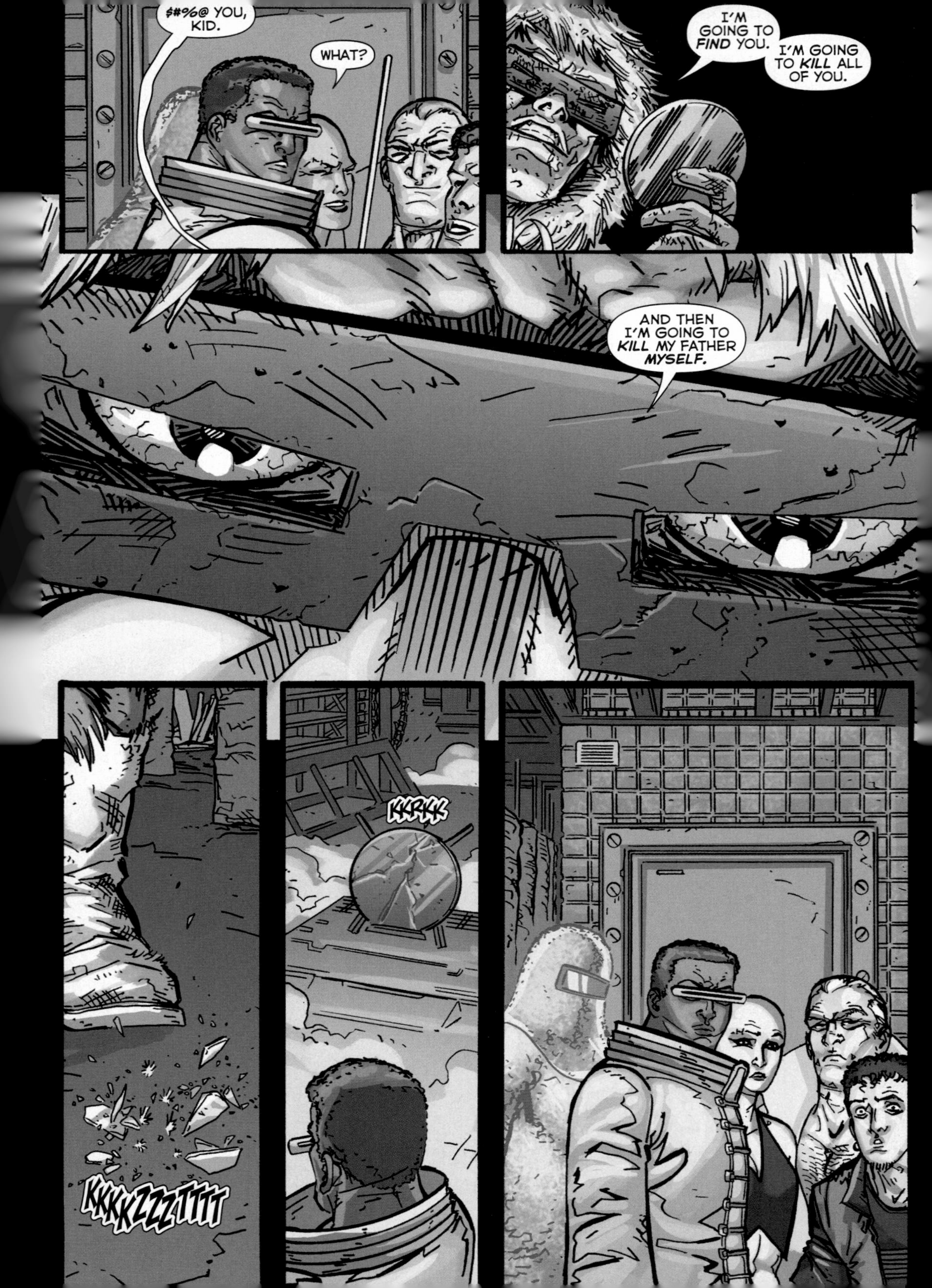
$#%@ YOU, KID.
WHAT?
I'M GOING TO *FIND* YOU.
I'M GOING TO *KILL* ALL OF YOU.
AND THEN I'M GOING TO *KILL* MY FATHER *MYSELF.*
KKKKZZZTTTT
KKRKK

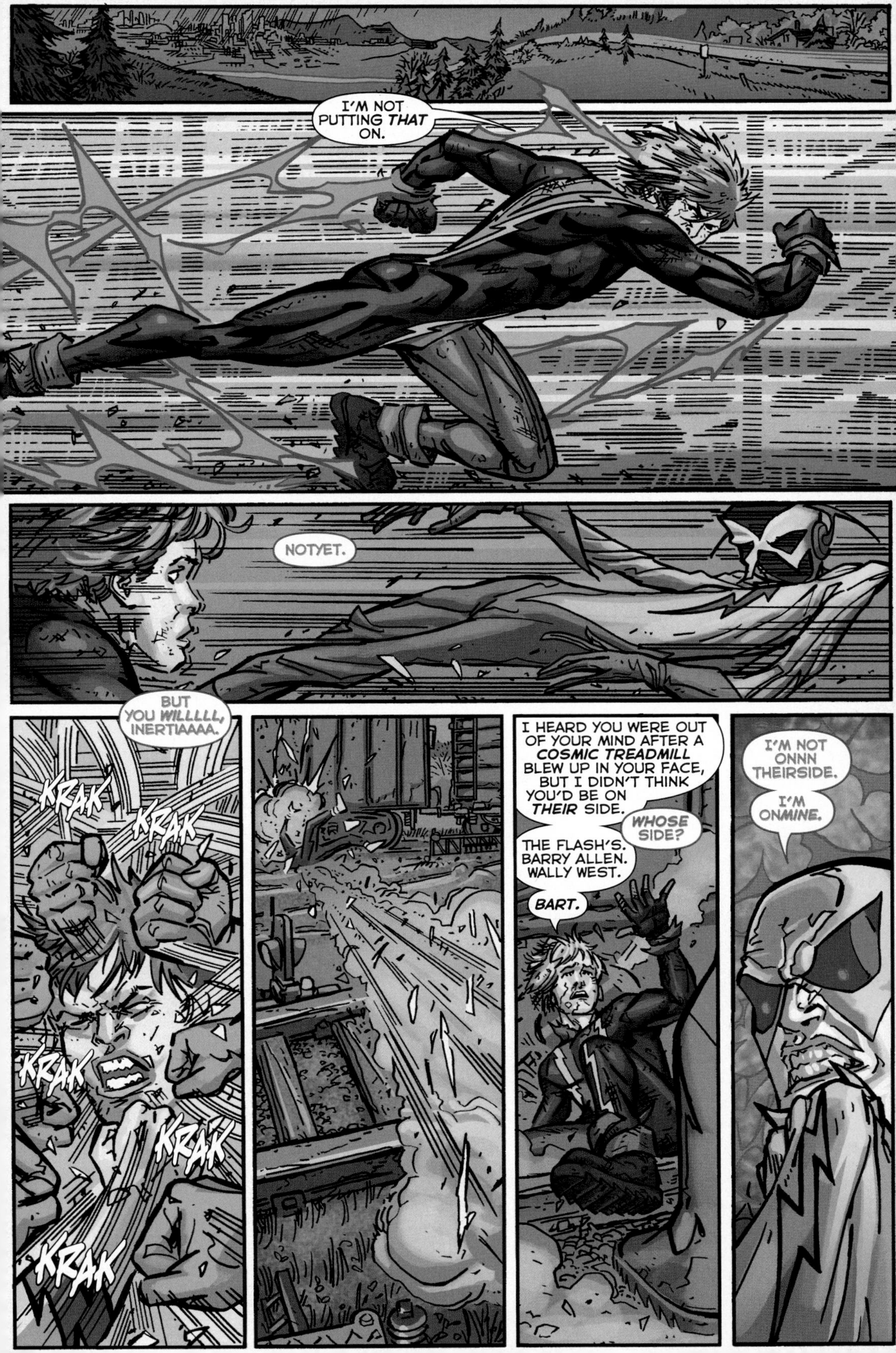
I'M NOT PUTTING THAT ON.
NOTYET.
BUT YOU WILLLLL, INERTIAAAA.
KRAK
KRAK
KRAK
KRAK
KRAK
I HEARD YOU WERE OUT OF YOUR MIND AFTER A COSMIC TREADMILL BLEW UP IN YOUR FACE, BUT I DIDN'T THINK YOU'D BE ON THEIR SIDE.
WHOSE SIDE?
THE FLASH'S. BARRY ALLEN. WALLY WEST.
BART.
I'M NOT ONNN THEIRSIDE.
I'M ONMINE.

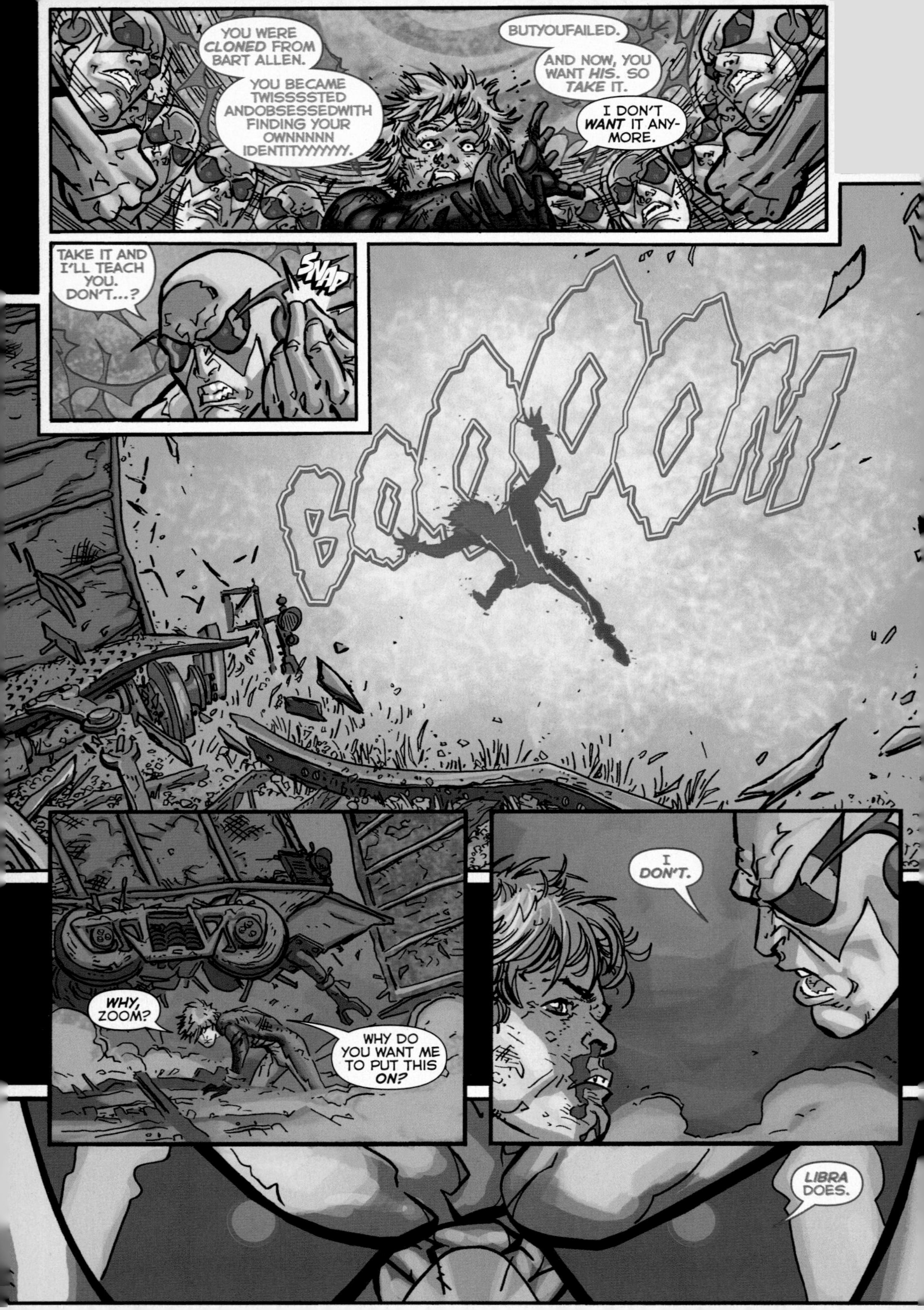
YOU WERE CLONED FROM BART ALLEN.
YOU BECAME TWISSSSTED ANDOBSESSEDWITH FINDING YOUR OWNNNNN IDENTITYYYYYYY.
BUTYOUFAILED.
AND NOW, YOU WANT HIS. SO TAKE IT.
I DON'T WANT IT ANY-MORE.
TAKE IT AND I'LL TEACH YOU. DON'T...?
SNAP
BOOOOOM
WHY, ZOOM?
WHY DO YOU WANT ME TO PUT THIS ON?
I DON'T.
LIBRA DOES.

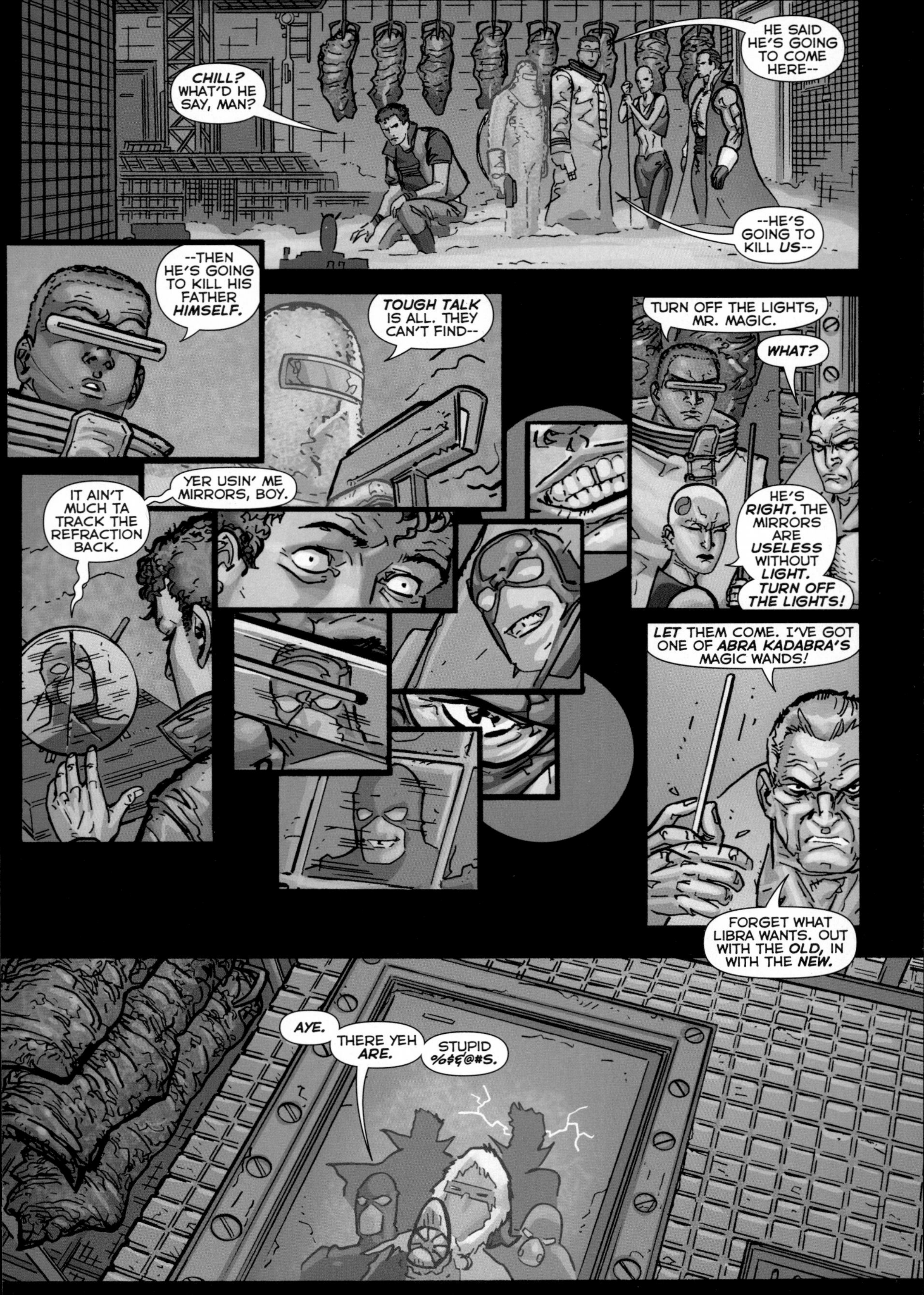

CHILL? WHAT'D HE SAY, MAN?
HE SAID HE'S GOING TO COME HERE--
--HE'S GOING TO KILL US--
--THEN HE'S GOING TO KILL HIS FATHER HIMSELF.
TOUGH TALK IS ALL. THEY CAN'T FIND--
YER USIN' ME MIRRORS, BOY.
IT AIN'T MUCH TA TRACK THE REFRACTION BACK.
TURN OFF THE LIGHTS, MR. MAGIC.
WHAT?
HE'S RIGHT. THE MIRRORS ARE USELESS WITHOUT LIGHT. TURN OFF THE LIGHTS!
LET THEM COME. I'VE GOT ONE OF ABRA KADABRA'S MAGIC WANDS!
FORGET WHAT LIBRA WANTS. OUT WITH THE OLD, IN WITH THE NEW.
AYE.
THERE YEH ARE.
STUPID %$&@#S.

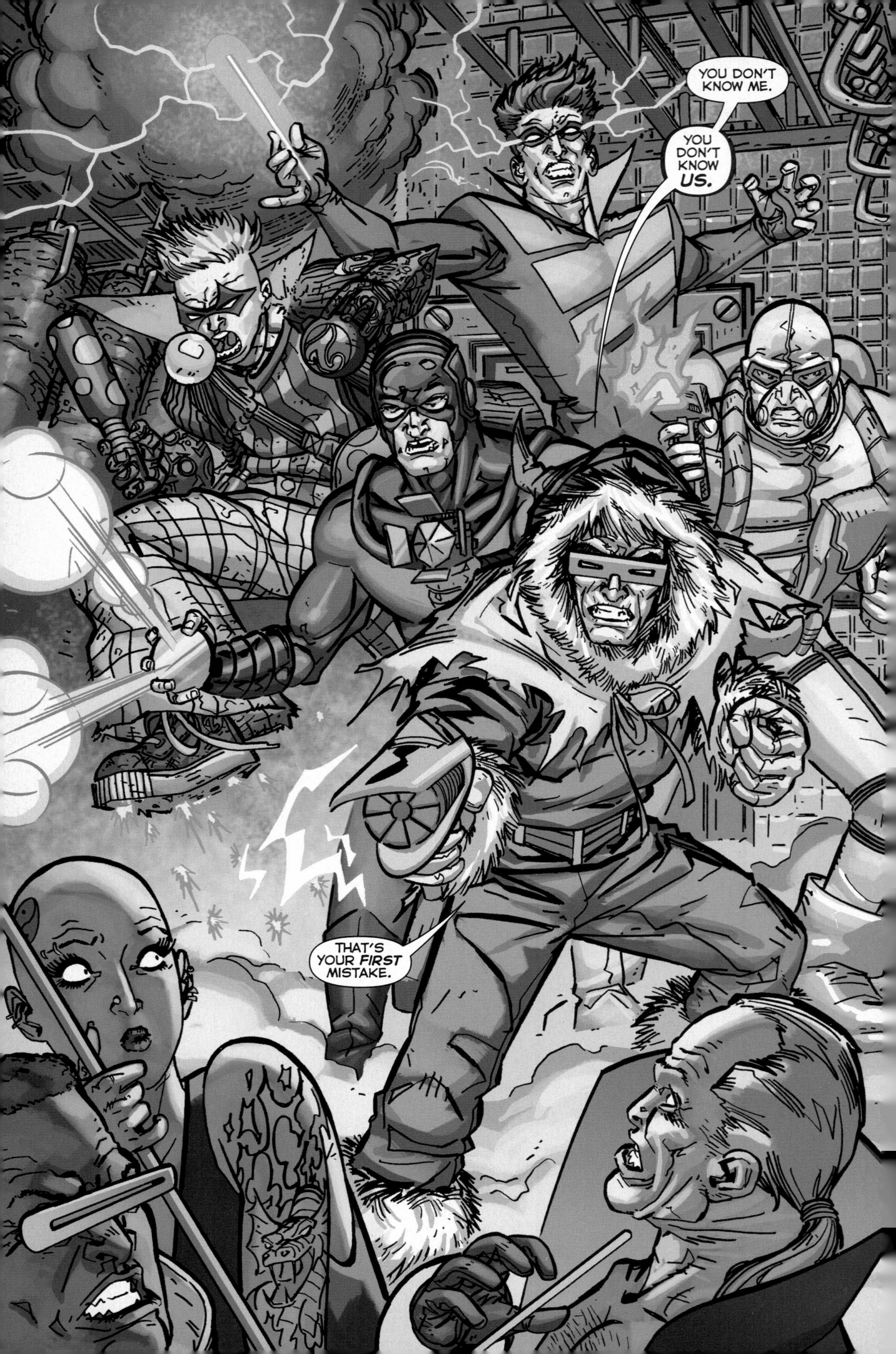
YOU DON'T KNOW ME.
YOU DON'T KNOW US.
THAT'S YOUR FIRST MISTAKE.

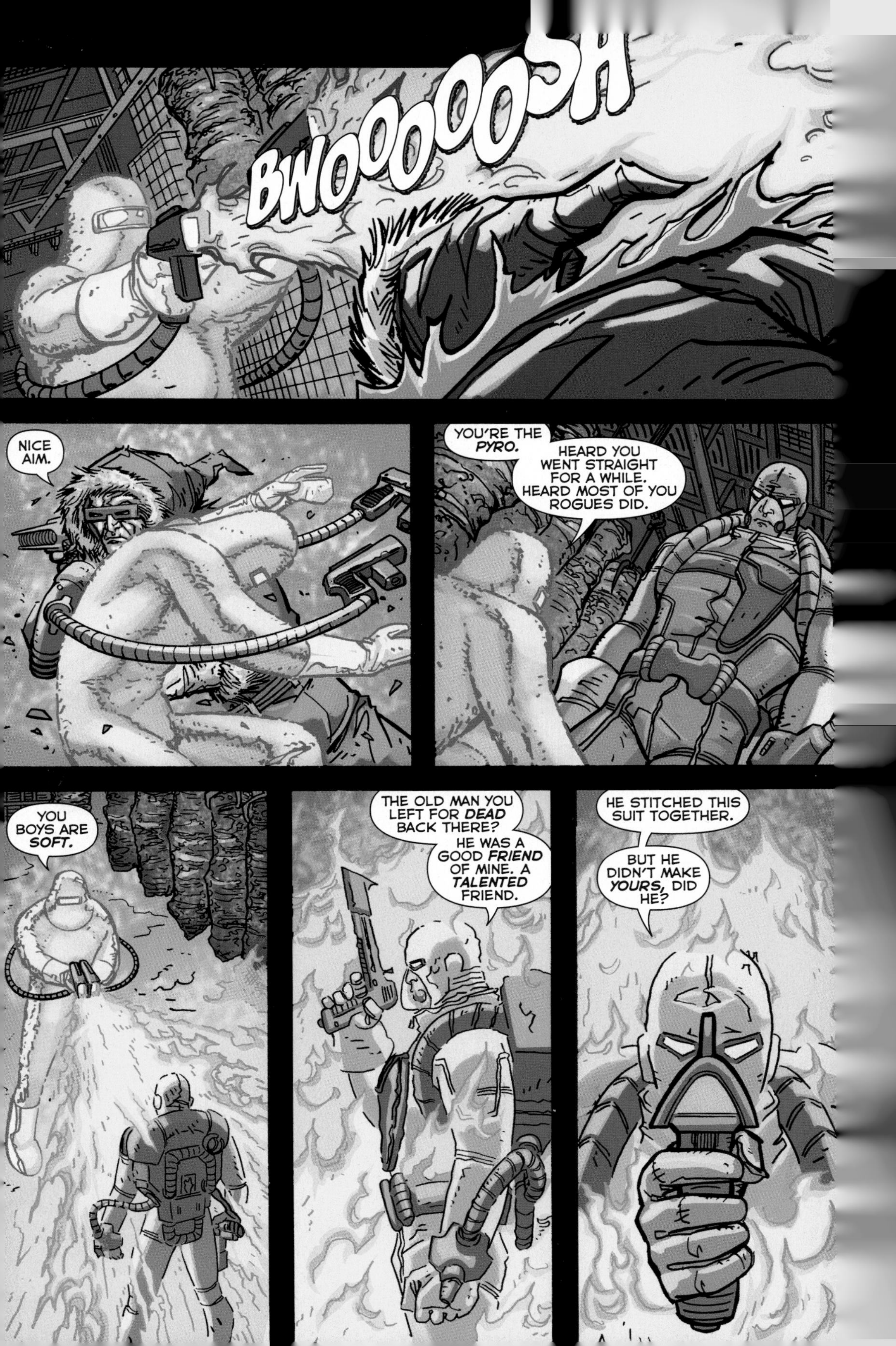
BWOOOOOOSH
NICE AIM.
YOU'RE THE PYRO.
HEARD YOU WENT STRAIGHT FOR A WHILE. HEARD MOST OF YOU ROGUES DID.
YOU BOYS ARE SOFT.
THE OLD MAN YOU LEFT FOR DEAD BACK THERE?
HE WAS A GOOD FRIEND OF MINE. A TALENTED FRIEND.
HE STITCHED THIS SUIT TOGETHER.
BUT HE DIDN'T MAKE YOURS, DID HE?

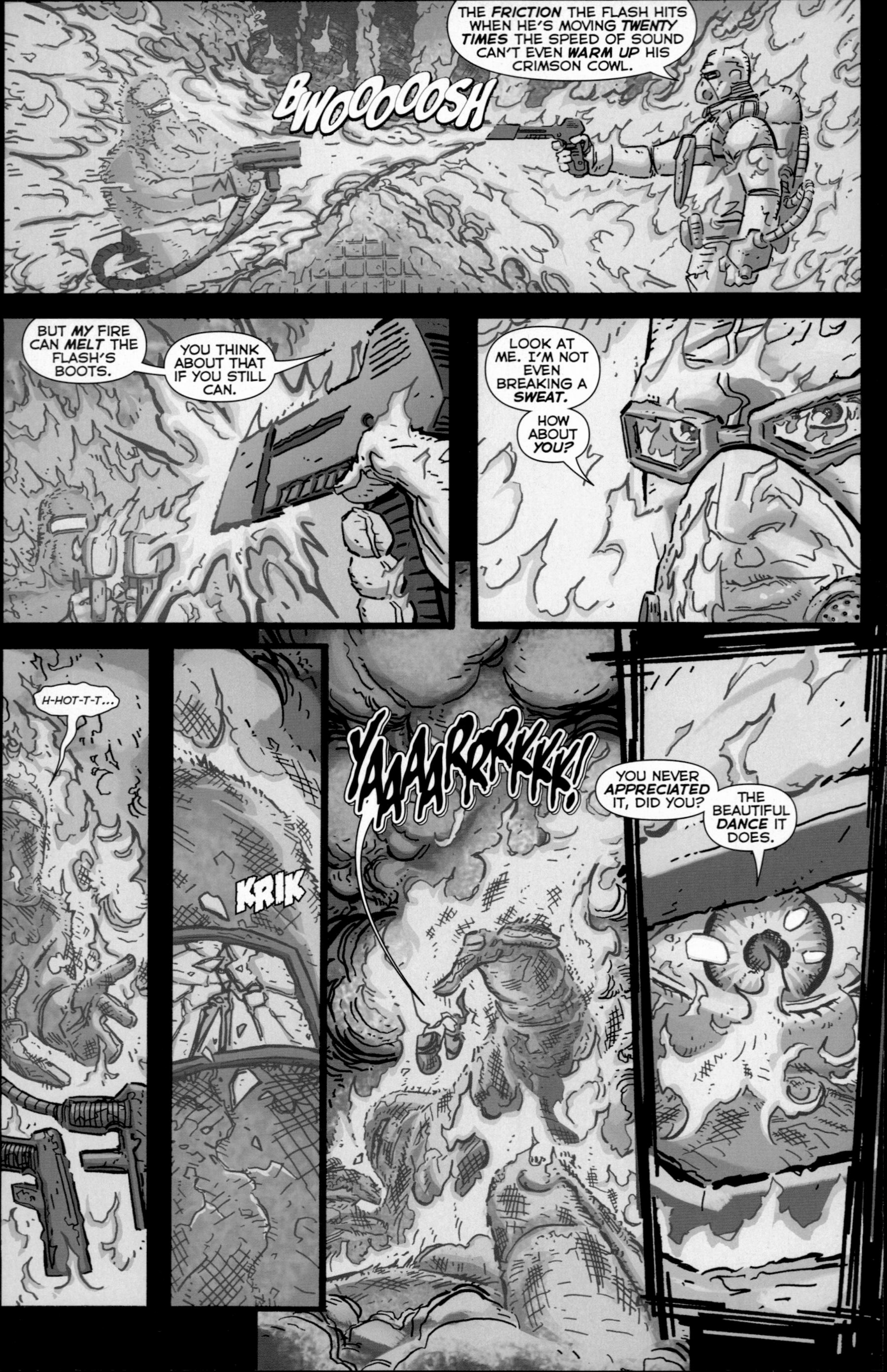
THE FRICTION THE FLASH HITS WHEN HE'S MOVING TWENTY TIMES THE SPEED OF SOUND CAN'T EVEN WARM UP HIS CRIMSON COWL.
BWOOOOOOSH
BUT MY FIRE CAN MELT THE FLASH'S BOOTS.
YOU THINK ABOUT THAT IF YOU STILL CAN.
LOOK AT ME. I'M NOT EVEN BREAKING A SWEAT.
HOW ABOUT YOU?
H-HOT-T-T...
KRIK
YAAAARRRKKK!
YOU NEVER APPRECIATED IT, DID YOU?
THE BEAUTIFUL DANCE IT DOES.

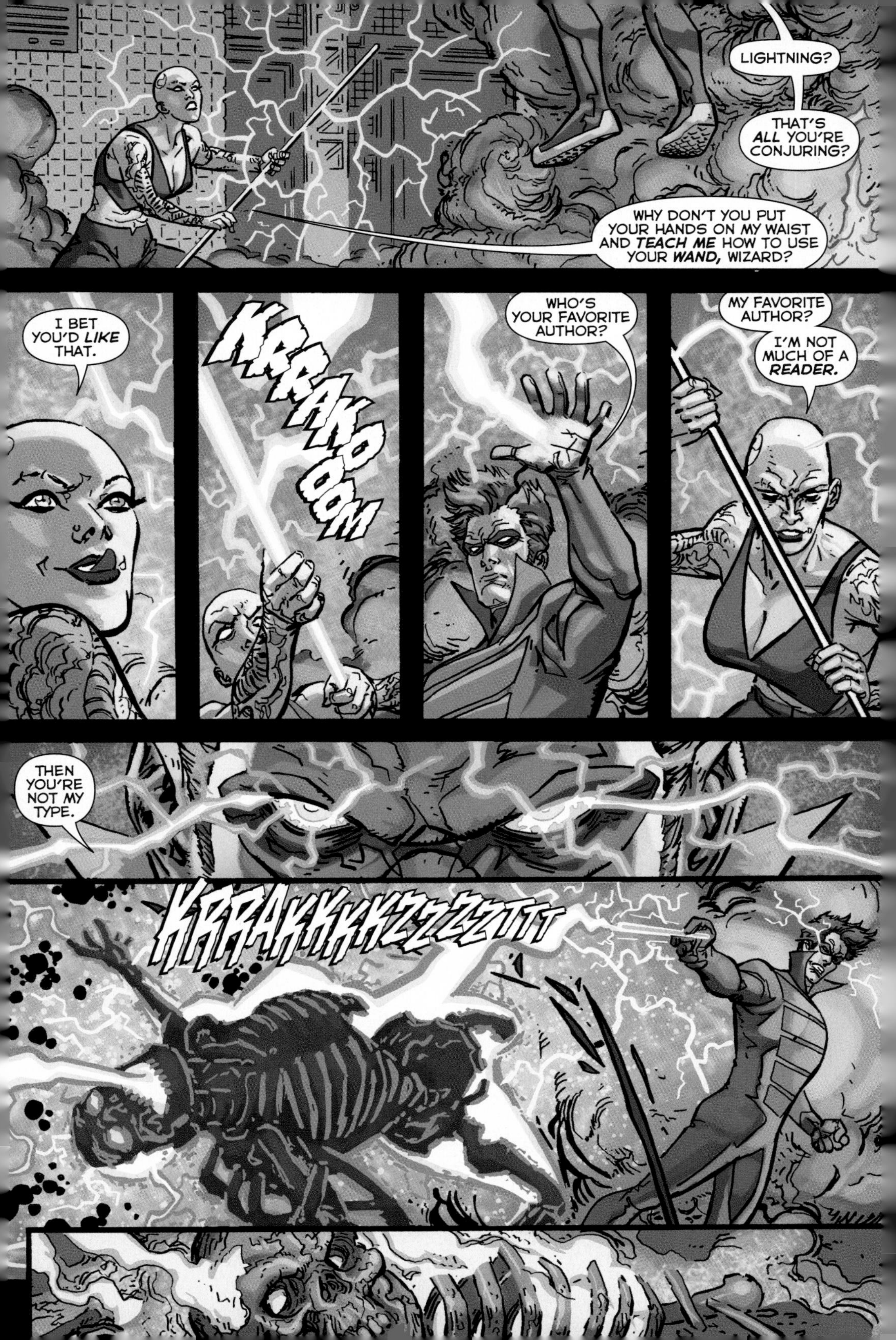
LIGHTNING?
THAT'S ALL YOU'RE CONJURING?
WHY DON'T YOU PUT YOUR HANDS ON MY WAIST AND TEACH ME HOW TO USE YOUR WAND, WIZARD?
I BET YOU'D LIKE THAT.
KRRAKOOOM
WHO'S YOUR FAVORITE AUTHOR?
MY FAVORITE AUTHOR?
I'M NOT MUCH OF A READER.
THEN YOU'RE NOT MY TYPE.
KRRAKKKKKZZZZZTTTT

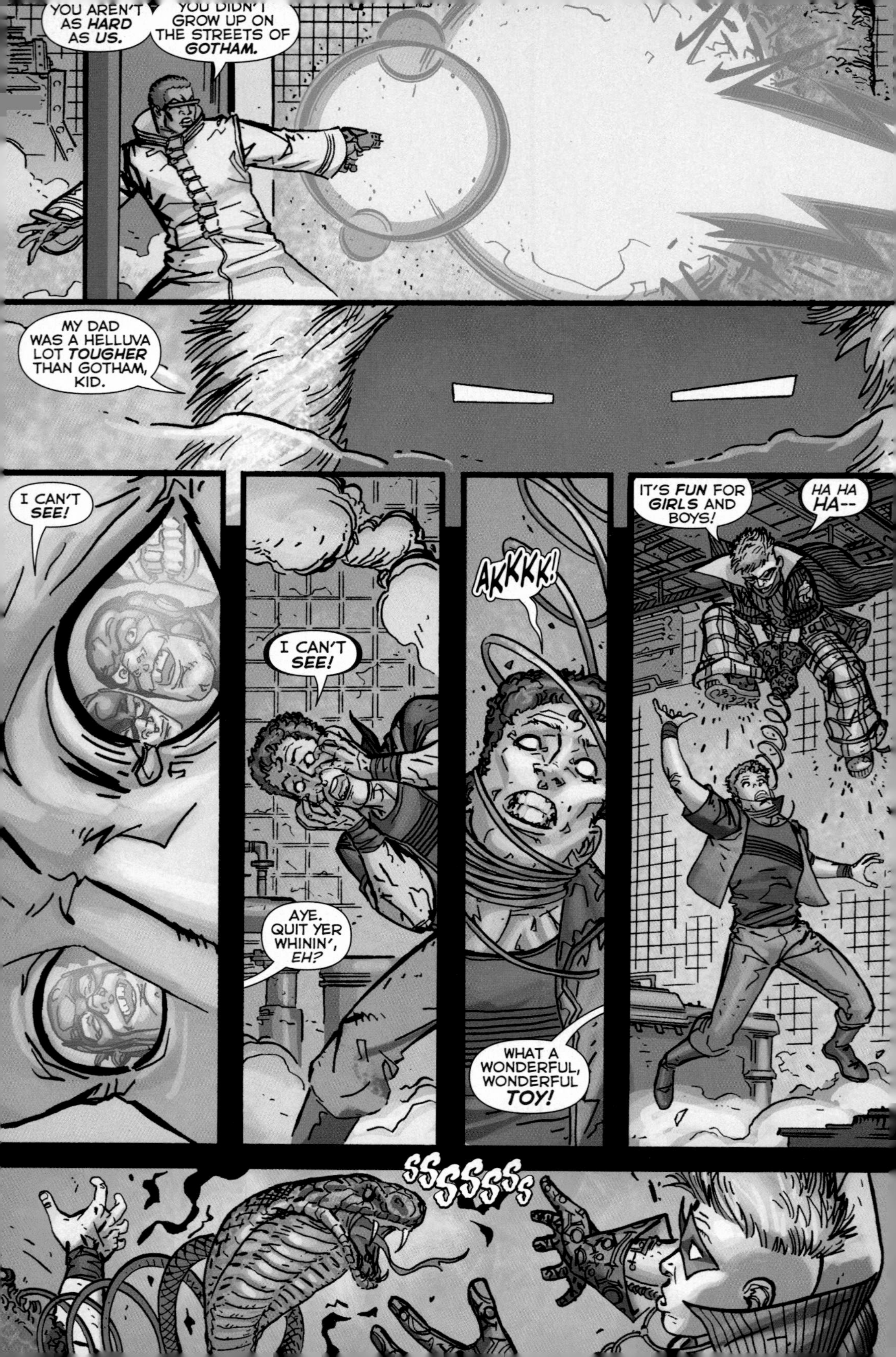
YOU AREN'T AS HARD AS US.
YOU DIDN'T GROW UP ON THE STREETS OF GOTHAM.
MY DAD WAS A HELLUVA LOT TOUGHER THAN GOTHAM, KID.
I CAN'T SEE!
I CAN'T SEE!
AYE. QUIT YER WHININ', EH?
AKKKK!
WHAT A WONDERFUL, WONDERFUL TOY!
IT'S FUN FOR GIRLS AND BOYS!
HA HA HA--
SSSSSSSS

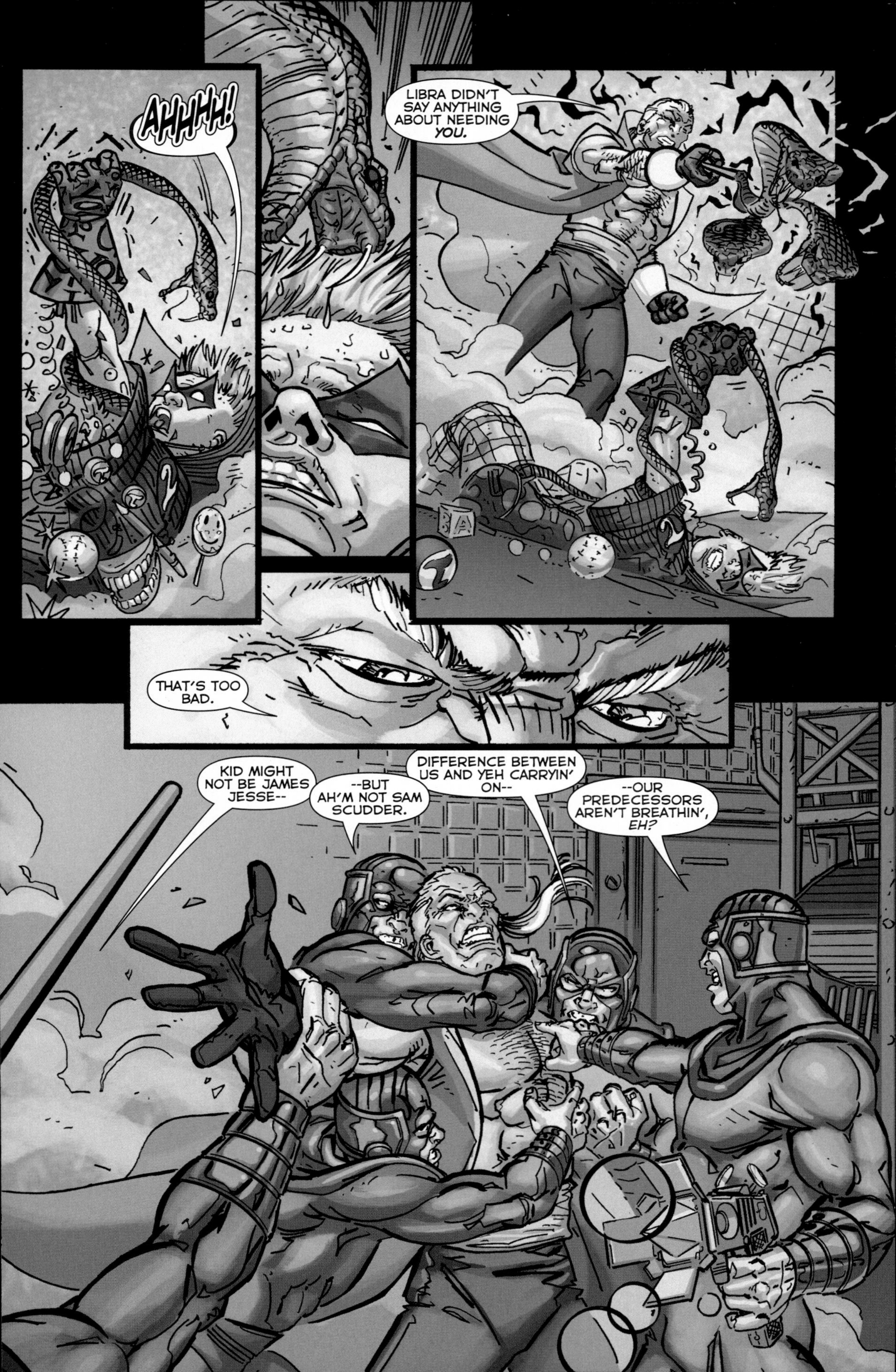
AHHHH!
LIBRA DIDN'T SAY ANYTHING ABOUT NEEDING *YOU.*
THAT'S TOO BAD.
KID MIGHT NOT BE JAMES JESSE--
--BUT AH'M NOT SAM SCUDDER.
DIFFERENCE BETWEEN US AND YEH CARRYIN' ON--
--OUR PREDECESSORS AREN'T BREATHIN', *EH?*

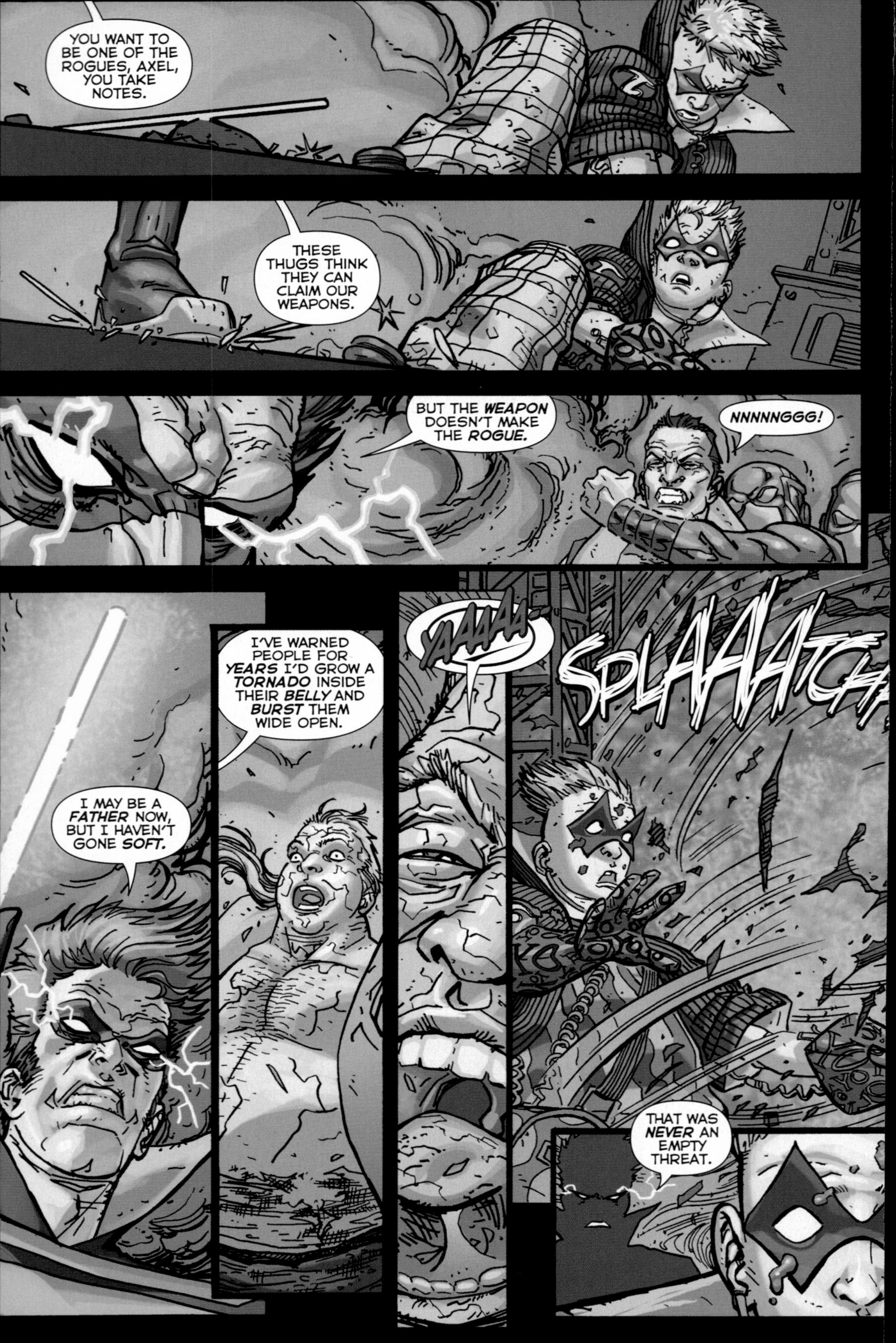
YOU WANT TO BE ONE OF THE ROGUES, AXEL, YOU TAKE NOTES.
THESE THUGS THINK THEY CAN CLAIM OUR WEAPONS.
BUT THE WEAPON DOESN'T MAKE THE ROGUE.
NNNNNGGG!
I MAY BE A FATHER NOW, BUT I HAVEN'T GONE SOFT.
I'VE WARNED PEOPLE FOR YEARS I'D GROW A TORNADO INSIDE THEIR BELLY AND BURST THEM WIDE OPEN.
YAAAA
SPLAAATCH
THAT WAS NEVER AN EMPTY THREAT.

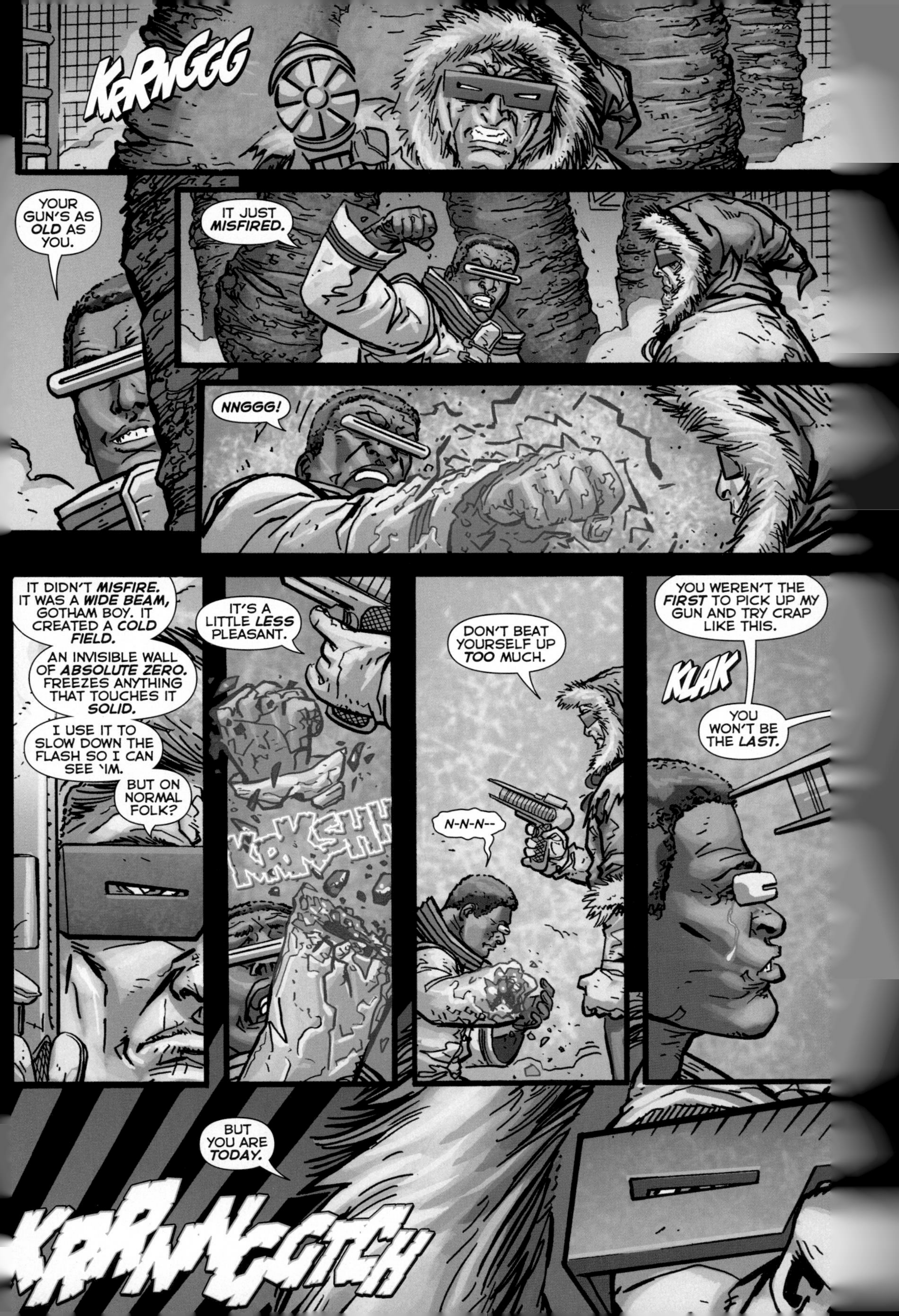
KRRNGGG
YOUR GUN'S AS OLD AS YOU.
IT JUST MISFIRED.
NNGGG!
IT DIDN'T MISFIRE. IT WAS A WIDE BEAM, GOTHAM BOY. IT CREATED A COLD FIELD.
AN INVISIBLE WALL OF ABSOLUTE ZERO. FREEZES ANYTHING THAT TOUCHES IT SOLID.
I USE IT TO SLOW DOWN THE FLASH SO I CAN SEE 'IM.
BUT ON NORMAL FOLK?
IT'S A LITTLE LESS PLEASANT.
KRKSHH
DON'T BEAT YOURSELF UP TOO MUCH.
N-N-N--
YOU WEREN'T THE FIRST TO PICK UP MY GUN AND TRY CRAP LIKE THIS.
KLAK
YOU WON'T BE THE LAST.
BUT YOU ARE TODAY.
KRRNGGTCH

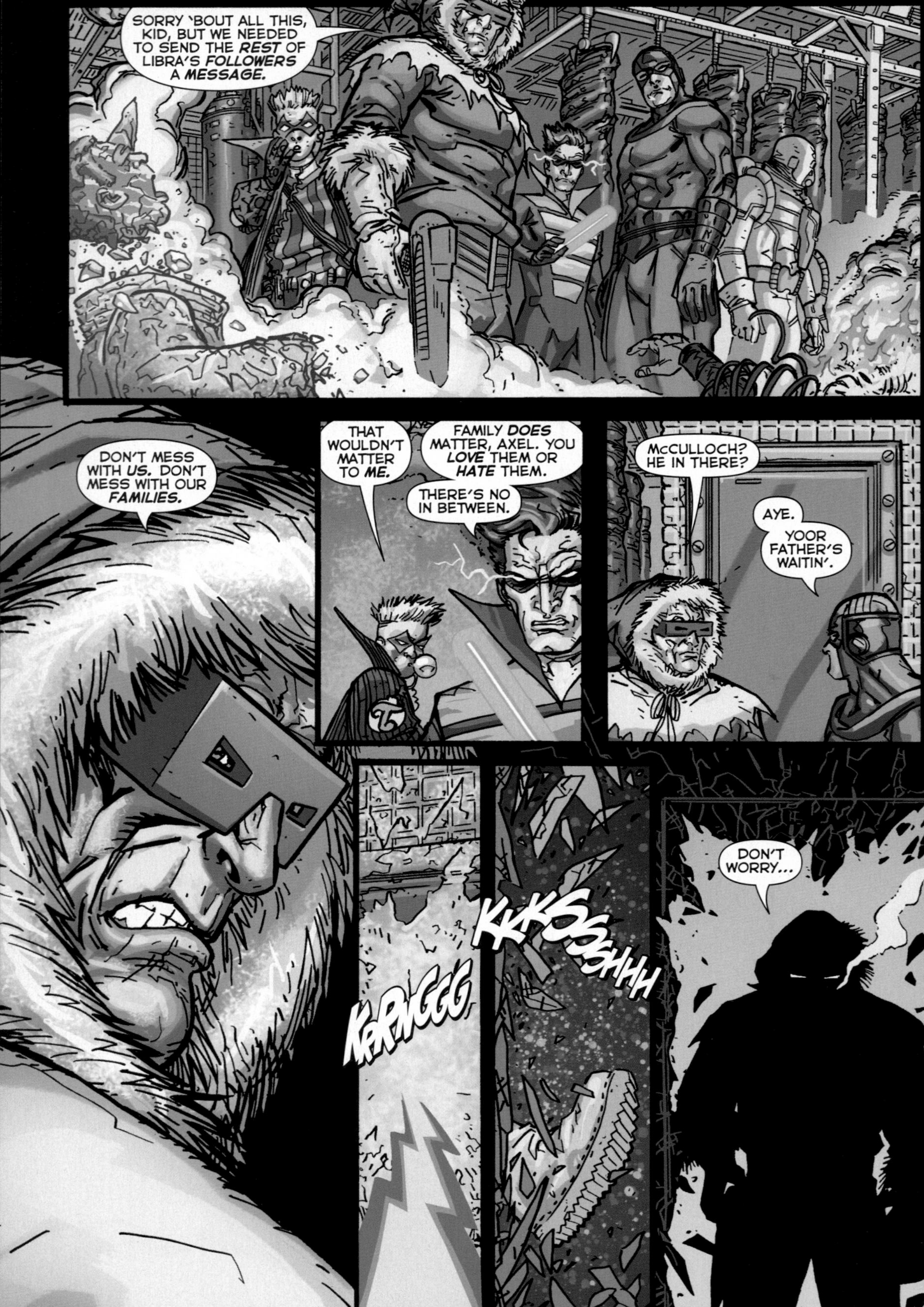
SORRY 'BOUT ALL THIS, KID, BUT WE NEEDED TO SEND THE REST OF LIBRA'S FOLLOWERS A MESSAGE.
DON'T MESS WITH US. DON'T MESS WITH OUR FAMILIES.
THAT WOULDN'T MATTER TO ME.
FAMILY DOES MATTER, AXEL. YOU LOVE THEM OR HATE THEM.
THERE'S NO IN BETWEEN.
McCULLOCH? HE IN THERE?
AYE.
YOOR FATHER'S WAITIN'.
KRRNGGG
KKKSSSHHH
DON'T WORRY...

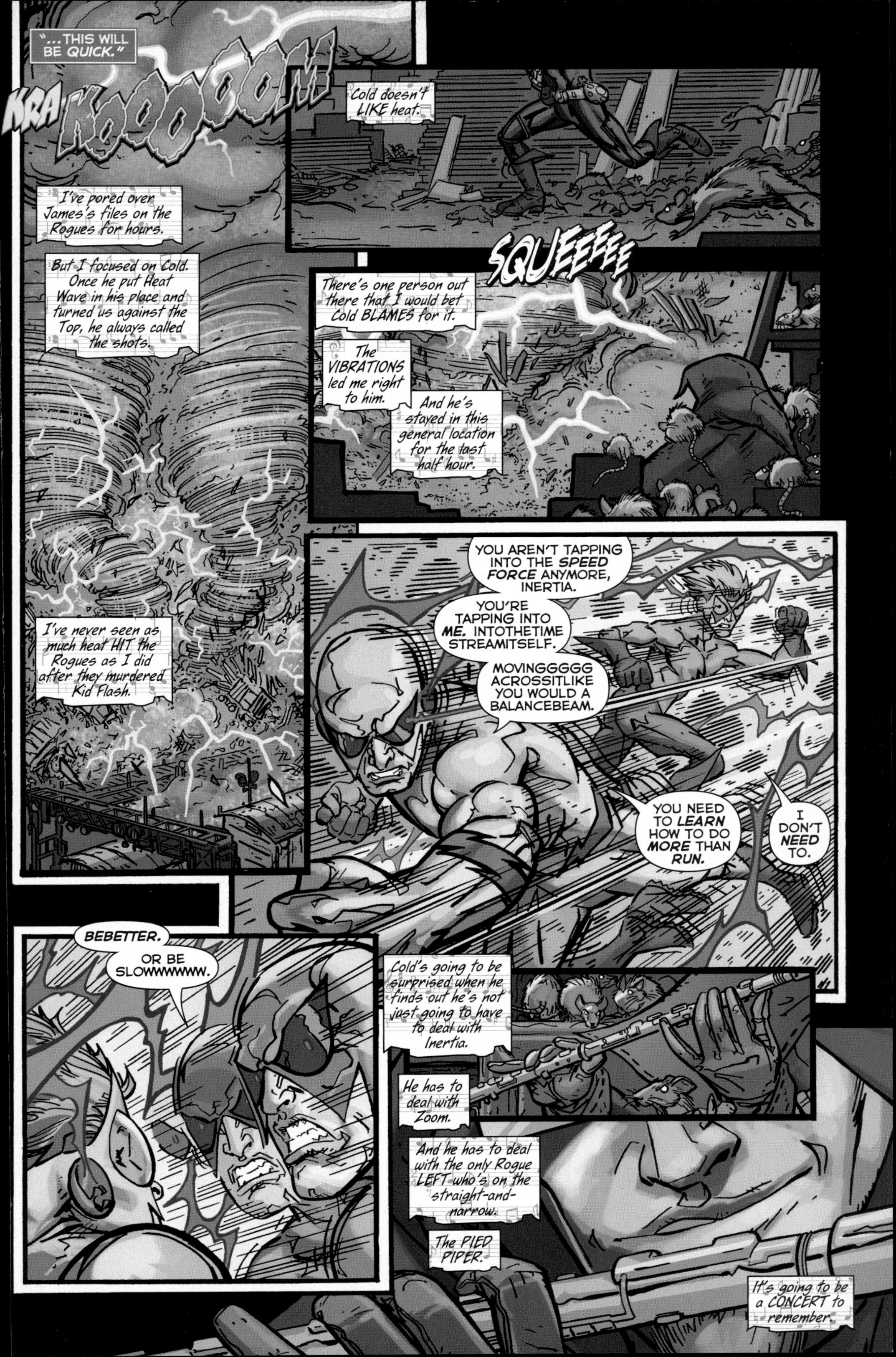
"...THIS WILL BE QUICK."
KRAKOOOOOOM
Cold doesn't LIKE heat.
I've pored over James's files on the Rogues for hours.
But I focused on Cold. Once he put Heat Wave in his place and turned us against the Top, he always called the shots.
SQUEEEEEE
There's one person out there that I would bet Cold BLAMES for it.
The VIBRATIONS led me right to him.
And he's stayed in this general location for the last half hour.
I've never seen as much heat HIT the Rogues as I did after they murdered Kid Flash.
YOU AREN'T TAPPING INTO THE SPEED FORCE ANYMORE, INERTIA.
YOU'RE TAPPING INTO ME. INTOTHETIME STREAMITSELF.
MOVINGGGGG ACROSSITLIKE YOU WOULD A BALANCEBEAM.
YOU NEED TO LEARN HOW TO DO MORE THAN RUN.
I DON'T NEED TO.
BEBETTER.
OR BE SLOWWWWWW.
Cold's going to be surprised when he finds out he's not just going to have to deal with Inertia.
He has to deal with Zoom.
And he has to deal with the only Rogue LEFT who's on the straight-and-narrow.
The PIED PIPER.
It's going to be a CONCERT to remember.

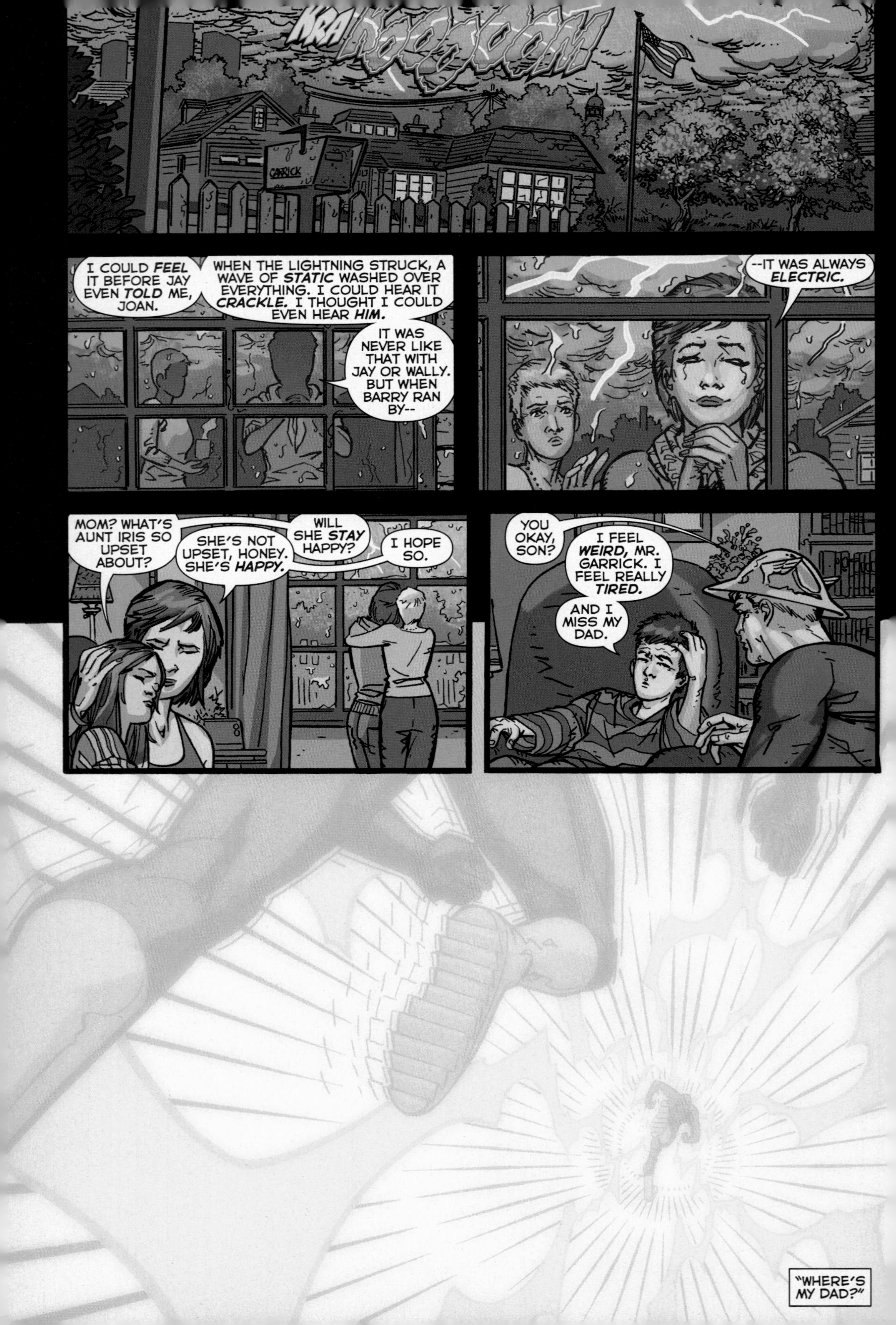
KRA BOOOOOOM
GARRICK
I COULD FEEL IT BEFORE JAY EVEN TOLD ME, JOAN.
WHEN THE LIGHTNING STRUCK, A WAVE OF STATIC WASHED OVER EVERYTHING. I COULD HEAR IT CRACKLE. I THOUGHT I COULD EVEN HEAR HIM.
IT WAS NEVER LIKE THAT WITH JAY OR WALLY. BUT WHEN BARRY RAN BY--
--IT WAS ALWAYS ELECTRIC.
MOM? WHAT'S AUNT IRIS SO UPSET ABOUT?
SHE'S NOT UPSET, HONEY. SHE'S HAPPY.
WILL SHE STAY HAPPY?
I HOPE SO.
YOU OKAY, SON?
I FEEL WEIRD, MR. GARRICK. I FEEL REALLY TIRED.
AND I MISS MY DAD.
"WHERE'S MY DAD?"

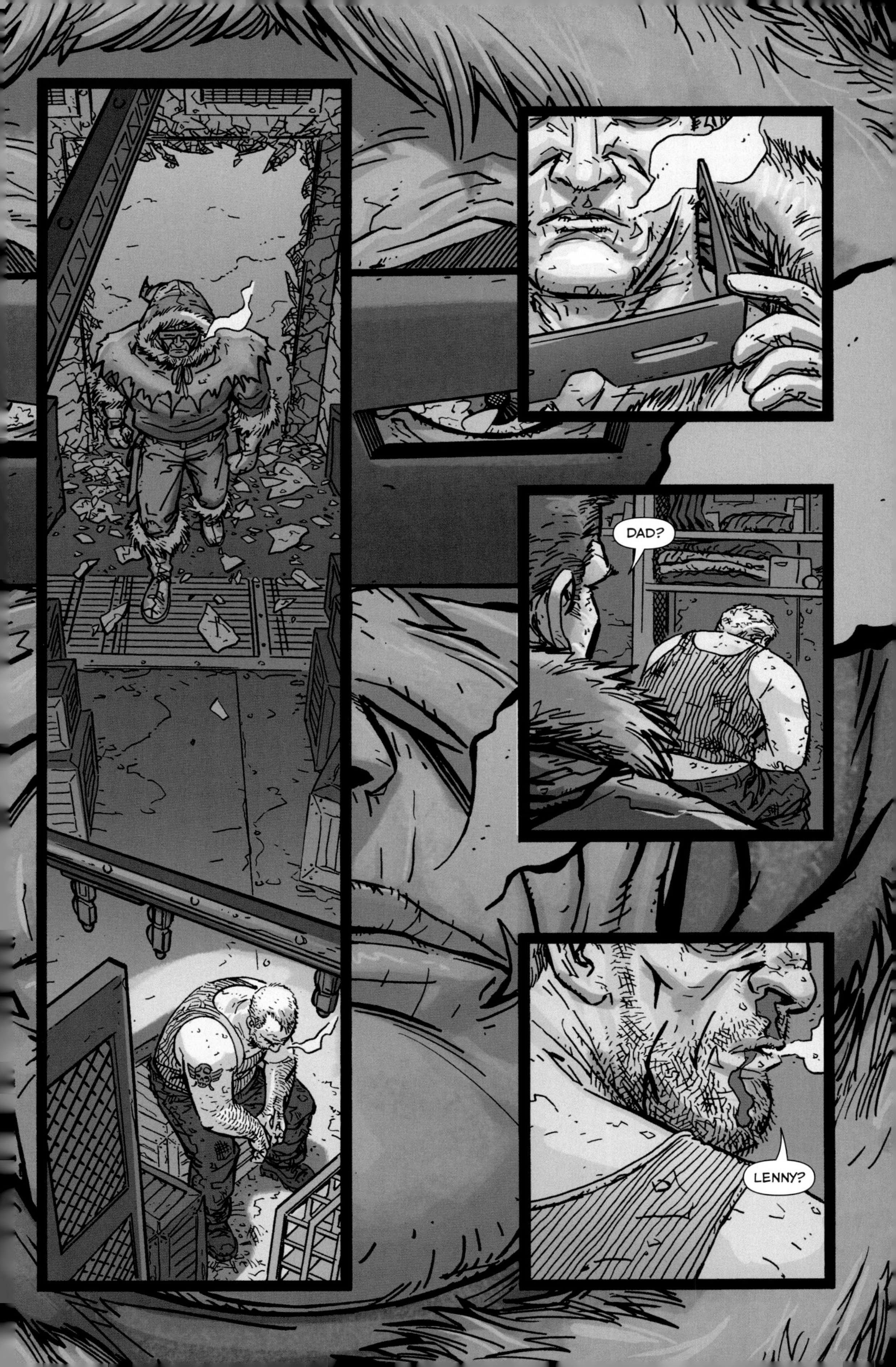
DAD?
LENNY?

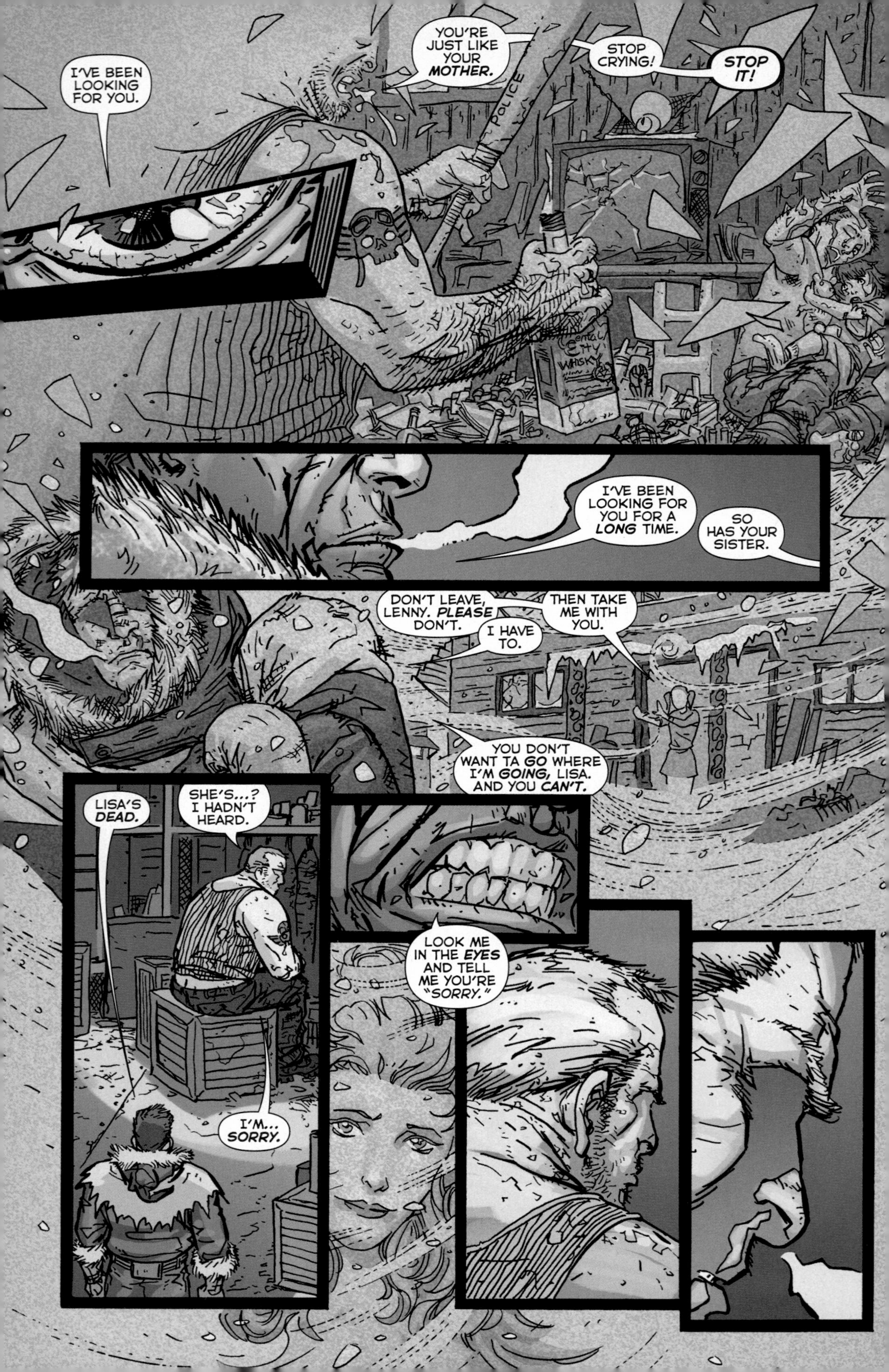
I'VE BEEN LOOKING FOR YOU.
YOU'RE JUST LIKE YOUR MOTHER.
STOP CRYING!
STOP IT!
I'VE BEEN LOOKING FOR YOU FOR A LONG TIME.
SO HAS YOUR SISTER.
DON'T LEAVE, LENNY. PLEASE DON'T.
I HAVE TO.
THEN TAKE ME WITH YOU.
YOU DON'T WANT TA GO WHERE I'M GOING, LISA. AND YOU CAN'T.
LISA'S DEAD.
SHE'S...? I HADN'T HEARD.
I'M... SORRY.
LOOK ME IN THE EYES AND TELL ME YOU'RE "SORRY."

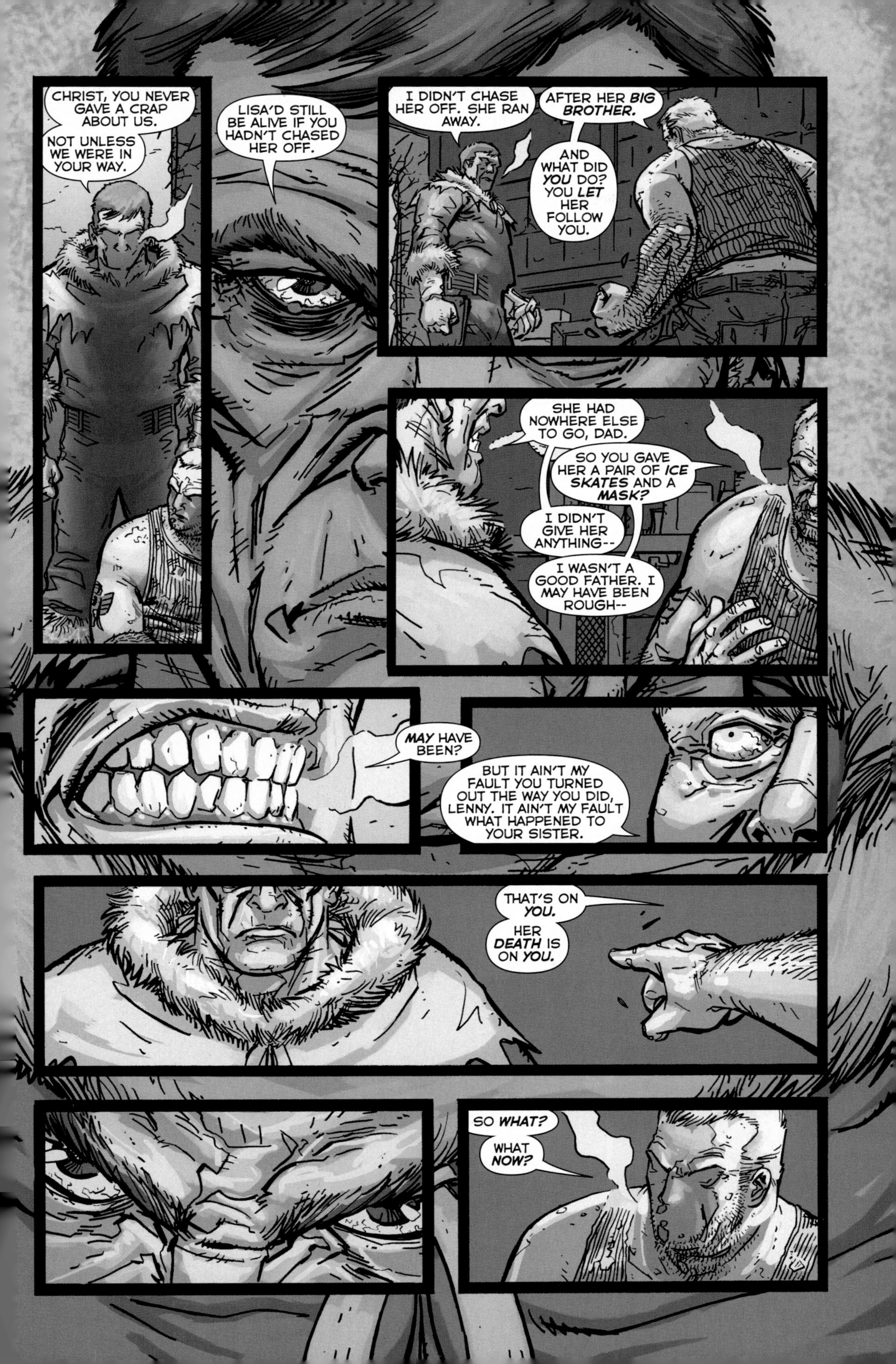
CHRIST, YOU NEVER GAVE A CRAP ABOUT US.
NOT UNLESS WE WERE IN YOUR WAY.
LISA'D STILL BE ALIVE IF YOU HADN'T CHASED HER OFF.
I DIDN'T CHASE HER OFF. SHE RAN AWAY.
AFTER HER BIG BROTHER.
AND WHAT DID YOU DO? YOU LET HER FOLLOW YOU.
SHE HAD NOWHERE ELSE TO GO, DAD.
SO YOU GAVE HER A PAIR OF ICE SKATES AND A MASK?
I DIDN'T GIVE HER ANYTHING--
I WASN'T A GOOD FATHER. I MAY HAVE BEEN ROUGH--
MAY HAVE BEEN?
BUT IT AIN'T MY FAULT YOU TURNED OUT THE WAY YOU DID, LENNY. IT AIN'T MY FAULT WHAT HAPPENED TO YOUR SISTER.
THAT'S ON YOU.
HER DEATH IS ON YOU.
SO WHAT?
WHAT NOW?

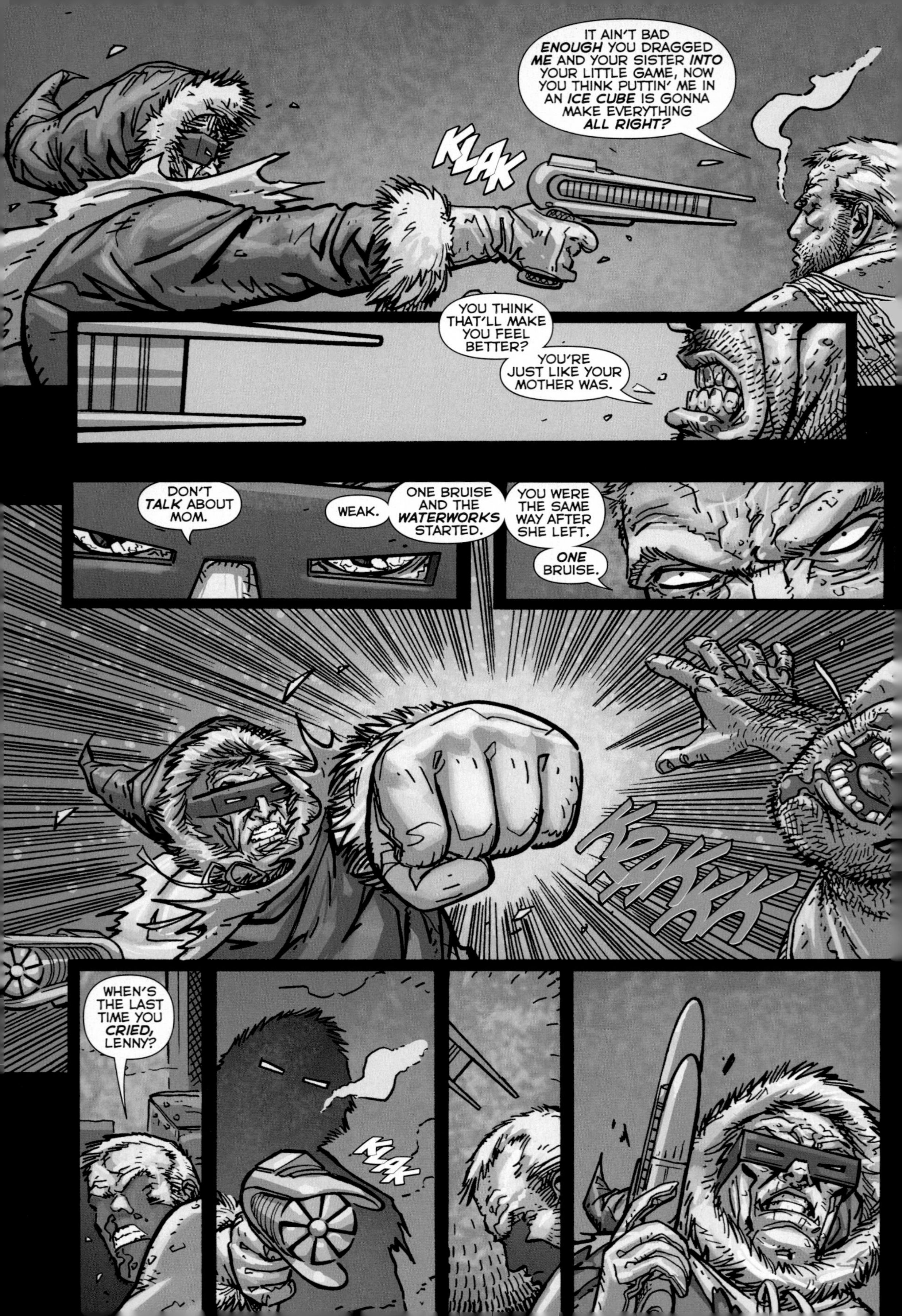
IT AIN'T BAD ENOUGH YOU DRAGGED ME AND YOUR SISTER INTO YOUR LITTLE GAME, NOW YOU THINK PUTTIN' ME IN AN ICE CUBE IS GONNA MAKE EVERYTHING ALL RIGHT?
KLAK
YOU THINK THAT'LL MAKE YOU FEEL BETTER?
YOU'RE JUST LIKE YOUR MOTHER WAS.
DON'T TALK ABOUT MOM.
WEAK.
ONE BRUISE AND THE WATERWORKS STARTED.
YOU WERE THE SAME WAY AFTER SHE LEFT.
ONE BRUISE.
KRAKKK
WHEN'S THE LAST TIME YOU CRIED, LENNY?
KLAK

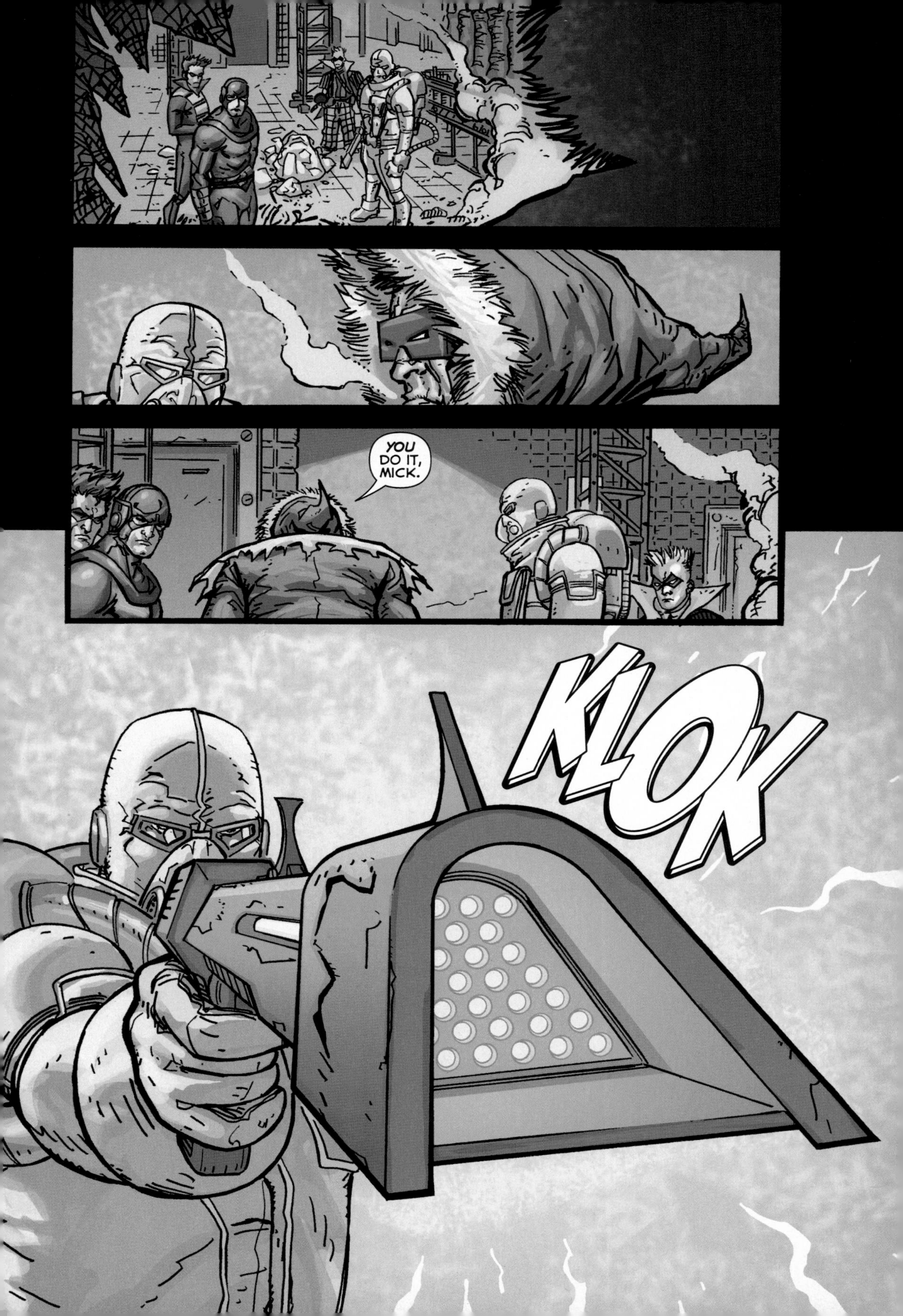
YOU DO IT, MICK.
KLOK

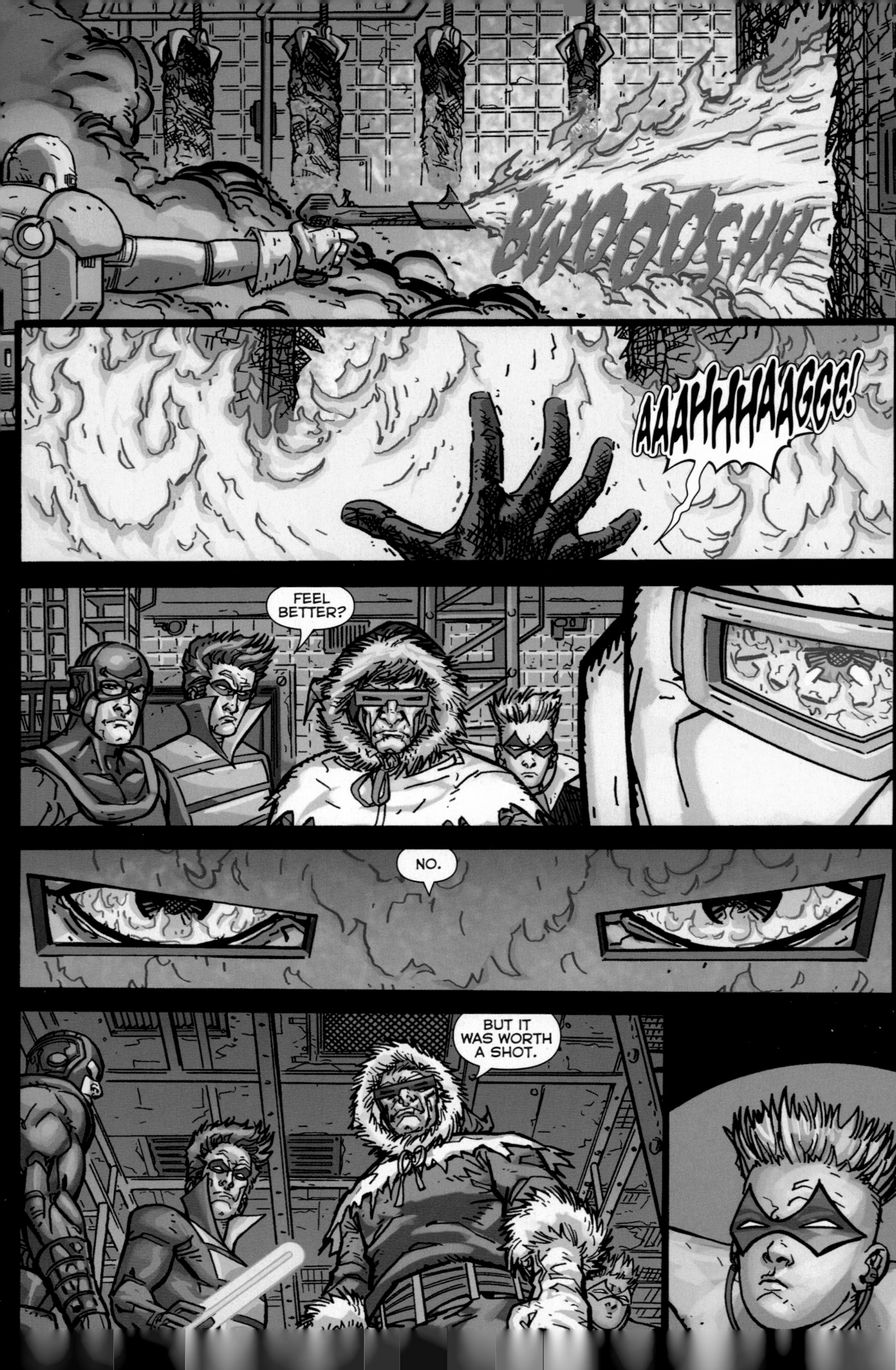
BWOOOSHH
AAAHHHAAGGG!
FEEL BETTER?
NO.
BUT IT WAS WORTH A SHOT.

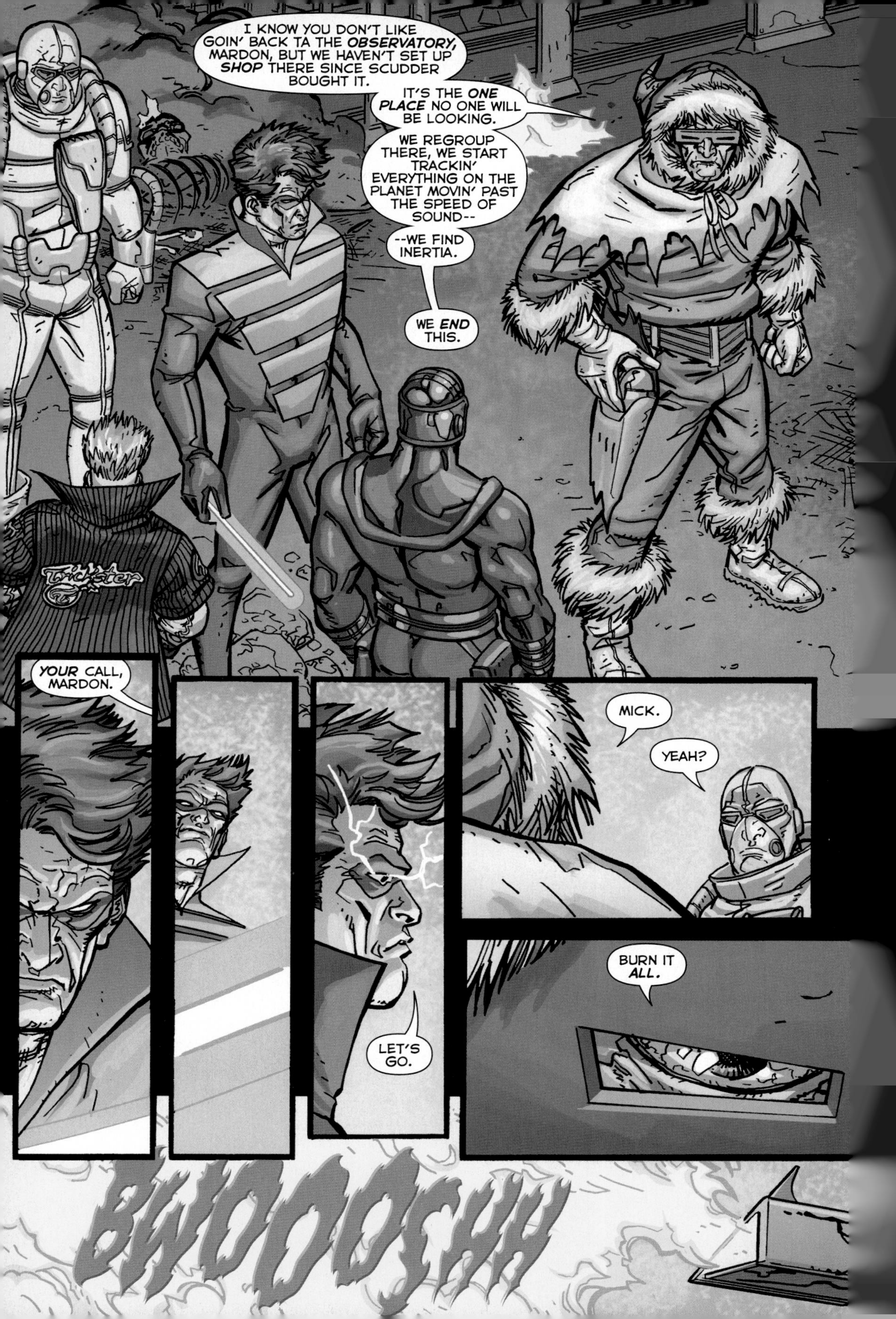
I KNOW YOU DON'T LIKE GOIN' BACK TA THE **OBSERVATORY,** MARDON, BUT WE HAVEN'T SET UP **SHOP** THERE SINCE SCUDDER BOUGHT IT.
IT'S THE **ONE PLACE** NO ONE WILL BE LOOKING.
WE REGROUP THERE, WE START TRACKIN' EVERYTHING ON THE PLANET MOVIN' PAST THE SPEED OF SOUND--
--WE FIND INERTIA.
WE **END** THIS.
YOUR CALL, MARDON.
LET'S GO.
MICK.
YEAH?
BURN IT **ALL.**
BWOOOSHH

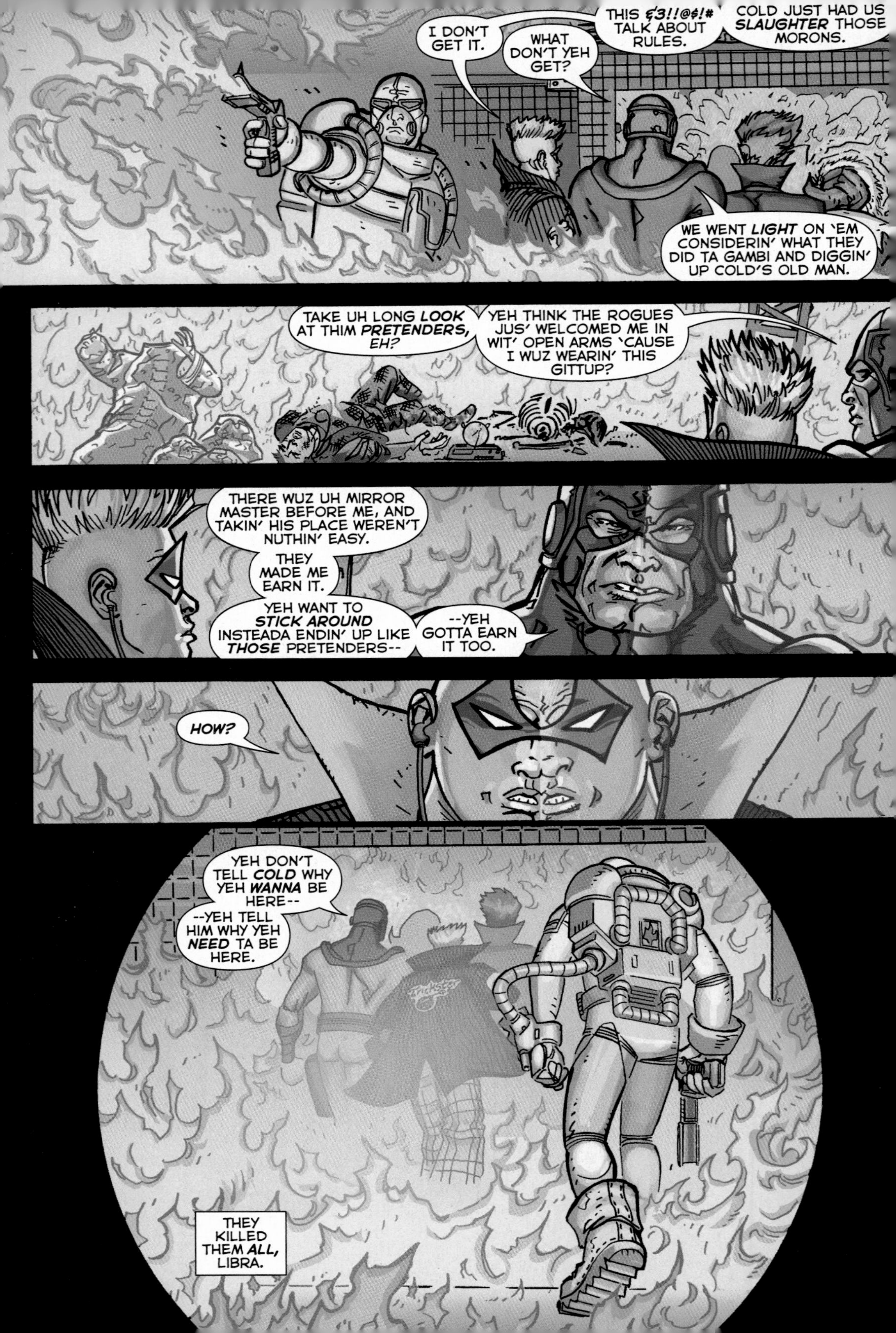
I DON'T GET IT.
WHAT DON'T YEH GET?
THIS €3!!@$!# TALK ABOUT RULES.
COLD JUST HAD US SLAUGHTER THOSE MORONS.
WE WENT LIGHT ON 'EM CONSIDERIN' WHAT THEY DID TA GAMBI AND DIGGIN' UP COLD'S OLD MAN.
TAKE UH LONG LOOK AT THIM PRETENDERS, EH?
YEH THINK THE ROGUES JUS' WELCOMED ME IN WIT' OPEN ARMS 'CAUSE I WUZ WEARIN' THIS GITTUP?
THERE WUZ UH MIRROR MASTER BEFORE ME, AND TAKIN' HIS PLACE WEREN'T NUTHIN' EASY.
THEY MADE ME EARN IT.
YEH WANT TO STICK AROUND INSTEADA ENDIN' UP LIKE THOSE PRETENDERS--
--YEH GOTTA EARN IT TOO.
HOW?
YEH DON'T TELL COLD WHY YEH WANNA BE HERE--
--YEH TELL HIM WHY YEH NEED TA BE HERE.
THEY KILLED THEM ALL, LIBRA.

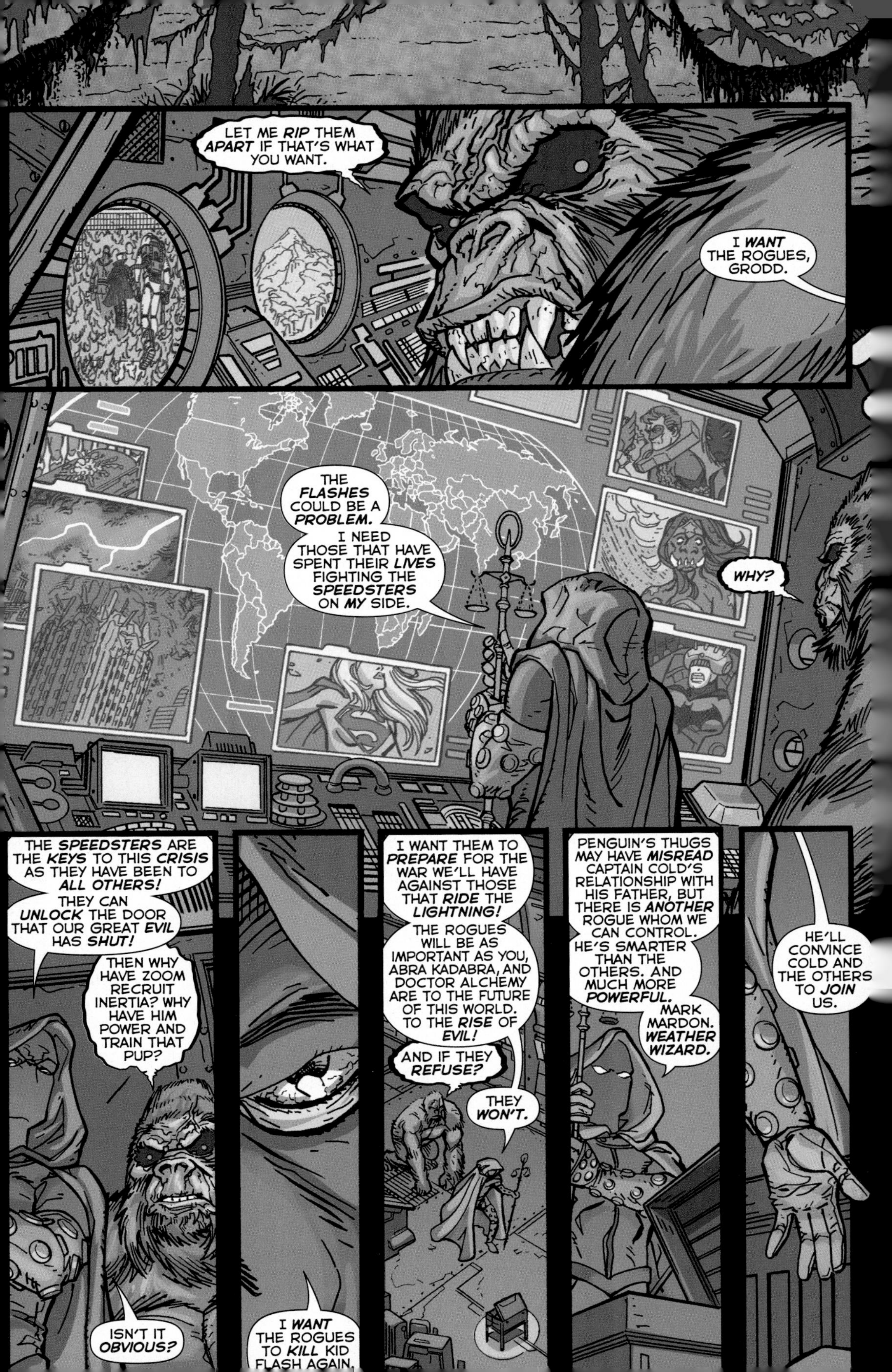

LET ME RIP THEM APART IF THAT'S WHAT YOU WANT.
I WANT THE ROGUES, GRODD.
THE FLASHES COULD BE A PROBLEM.
I NEED THOSE THAT HAVE SPENT THEIR LIVES FIGHTING THE SPEEDSTERS ON MY SIDE.
WHY?
THE SPEEDSTERS ARE THE KEYS TO THIS CRISIS AS THEY HAVE BEEN TO ALL OTHERS!
THEY CAN UNLOCK THE DOOR THAT OUR GREAT EVIL HAS SHUT!
THEN WHY HAVE ZOOM RECRUIT INERTIA? WHY HAVE HIM POWER AND TRAIN THAT PUP?
ISN'T IT OBVIOUS?
I WANT THE ROGUES TO KILL KID FLASH AGAIN.
I WANT THEM TO PREPARE FOR THE WAR WE'LL HAVE AGAINST THOSE THAT RIDE THE LIGHTNING!
THE ROGUES WILL BE AS IMPORTANT AS YOU, ABRA KADABRA, AND DOCTOR ALCHEMY ARE TO THE FUTURE OF THIS WORLD. TO THE RISE OF EVIL!
AND IF THEY REFUSE?
THEY WON'T.
PENGUIN'S THUGS MAY HAVE MISREAD CAPTAIN COLD'S RELATIONSHIP WITH HIS FATHER, BUT THERE IS ANOTHER ROGUE WHOM WE CAN CONTROL.
HE'S SMARTER THAN THE OTHERS. AND MUCH MORE POWERFUL.
MARK MARDON. WEATHER WIZARD.
HE'LL CONVINCE COLD AND THE OTHERS TO JOIN US.

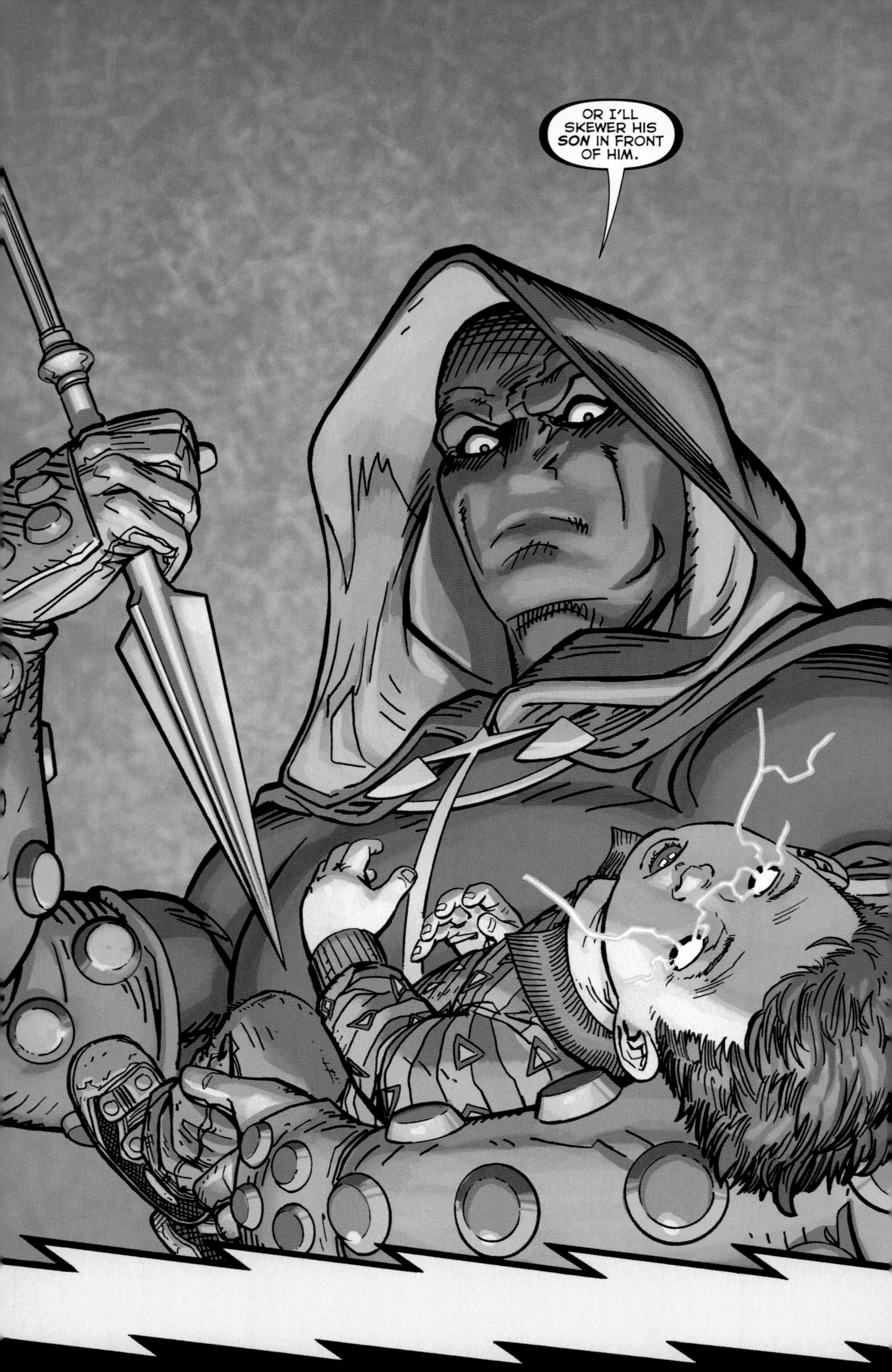
OR I'LL SKEWER HIS SON IN FRONT OF HIM.

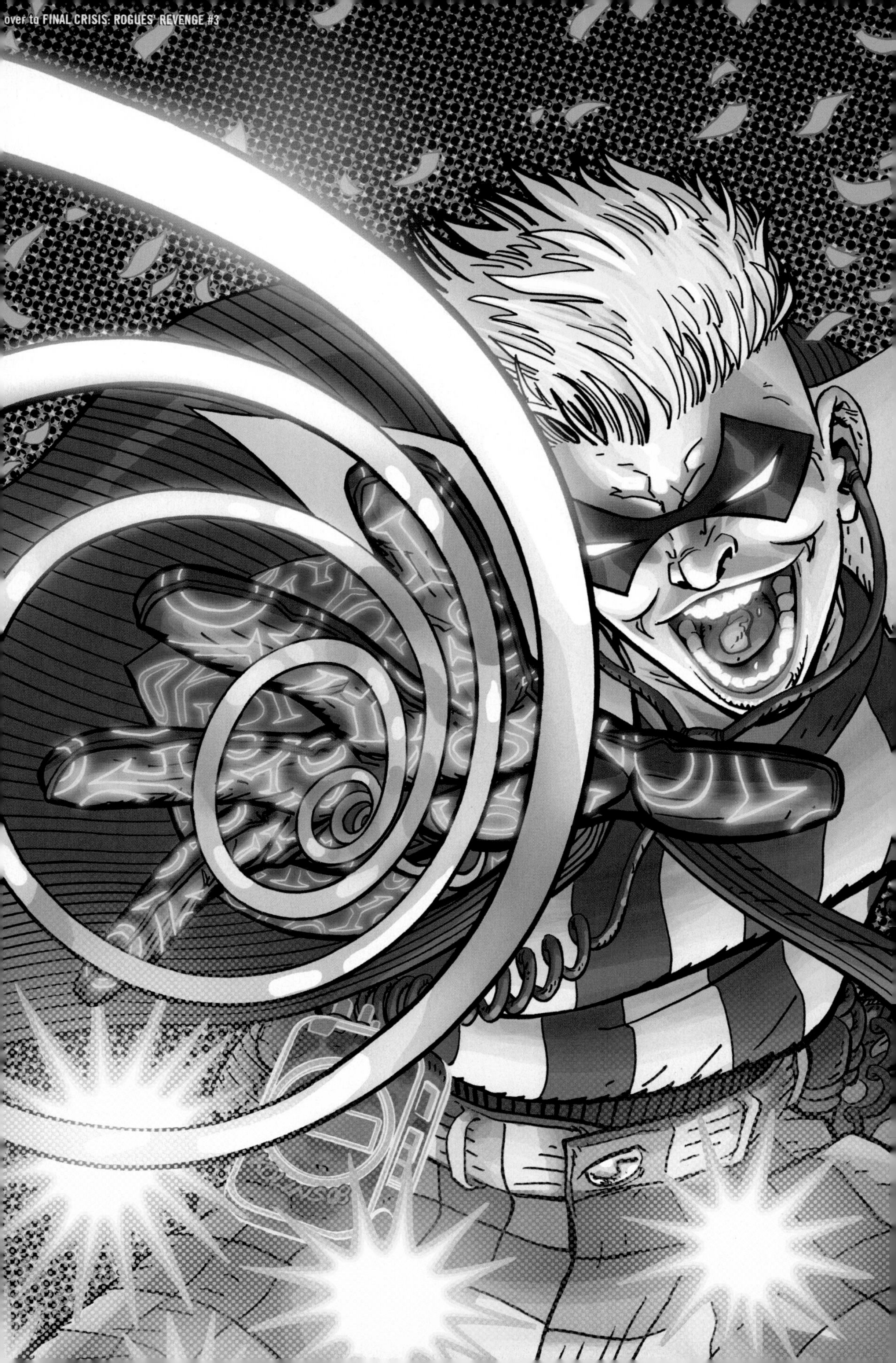
over to FINAL CRISIS: ROGUES' REVENGE #3

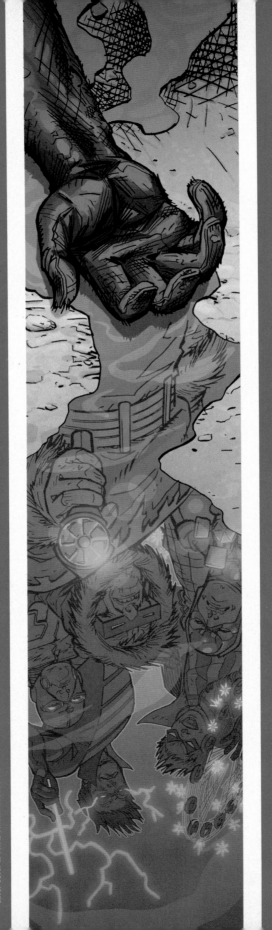

Silver cover to FINAL CRISIS: ROGUES' REVENGE #3

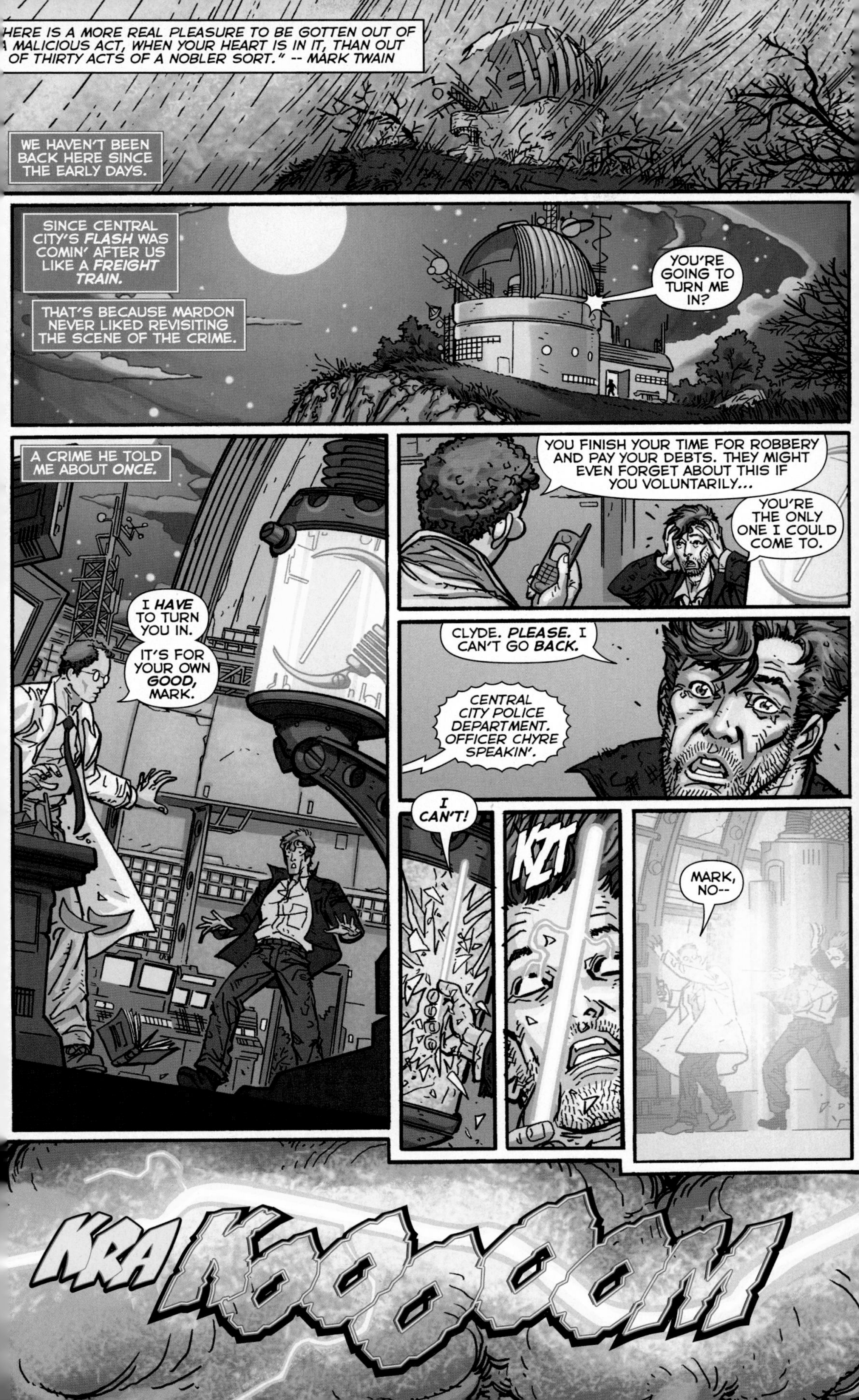
"THERE IS A MORE REAL PLEASURE TO BE GOTTEN OUT OF A MALICIOUS ACT, WHEN YOUR HEART IS IN IT, THAN OUT OF THIRTY ACTS OF A NOBLER SORT." -- MARK TWAIN
WE HAVEN'T BEEN BACK HERE SINCE THE EARLY DAYS.
SINCE CENTRAL CITY'S FLASH WAS COMIN' AFTER US LIKE A FREIGHT TRAIN.
THAT'S BECAUSE MARDON NEVER LIKED REVISITING THE SCENE OF THE CRIME.
YOU'RE GOING TO TURN ME IN?
A CRIME HE TOLD ME ABOUT ONCE.
I HAVE TO TURN YOU IN.
IT'S FOR YOUR OWN GOOD, MARK.
YOU FINISH YOUR TIME FOR ROBBERY AND PAY YOUR DEBTS. THEY MIGHT EVEN FORGET ABOUT THIS IF YOU VOLUNTARILY...
YOU'RE THE ONLY ONE I COULD COME TO.
CLYDE. PLEASE. I CAN'T GO BACK.
CENTRAL CITY POLICE DEPARTMENT. OFFICER CHYRE SPEAKIN'.
I CAN'T!
KZT
MARK, NO--
KRAKOOOOOM

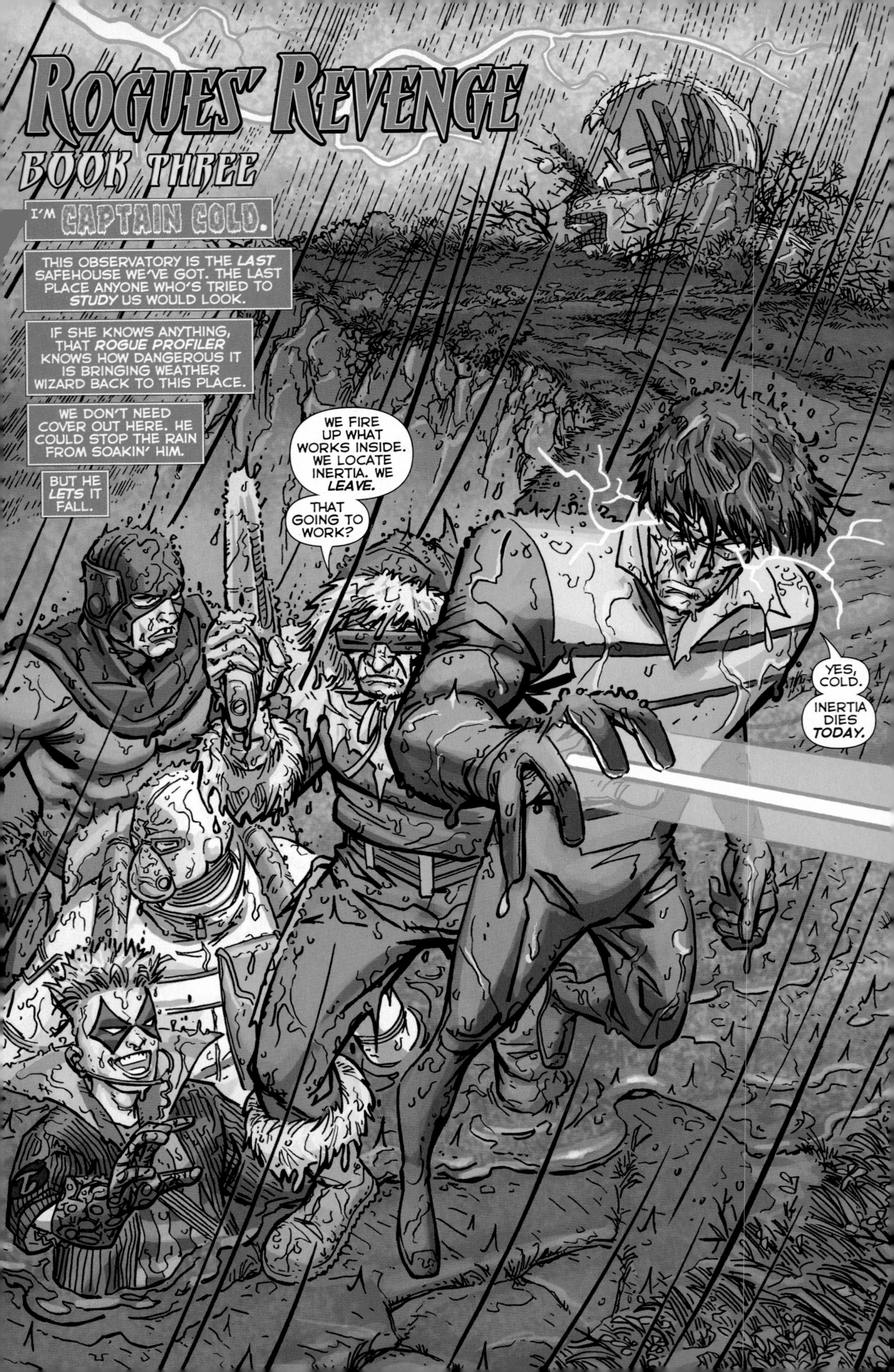
ROGUES' REVENGE
BOOK THREE
I'M CAPTAIN COLD.
THIS OBSERVATORY IS THE LAST SAFEHOUSE WE'VE GOT. THE LAST PLACE ANYONE WHO'S TRIED TO STUDY US WOULD LOOK.
IF SHE KNOWS ANYTHING, THAT ROGUE PROFILER KNOWS HOW DANGEROUS IT IS BRINGING WEATHER WIZARD BACK TO THIS PLACE.
WE DON'T NEED COVER OUT HERE. HE COULD STOP THE RAIN FROM SOAKIN' HIM.
BUT HE LETS IT FALL.
WE FIRE UP WHAT WORKS INSIDE. WE LOCATE INERTIA. WE LEAVE.
THAT GOING TO WORK?
YES, COLD.
INERTIA DIES TODAY.

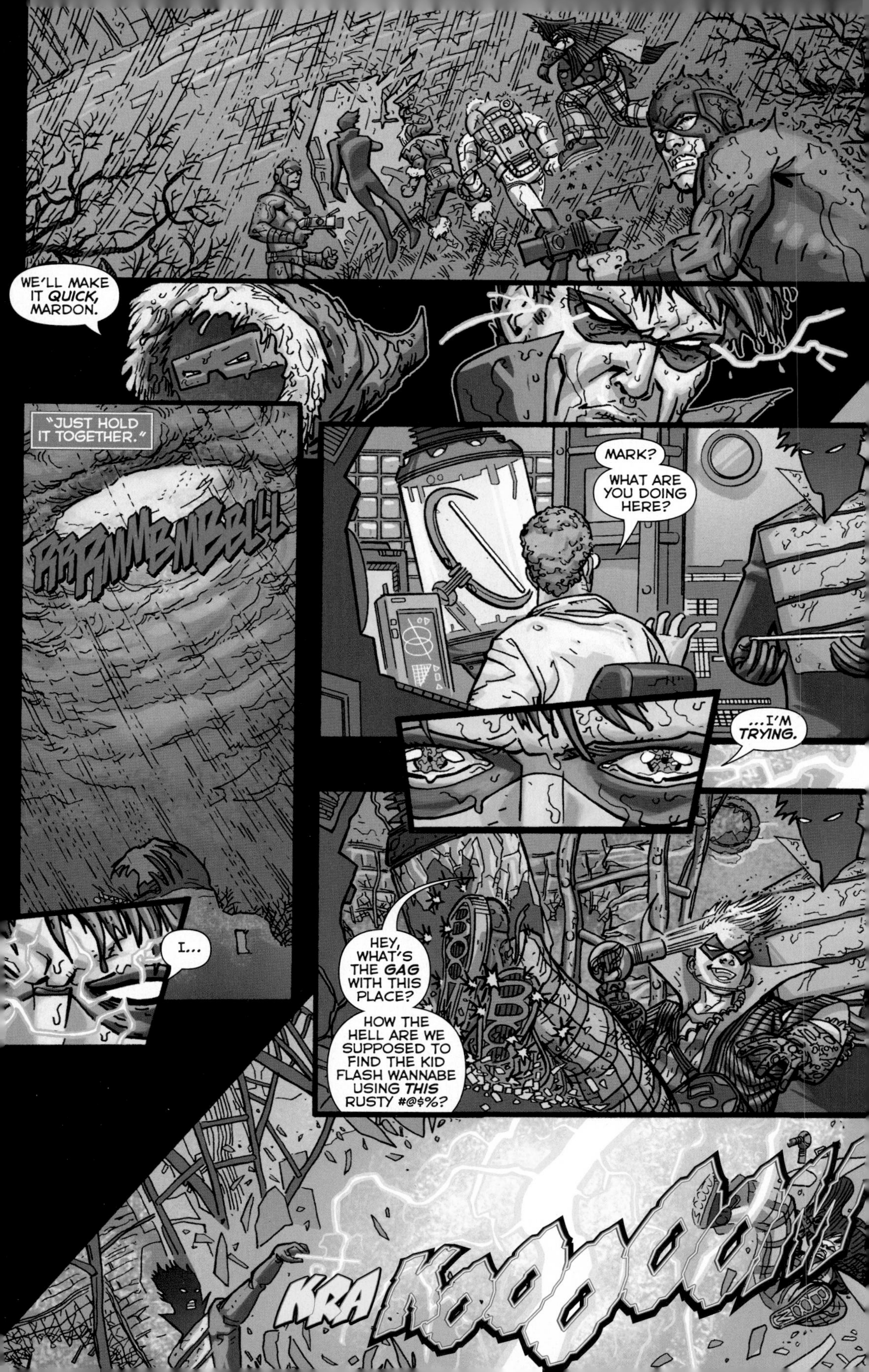

WE'LL MAKE IT QUICK, MARDON.
"JUST HOLD IT TOGETHER."
RRRMMBMBBLLL
MARK?
WHAT ARE YOU DOING HERE?
...I'M TRYING.
I...
HEY, WHAT'S THE GAG WITH THIS PLACE?
HOW THE HELL ARE WE SUPPOSED TO FIND THE KID FLASH WANNABE USING THIS RUSTY #@$%?
KRAKOOOOOM

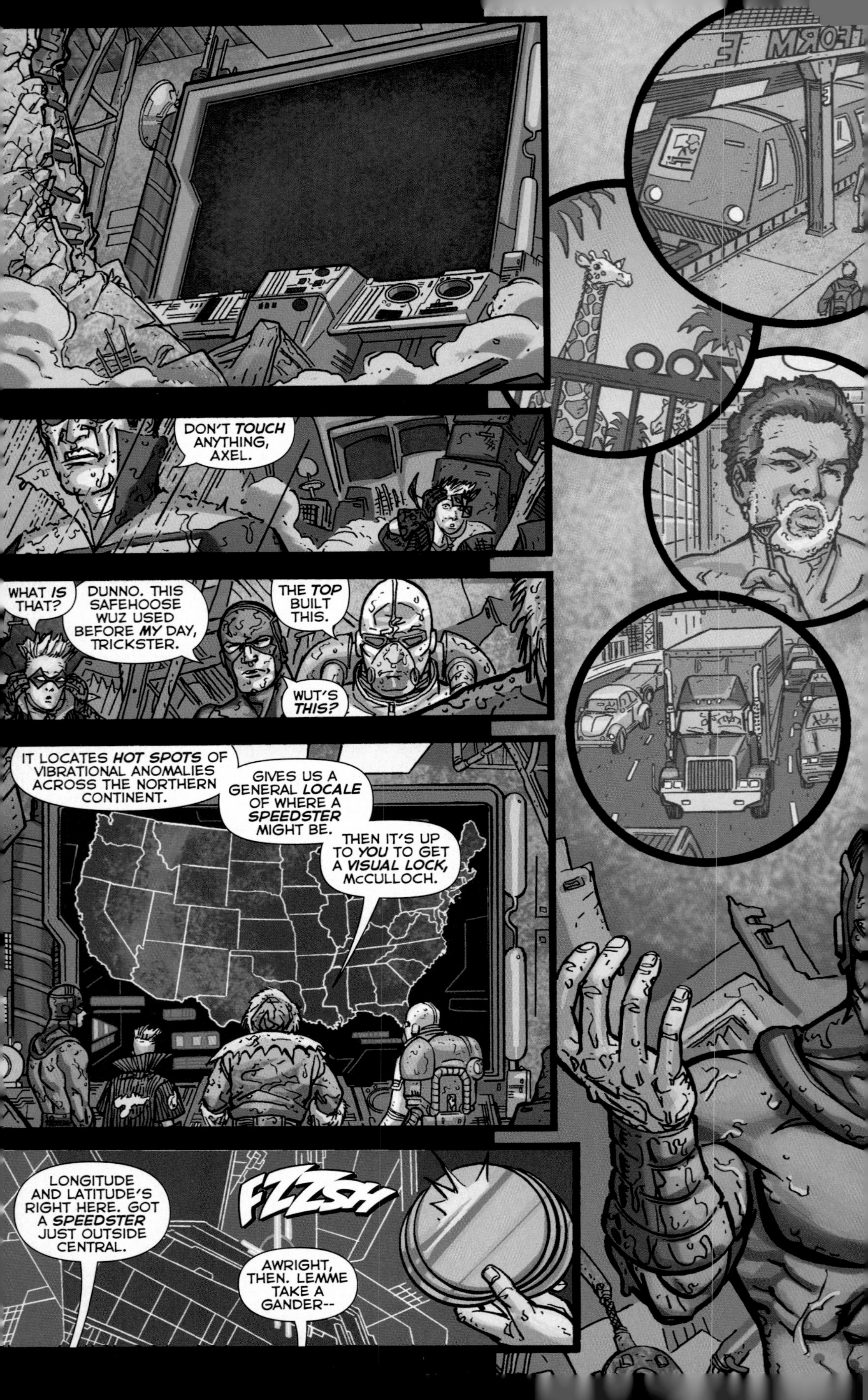
FORM E
ZOO
DON'T TOUCH ANYTHING, AXEL.
WHAT IS THAT?
DUNNO. THIS SAFEHOOSE WUZ USED BEFORE MY DAY, TRICKSTER.
THE TOP BUILT THIS.
WUT'S THIS?
IT LOCATES HOT SPOTS OF VIBRATIONAL ANOMALIES ACROSS THE NORTHERN CONTINENT.
GIVES US A GENERAL LOCALE OF WHERE A SPEEDSTER MIGHT BE.
THEN IT'S UP TO YOU TO GET A VISUAL LOCK, McCULLOCH.
LONGITUDE AND LATITUDE'S RIGHT HERE. GOT A SPEEDSTER JUST OUTSIDE CENTRAL.
FZZSH
AWRIGHT, THEN. LEMME TAKE A GANDER--

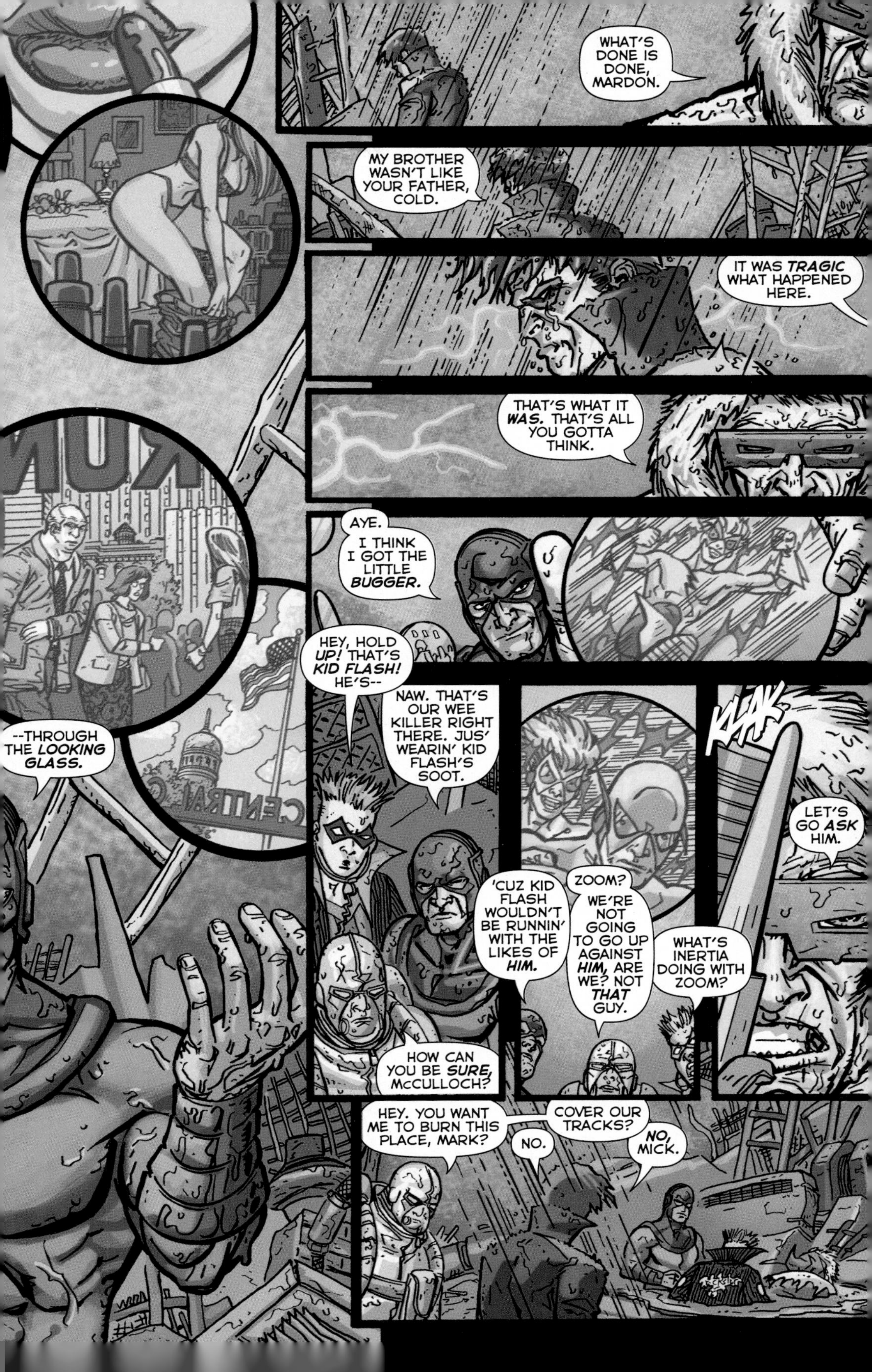

WHAT'S DONE IS DONE, MARDON.
MY BROTHER WASN'T LIKE YOUR FATHER, COLD.
IT WAS TRAGIC WHAT HAPPENED HERE.
THAT'S WHAT IT WAS. THAT'S ALL YOU GOTTA THINK.
--THROUGH THE LOOKING GLASS.
AYE. I THINK I GOT THE LITTLE BUGGER.
HEY, HOLD UP! THAT'S KID FLASH! HE'S--
NAW. THAT'S OUR WEE KILLER RIGHT THERE. JUS' WEARIN' KID FLASH'S SOOT.
'CUZ KID FLASH WOULDN'T BE RUNNIN' WITH THE LIKES OF HIM.
HOW CAN YOU BE SURE, McCULLOCH?
ZOOM?
WE'RE NOT GOING TO GO UP AGAINST HIM, ARE WE? NOT THAT GUY.
WHAT'S INERTIA DOING WITH ZOOM?
KLAK
LET'S GO ASK HIM.
HEY. YOU WANT ME TO BURN THIS PLACE, MARK?
COVER OUR TRACKS?
NO.
NO, MICK.

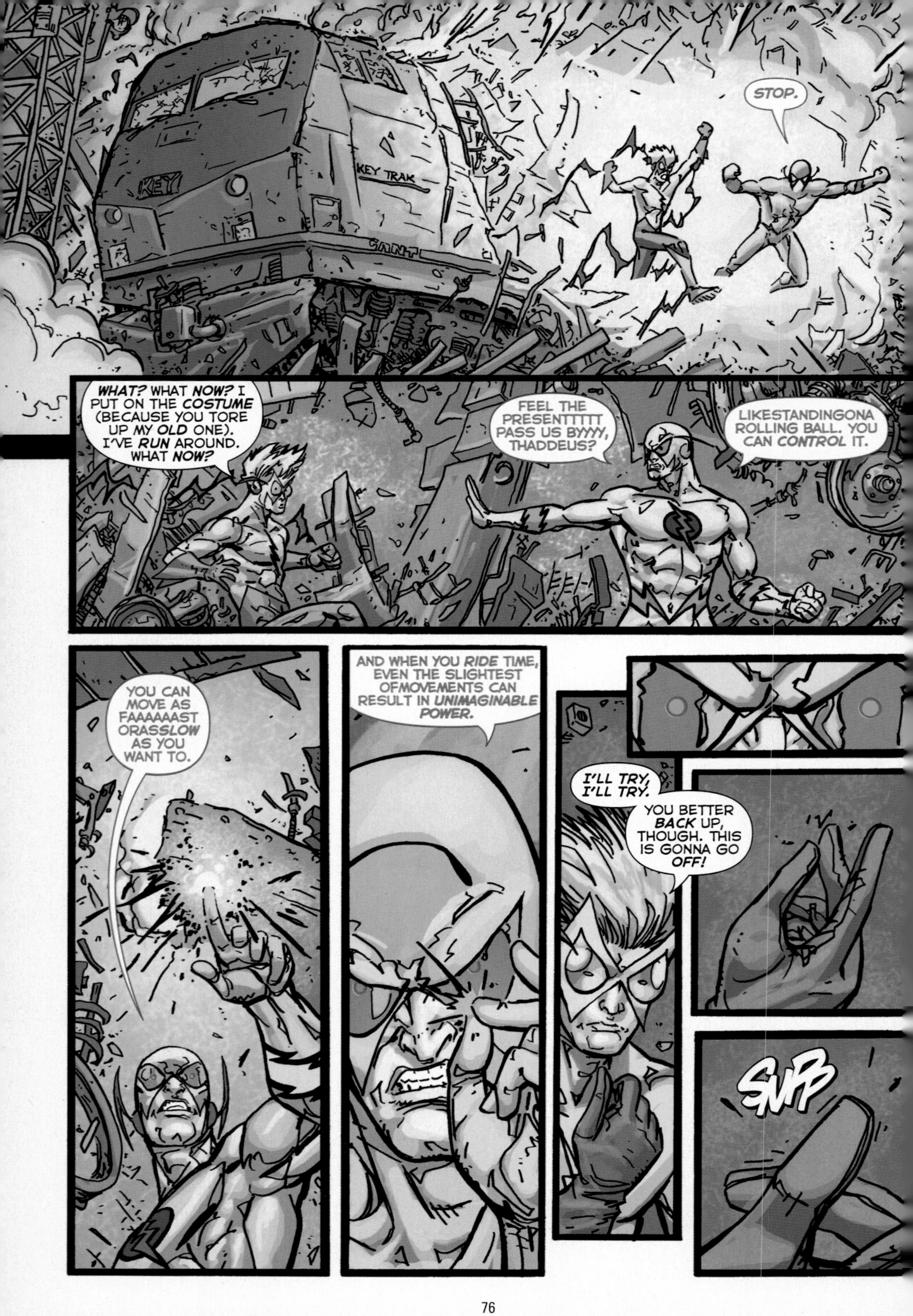

KEY TRAK
STOP.
WHAT? WHAT NOW? I PUT ON THE COSTUME (BECAUSE YOU TORE UP MY OLD ONE). I'VE RUN AROUND. WHAT NOW?
FEEL THE PRESENTTTTTT PASS US BYYYY, THADDEUS?
LIKESTANDINGONA ROLLING BALL. YOU CAN CONTROL IT.
YOU CAN MOVE AS FAAAAAAST ORASSLOW AS YOU WANT TO.
AND WHEN YOU RIDE TIME, EVEN THE SLIGHTEST OFMOVEMENTS CAN RESULT IN UNIMAGINABLE POWER.
I'LL TRY, I'LL TRY.
YOU BETTER BACK UP, THOUGH. THIS IS GONNA GO OFF!
SNP

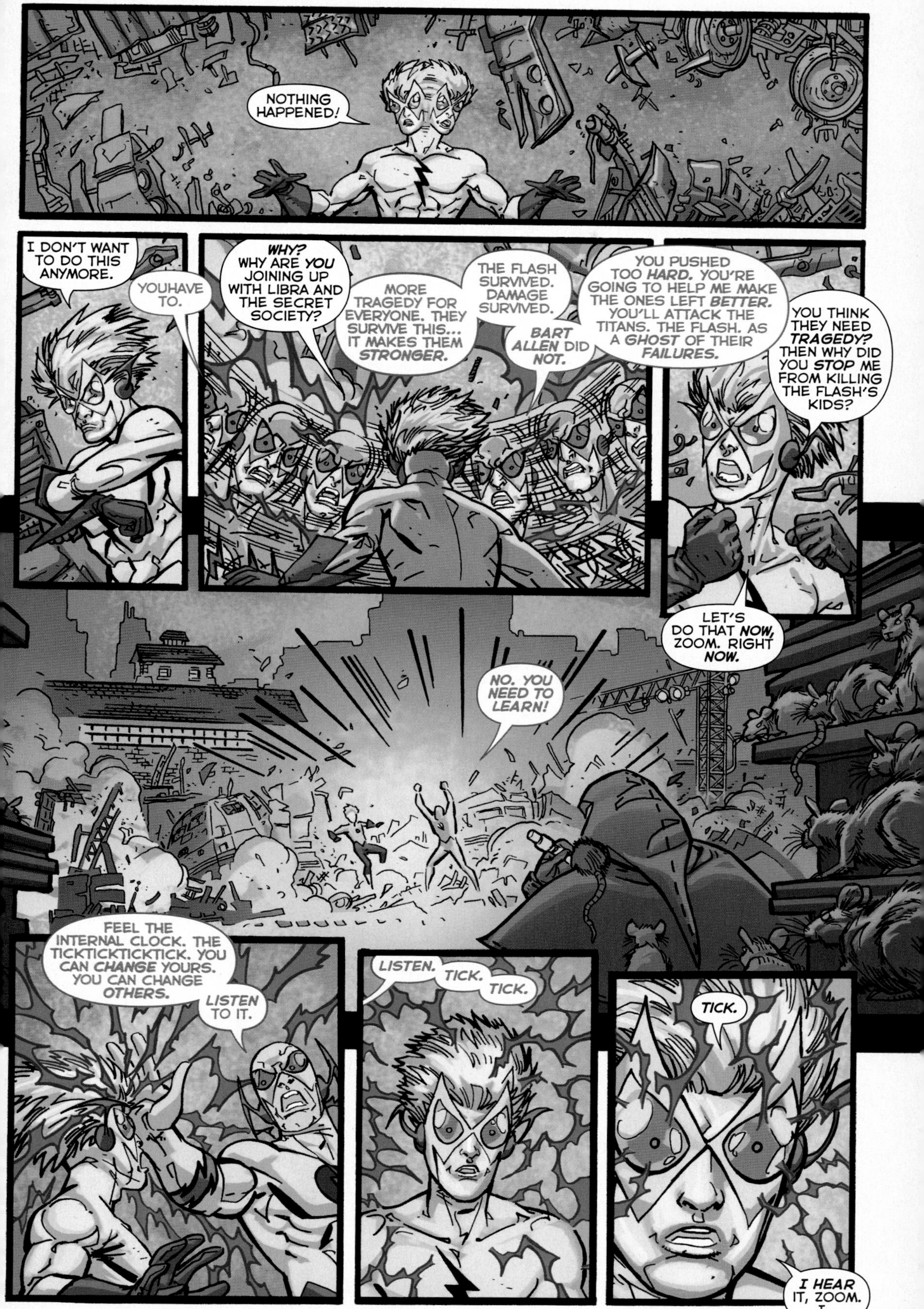

NOTHING HAPPENED!
I DON'T WANT TO DO THIS ANYMORE.
YOUHAVE TO.
WHY? WHY ARE YOU JOINING UP WITH LIBRA AND THE SECRET SOCIETY?
MORE TRAGEDY FOR EVERYONE. THEY SURVIVE THIS... IT MAKES THEM STRONGER.
THE FLASH SURVIVED. DAMAGE SURVIVED.
BART ALLEN DID NOT.
YOU PUSHED TOO HARD. YOU'RE GOING TO HELP ME MAKE THE ONES LEFT BETTER. YOU'LL ATTACK THE TITANS. THE FLASH. AS A GHOST OF THEIR FAILURES.
YOU THINK THEY NEED TRAGEDY? THEN WHY DID YOU STOP ME FROM KILLING THE FLASH'S KIDS?
LET'S DO THAT NOW, ZOOM. RIGHT NOW.
NO. YOU NEED TO LEARN!
FEEL THE INTERNAL CLOCK. THE TICKTICKTICKTICK. YOU CAN CHANGE YOURS. YOU CAN CHANGE OTHERS.
LISTEN TO IT.
LISTEN.
TICK.
TICK.
TICK.
I HEAR IT, ZOOM. I--

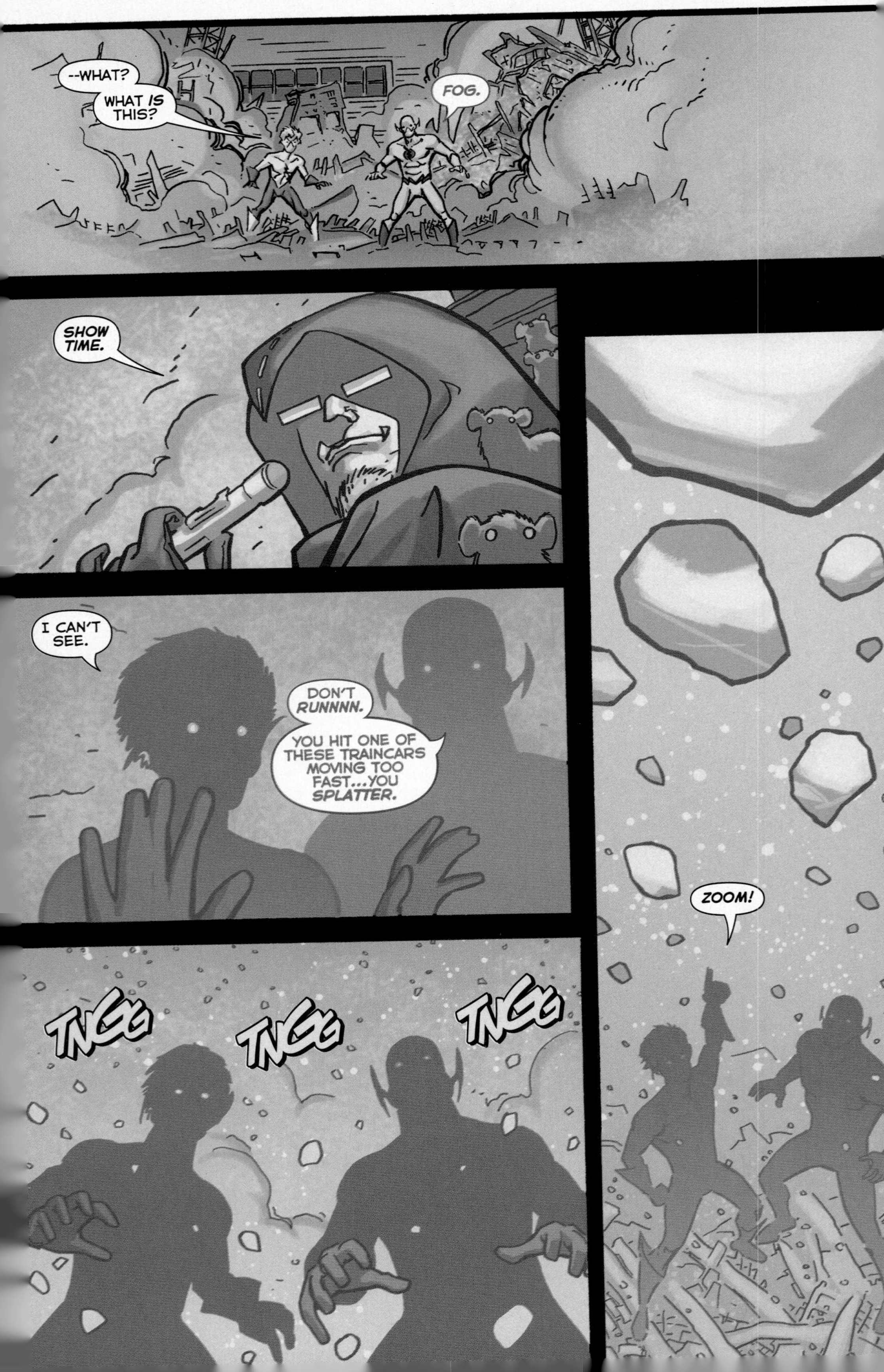
--WHAT?
WHAT IS THIS?
FOG.
SHOW TIME.
I CAN'T SEE.
DON'T RUNNNN.
YOU HIT ONE OF THESE TRAINCARS MOVING TOO FAST...YOU SPLATTER.
TNGG
TNGG
TNGG
ZOOM!

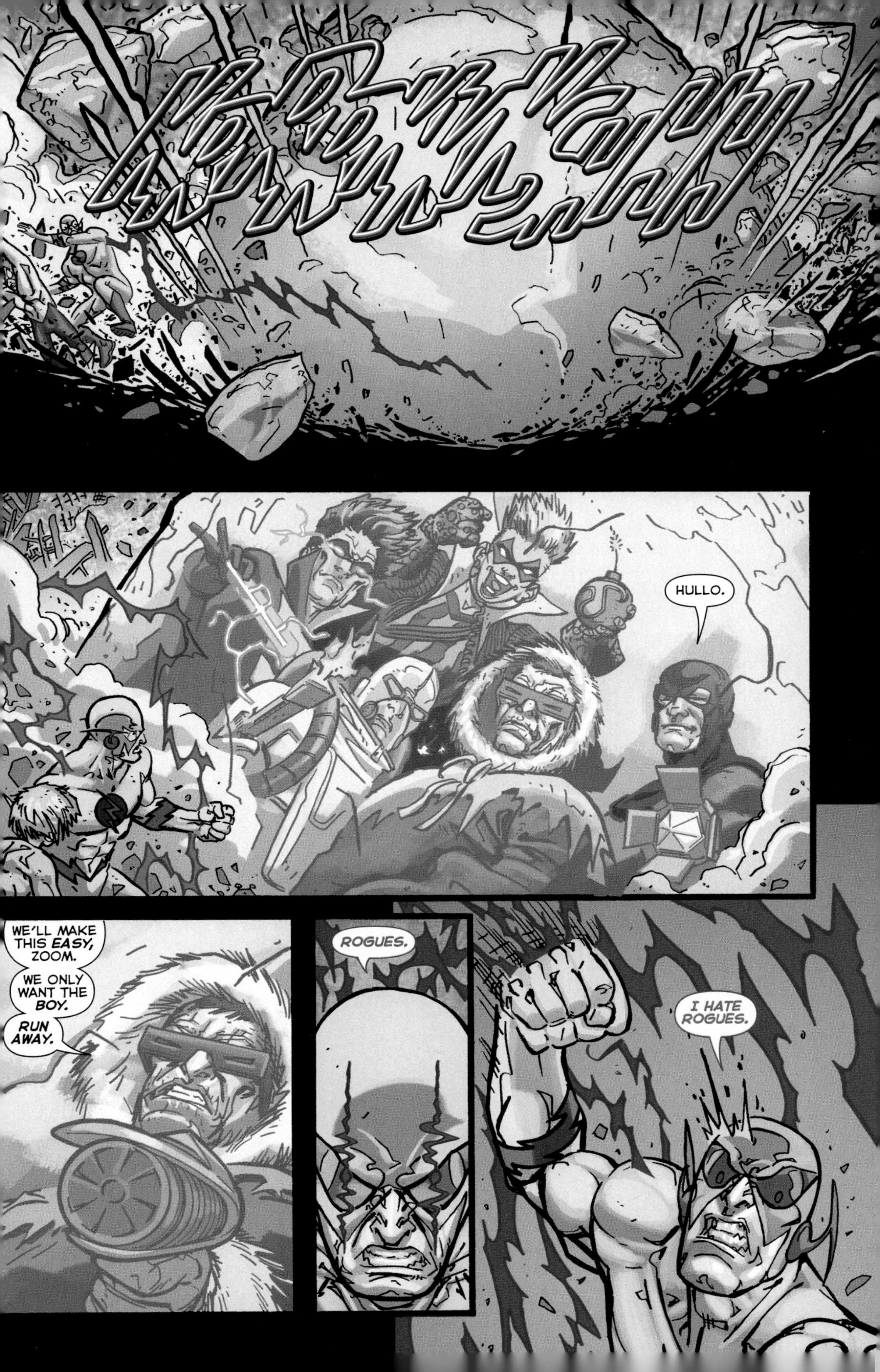
HULLO.
WE'LL MAKE THIS *EASY,* ZOOM.
WE ONLY WANT THE *BOY.*
RUN AWAY.
ROGUES.
I HATE ROGUES.

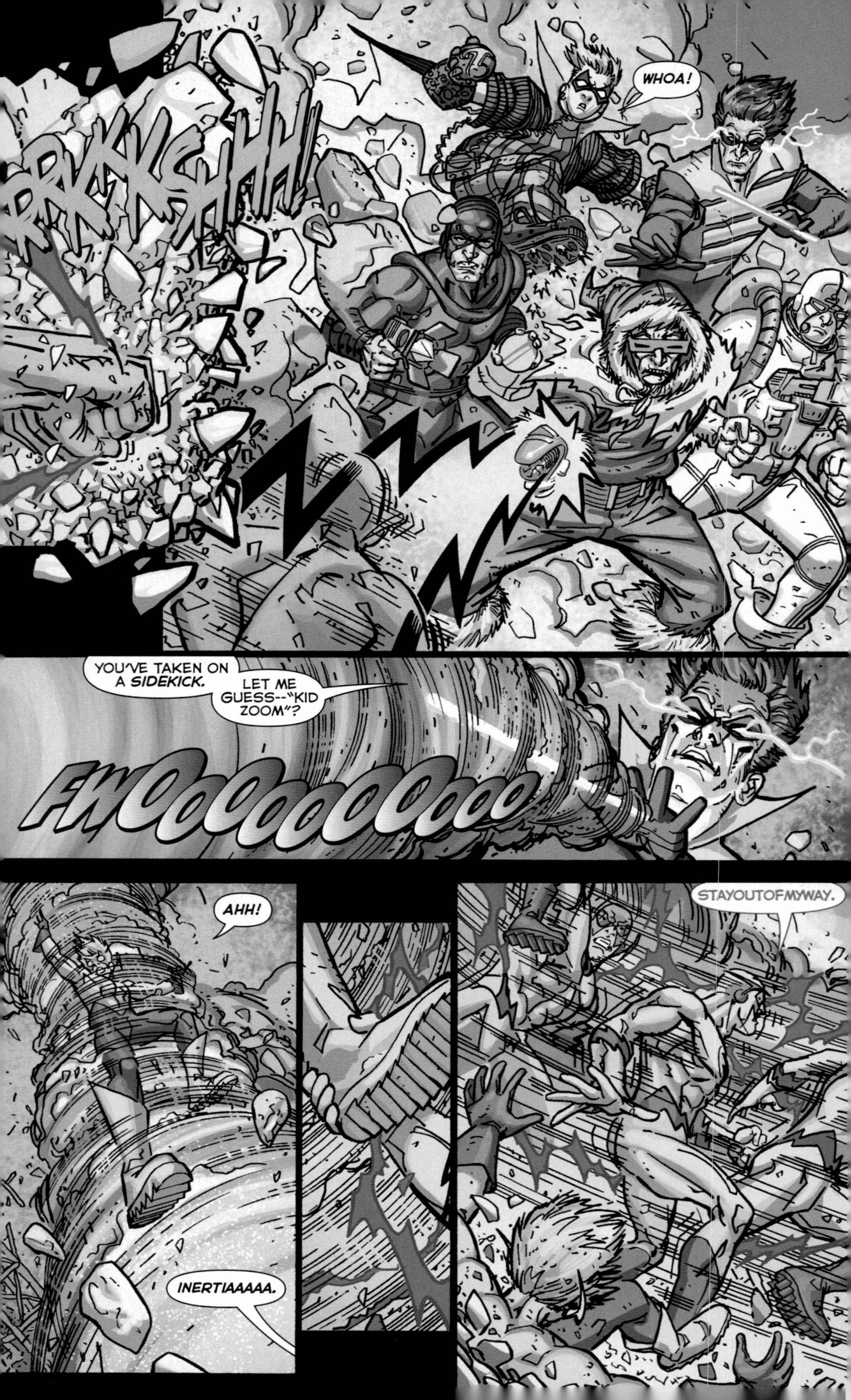
BRKKSHHH!
WHOA!
YOU'VE TAKEN ON A SIDEKICK.
LET ME GUESS--"KID ZOOM"?
FWOOOOOOOOOO
AHH!
INERTIAAAAA.
STAYOUTOFMYWAY.

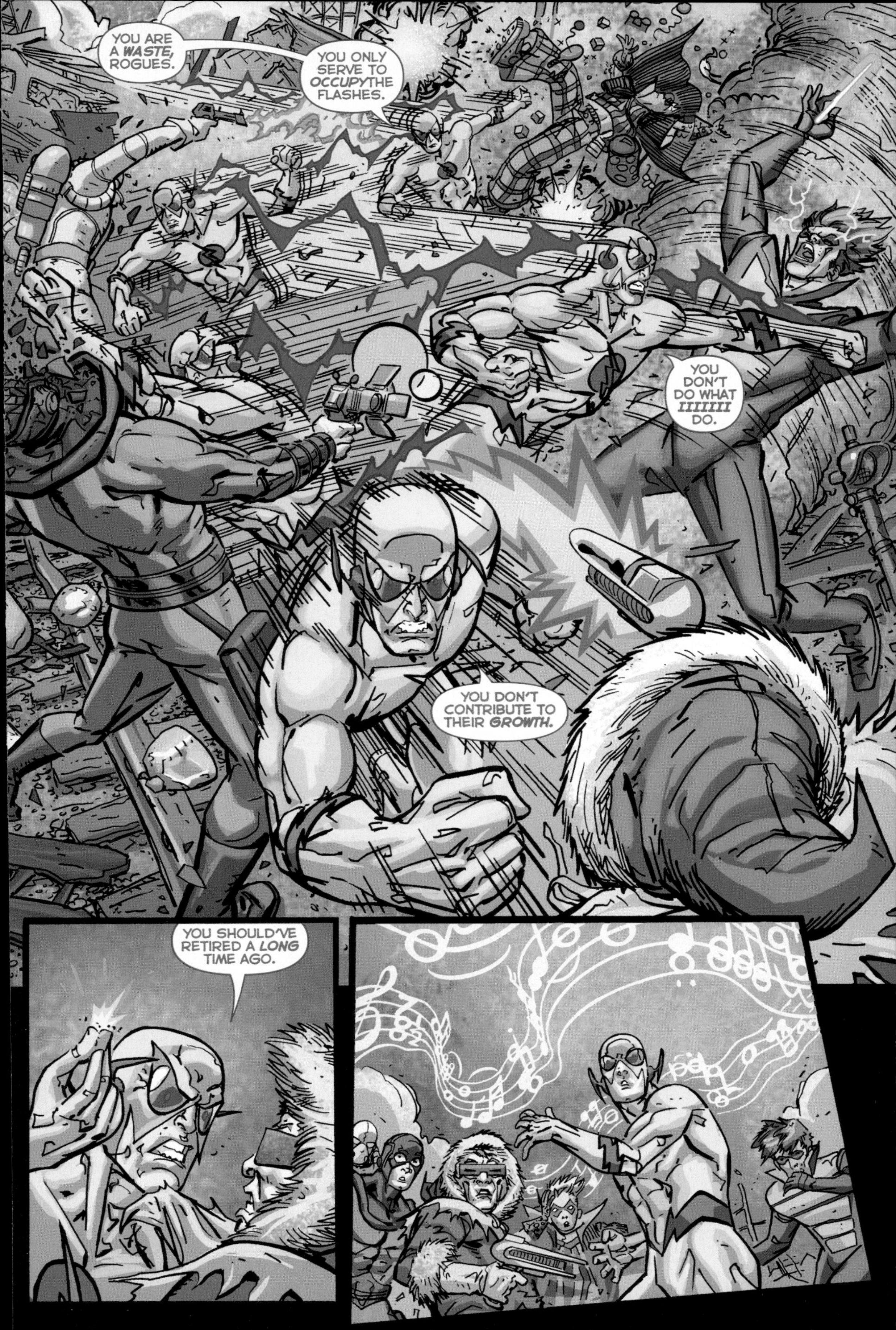
YOU ARE A WASTE, ROGUES.
YOU ONLY SERVE TO OCCUPY THE FLASHES.
YOU DON'T DO WHAT IIIIII DO.
YOU DON'T CONTRIBUTE TO THEIR GROWTH.
YOU SHOULD'VE RETIRED A LONG TIME AGO.

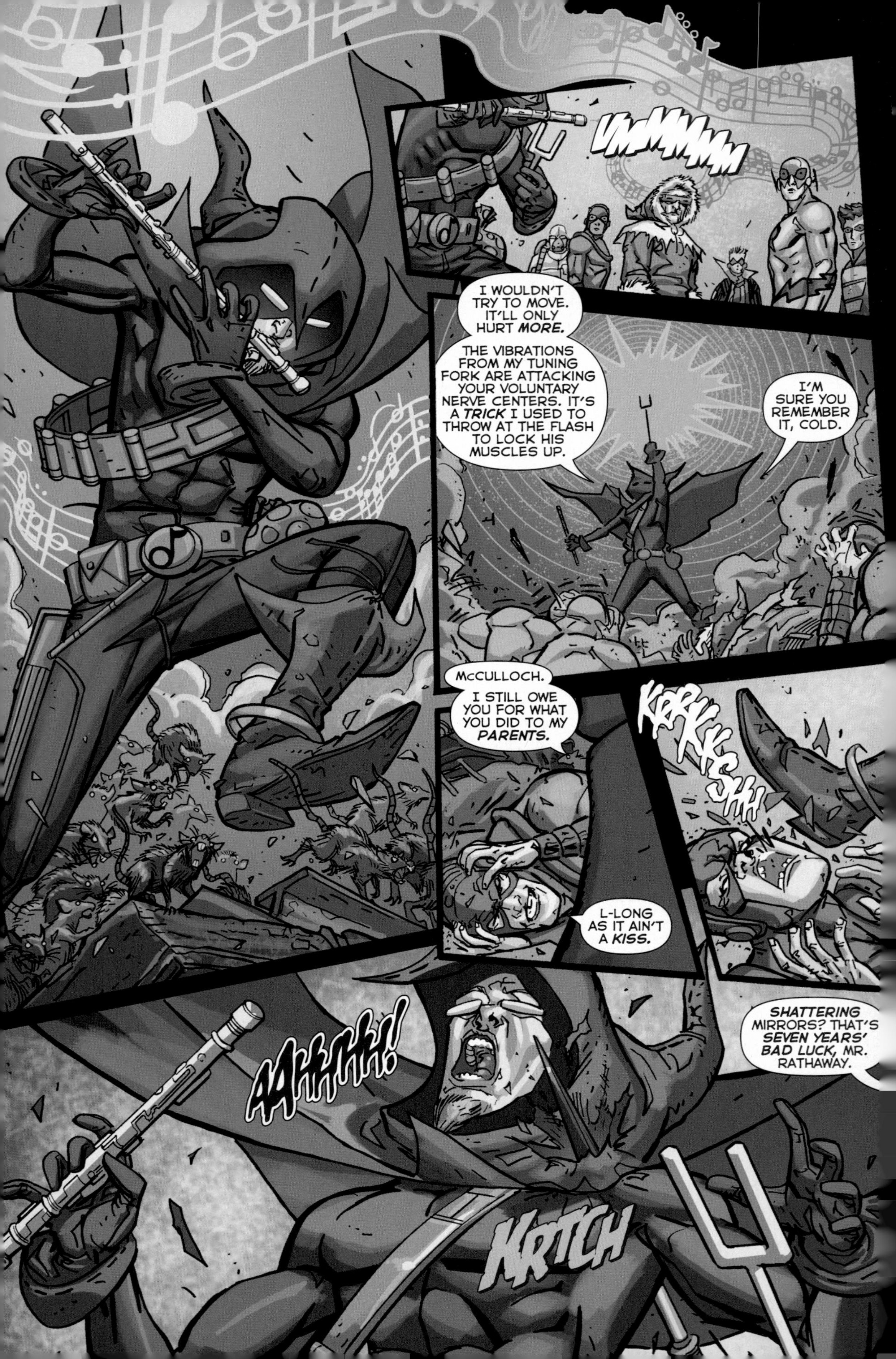

UMMMMMM
I WOULDN'T TRY TO MOVE. IT'LL ONLY HURT MORE.
THE VIBRATIONS FROM MY TUNING FORK ARE ATTACKING YOUR VOLUNTARY NERVE CENTERS. IT'S A TRICK I USED TO THROW AT THE FLASH TO LOCK HIS MUSCLES UP.
I'M SURE YOU REMEMBER IT, COLD.
McCULLOCH.
I STILL OWE YOU FOR WHAT YOU DID TO MY PARENTS.
L-LONG AS IT AIN'T A KISS.
KRKKSHH
AAHHHH!
SHATTERING MIRRORS? THAT'S SEVEN YEARS' BAD LUCK, MR. RATHAWAY.
KRTCH

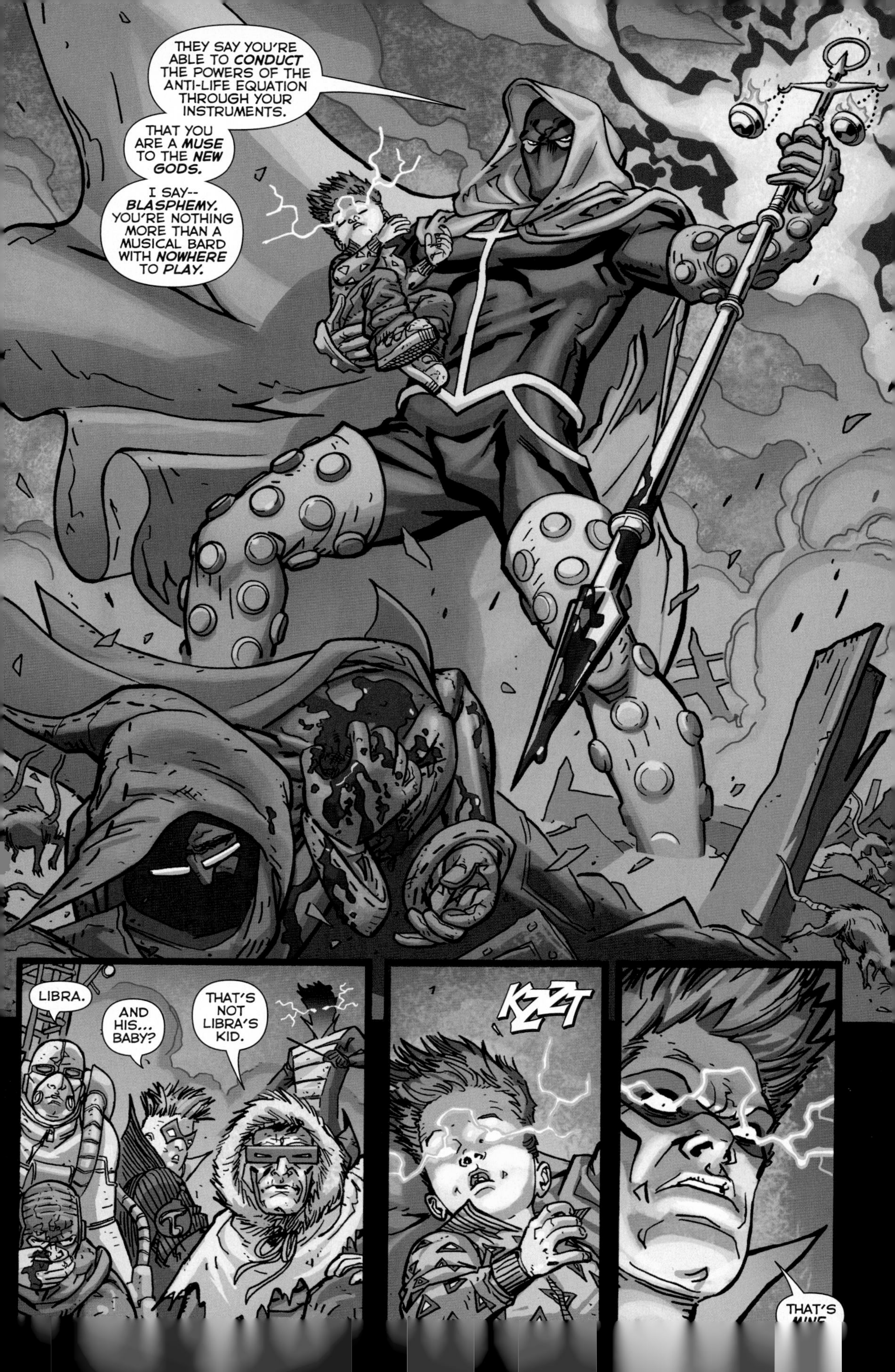
THEY SAY YOU'RE ABLE TO *CONDUCT* THE POWERS OF THE ANTI-LIFE EQUATION THROUGH YOUR INSTRUMENTS.
THAT YOU ARE A *MUSE* TO THE *NEW GODS.*
I SAY-- *BLASPHEMY.* YOU'RE NOTHING MORE THAN A MUSICAL BARD WITH *NOWHERE* TO *PLAY.*
LIBRA.
AND HIS... BABY?
THAT'S NOT LIBRA'S KID.
KZZZT
THAT'S

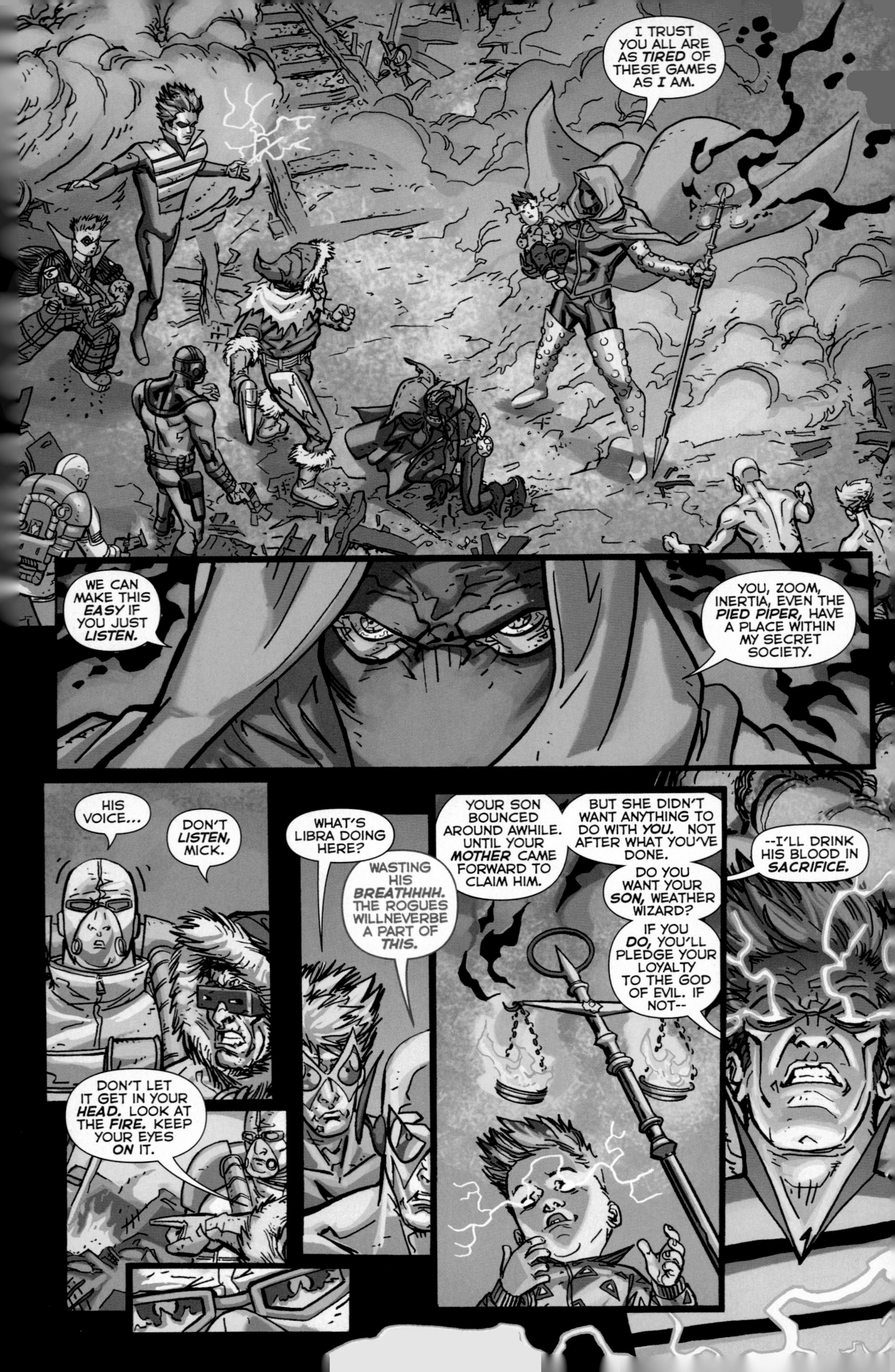
I TRUST YOU ALL ARE AS TIRED OF THESE GAMES AS I AM.
WE CAN MAKE THIS EASY IF YOU JUST LISTEN.
YOU, ZOOM, INERTIA, EVEN THE PIED PIPER, HAVE A PLACE WITHIN MY SECRET SOCIETY.
HIS VOICE...
DON'T LISTEN, MICK.
DON'T LET IT GET IN YOUR HEAD. LOOK AT THE FIRE. KEEP YOUR EYES ON IT.
WHAT'S LIBRA DOING HERE?
WASTING HIS BREATHHHH. THE ROGUES WILLNEVERBE A PART OF THIS.
YOUR SON BOUNCED AROUND AWHILE. UNTIL YOUR MOTHER CAME FORWARD TO CLAIM HIM.
BUT SHE DIDN'T WANT ANYTHING TO DO WITH YOU. NOT AFTER WHAT YOU'VE DONE.
DO YOU WANT YOUR SON, WEATHER WIZARD?
IF YOU DO, YOU'LL PLEDGE YOUR LOYALTY TO THE GOD OF EVIL. IF NOT--
--I'LL DRINK HIS BLOOD IN SACRIFICE.

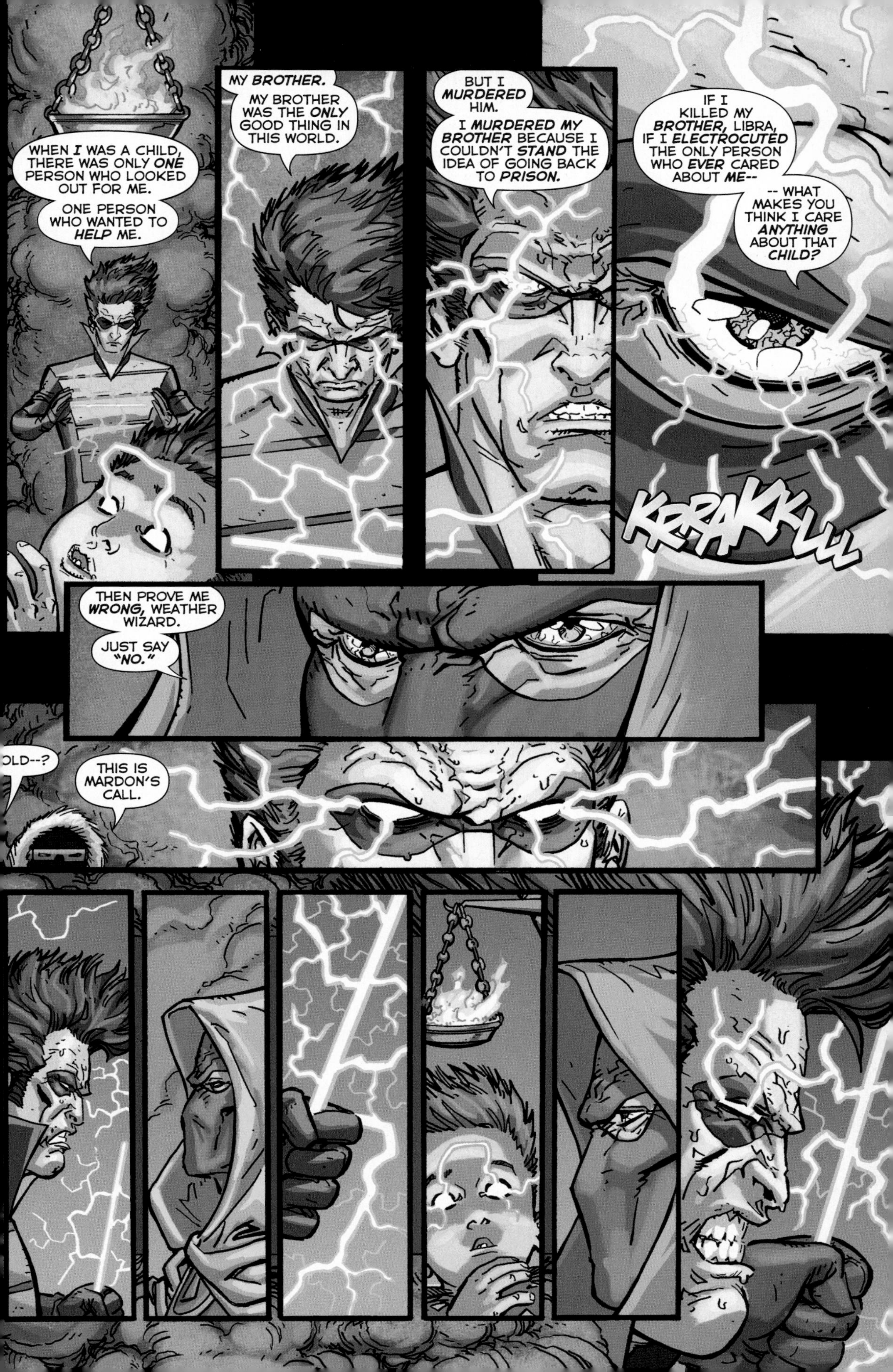

WHEN I WAS A CHILD, THERE WAS ONLY ONE PERSON WHO LOOKED OUT FOR ME.
ONE PERSON WHO WANTED TO HELP ME.
MY BROTHER.
MY BROTHER WAS THE ONLY GOOD THING IN THIS WORLD.
BUT I MURDERED HIM.
I MURDERED MY BROTHER BECAUSE I COULDN'T STAND THE IDEA OF GOING BACK TO PRISON.
IF I KILLED MY BROTHER, LIBRA, IF I ELECTROCUTED THE ONLY PERSON WHO EVER CARED ABOUT ME--
-- WHAT MAKES YOU THINK I CARE ANYTHING ABOUT THAT CHILD?
KRRAKKLLL
THEN PROVE ME WRONG, WEATHER WIZARD.
JUST SAY "NO."
OLD--?
THIS IS MARDON'S CALL.

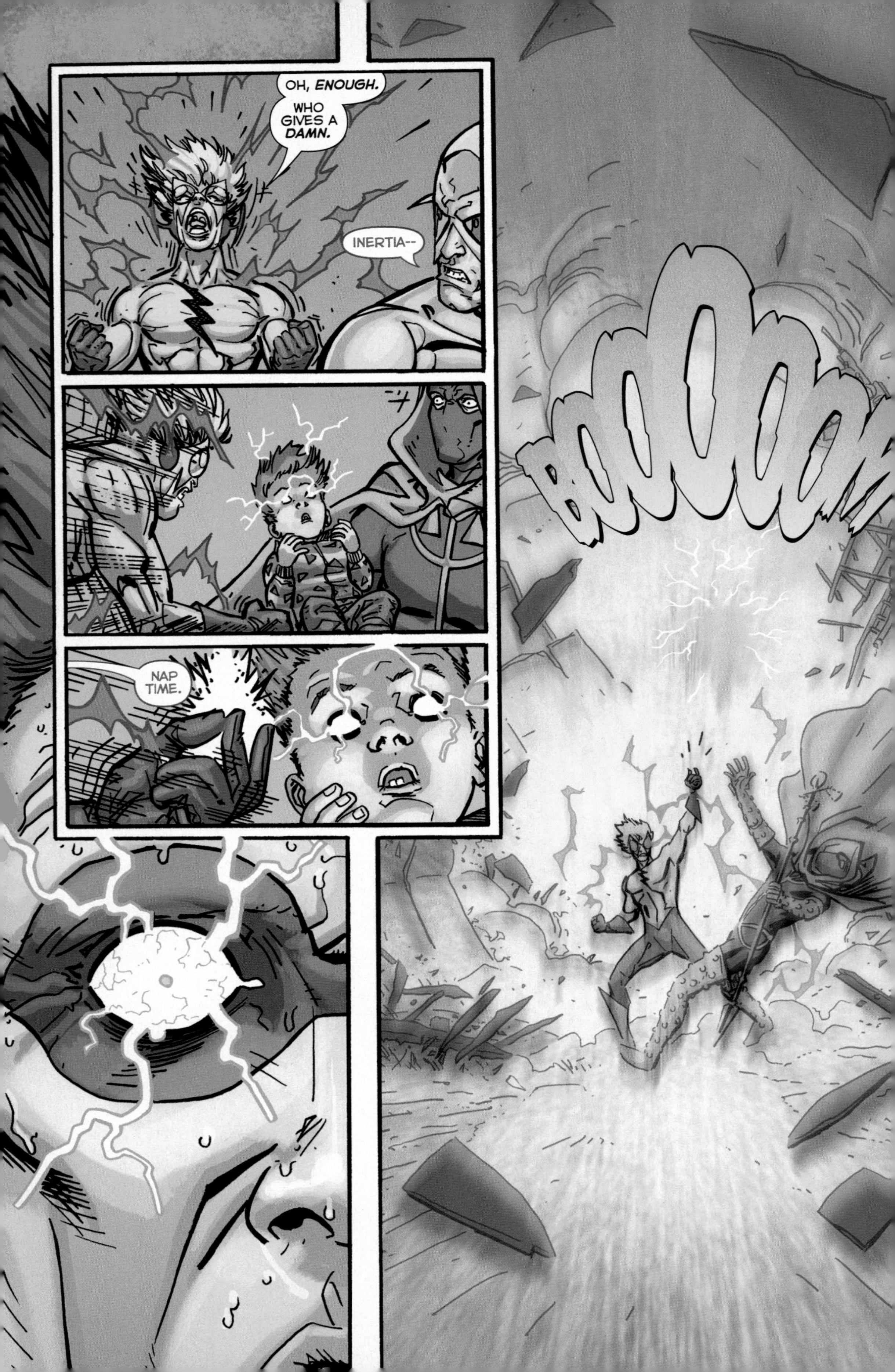
OH, ENOUGH.
WHO GIVES A DAMN.
INERTIA--
NAP TIME.
BOOOOOM

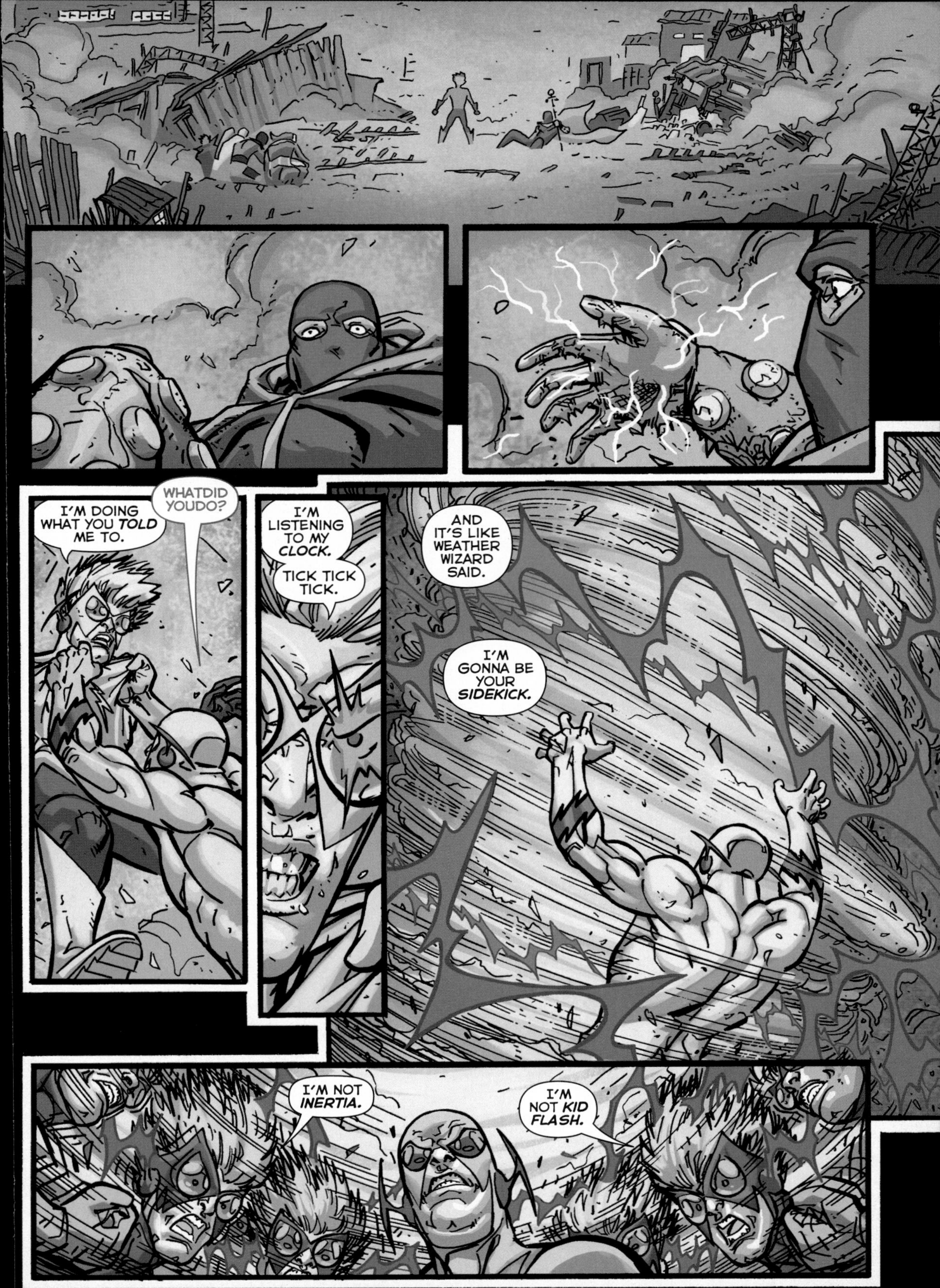
I'M DOING WHAT YOU TOLD ME TO.
WHATDID YOUDO?
I'M LISTENING TO MY CLOCK.
TICK TICK TICK.
AND IT'S LIKE WEATHER WIZARD SAID.
I'M GONNA BE YOUR SIDEKICK.
I'M NOT INERTIA.
I'M NOT KID FLASH.

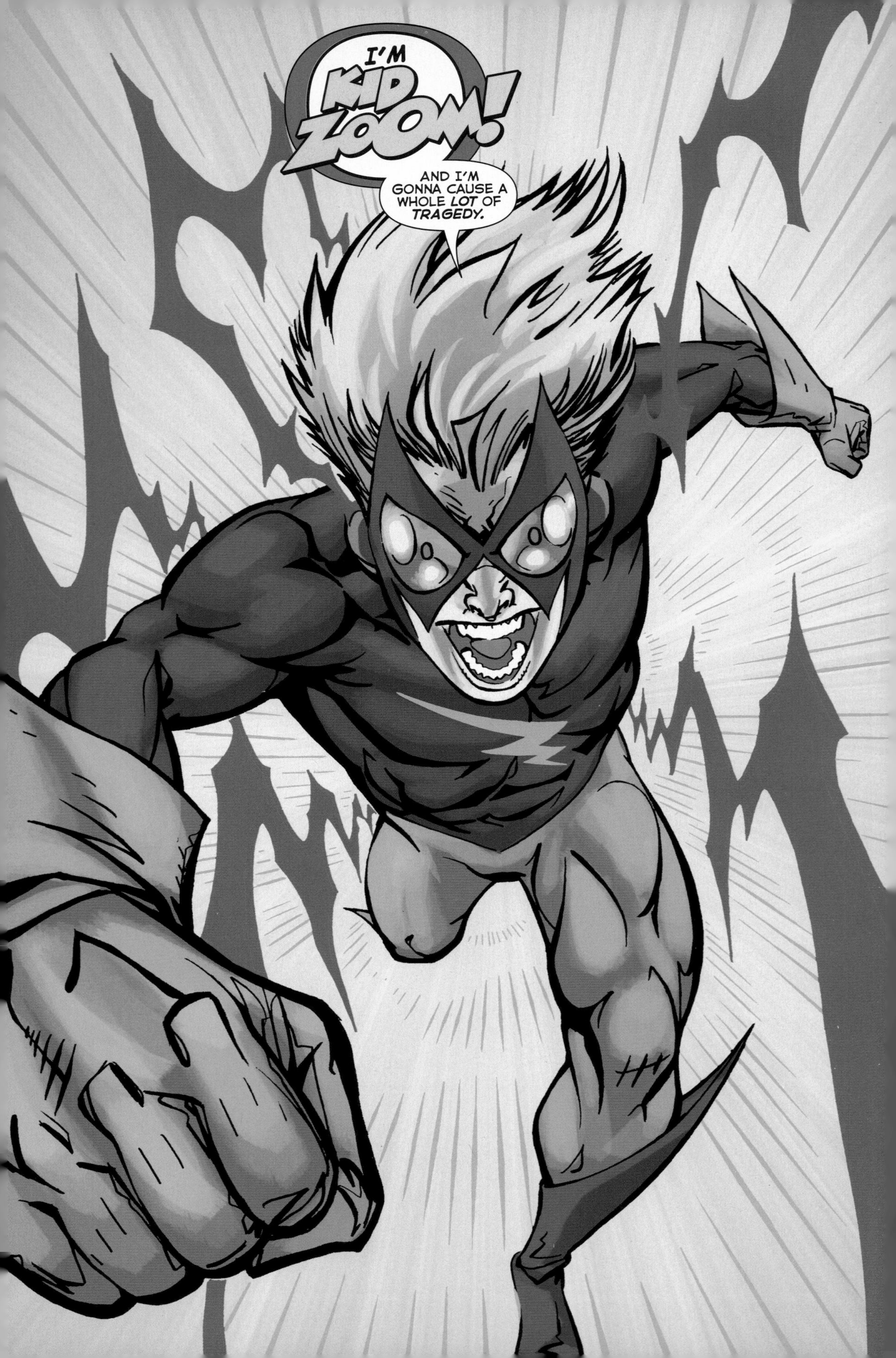
I'M KID ZOOM!
AND I'M GONNA CAUSE A WHOLE *LOT* OF *TRAGEDY.*

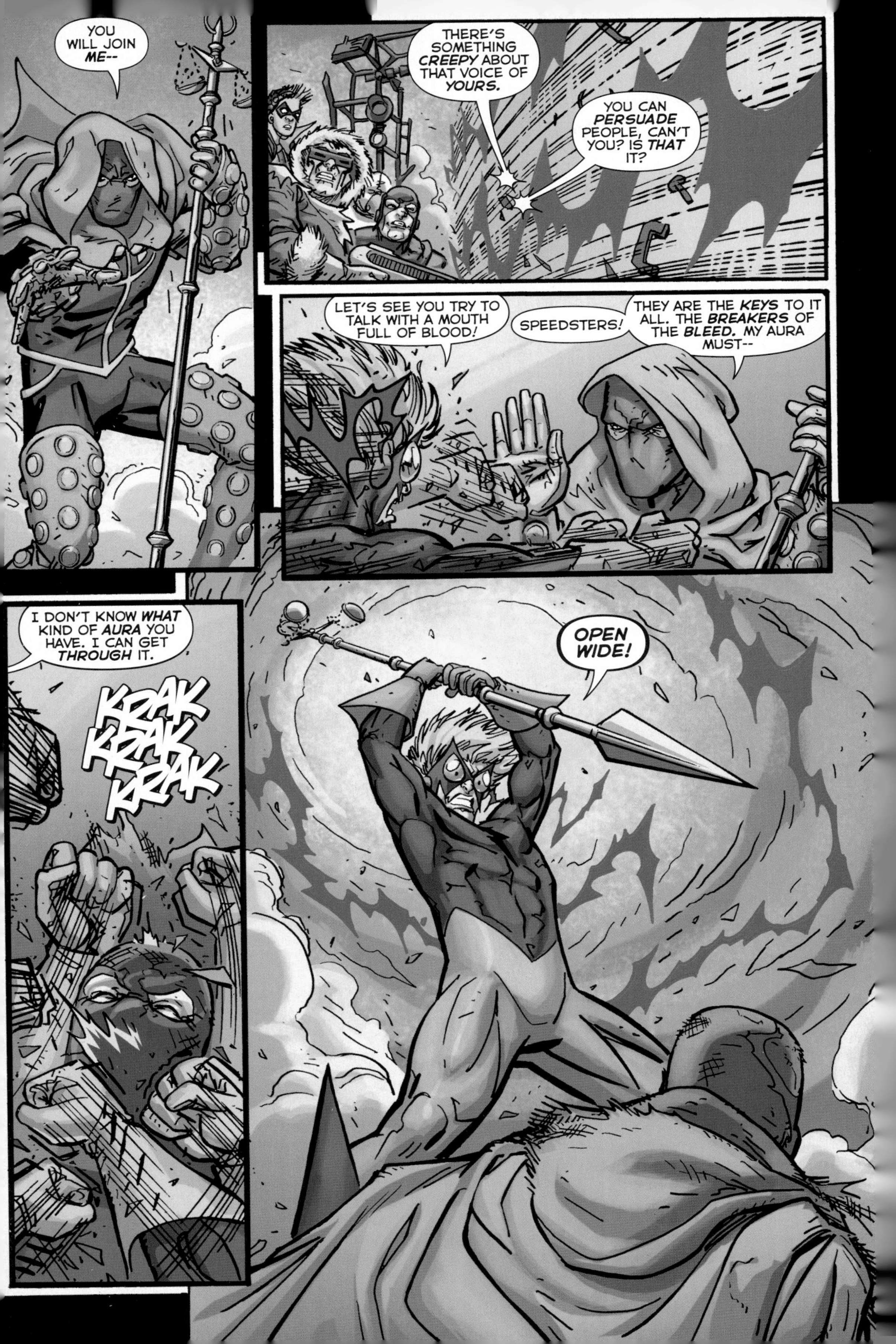
YOU WILL JOIN ME--
THERE'S SOMETHING CREEPY ABOUT THAT VOICE OF YOURS.
YOU CAN PERSUADE PEOPLE, CAN'T YOU? IS THAT IT?
LET'S SEE YOU TRY TO TALK WITH A MOUTH FULL OF BLOOD!
SPEEDSTERS!
THEY ARE THE KEYS TO IT ALL. THE BREAKERS OF THE BLEED. MY AURA MUST--
I DON'T KNOW WHAT KIND OF AURA YOU HAVE. I CAN GET THROUGH IT.
KRAK KRAK KRAK
OPEN WIDE!

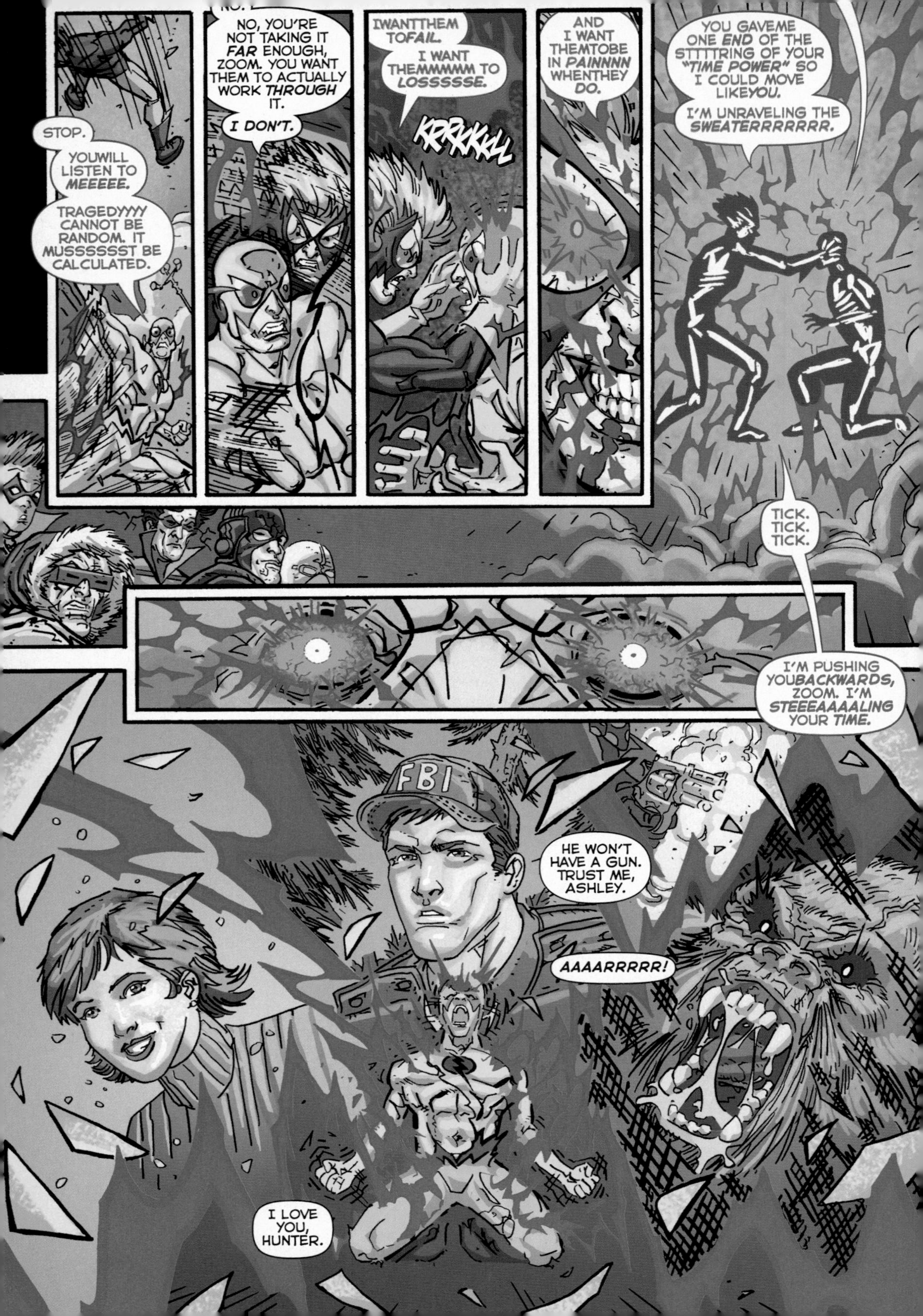

STOP.
YOUWILL LISTEN TO MEEEEE.
TRAGEDYYYY CANNOT BE RANDOM. IT MUSSSSSST BE CALCULATED.
NO, YOU'RE NOT TAKING IT FAR ENOUGH, ZOOM. YOU WANT THEM TO ACTUALLY WORK THROUGH IT.
I DON'T.
IWANTTHEM TOFAIL.
I WANT THEMMMMM TO LOSSSSSE.
KRRKKKLL
AND I WANT THEMTOBE IN PAINNNN WHENTHEY DO.
YOU GAVEME ONE END OF THE STTTTRING OF YOUR "TIME POWER" SO I COULD MOVE LIKEYOU.
I'M UNRAVELING THE SWEATERRRRRRR.
TICK. TICK. TICK.
I'M PUSHING YOUBACKWARDS, ZOOM. I'M STEEEAAAALING YOUR TIME.
FBI
HE WON'T HAVE A GUN. TRUST ME, ASHLEY.
AAAARRRRR!
I LOVE YOU, HUNTER.

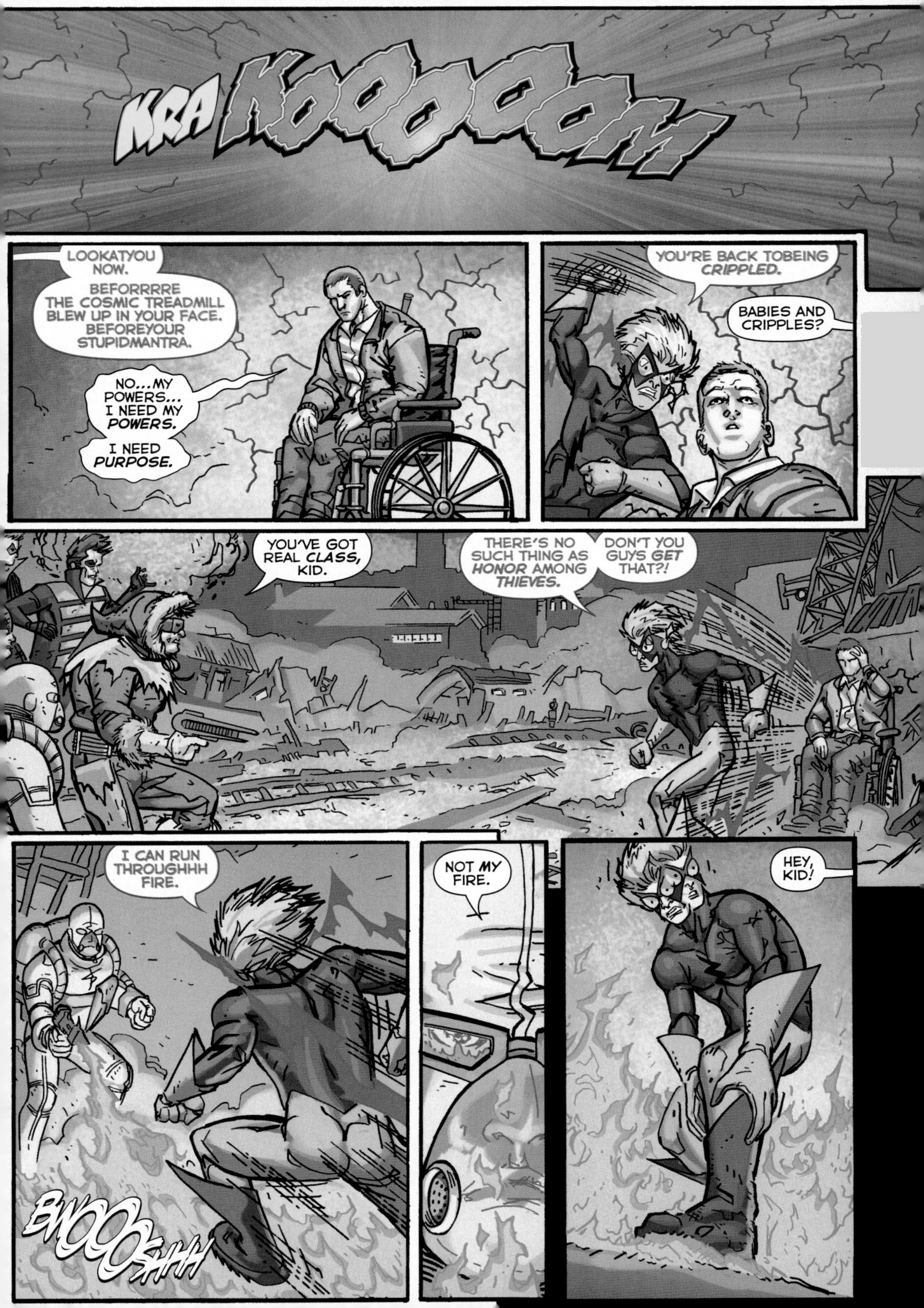
KRA KOOOOOOM
LOOKATYOU NOW.
BEFORRRRE THE COSMIC TREADMILL BLEW UP IN YOUR FACE. BEFOREYOUR STUPIDMANTRA.
NO...MY POWERS... I NEED MY POWERS.
I NEED PURPOSE.
YOU'RE BACK TOBEING CRIPPLED.
BABIES AND CRIPPLES?
YOU'VE GOT REAL CLASS, KID.
THERE'S NO SUCH THING AS HONOR AMONG THIEVES.
DON'T YOU GUYS GET THAT?!
I CAN RUN THROUGHHH FIRE.
BWOOOSHHH
NOT MY FIRE.
HEY, KID!

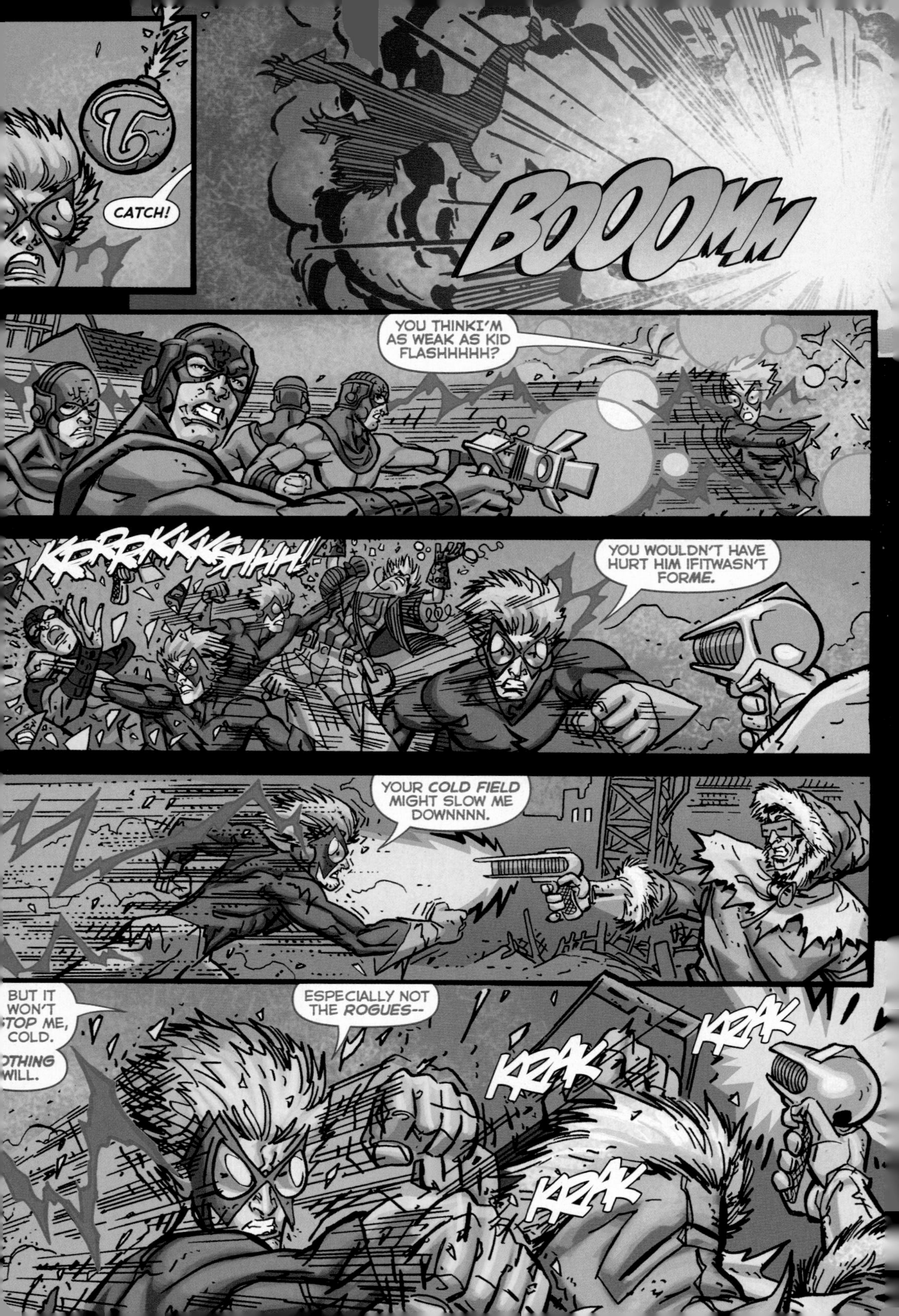
CATCH!
BOOOOMM
YOU THINK I'M AS WEAK AS KID FLASHHHHHH?
KRRRKKKSHHH!
YOU WOULDN'T HAVE HURT HIM IF IT WASN'T FOR ME.
YOUR COLD FIELD MIGHT SLOW ME DOWNNNN.
BUT IT WON'T STOP ME, COLD.
OTHING WILL.
ESPECIALLY NOT THE ROGUES--
KRAK
KRAK
KRAK

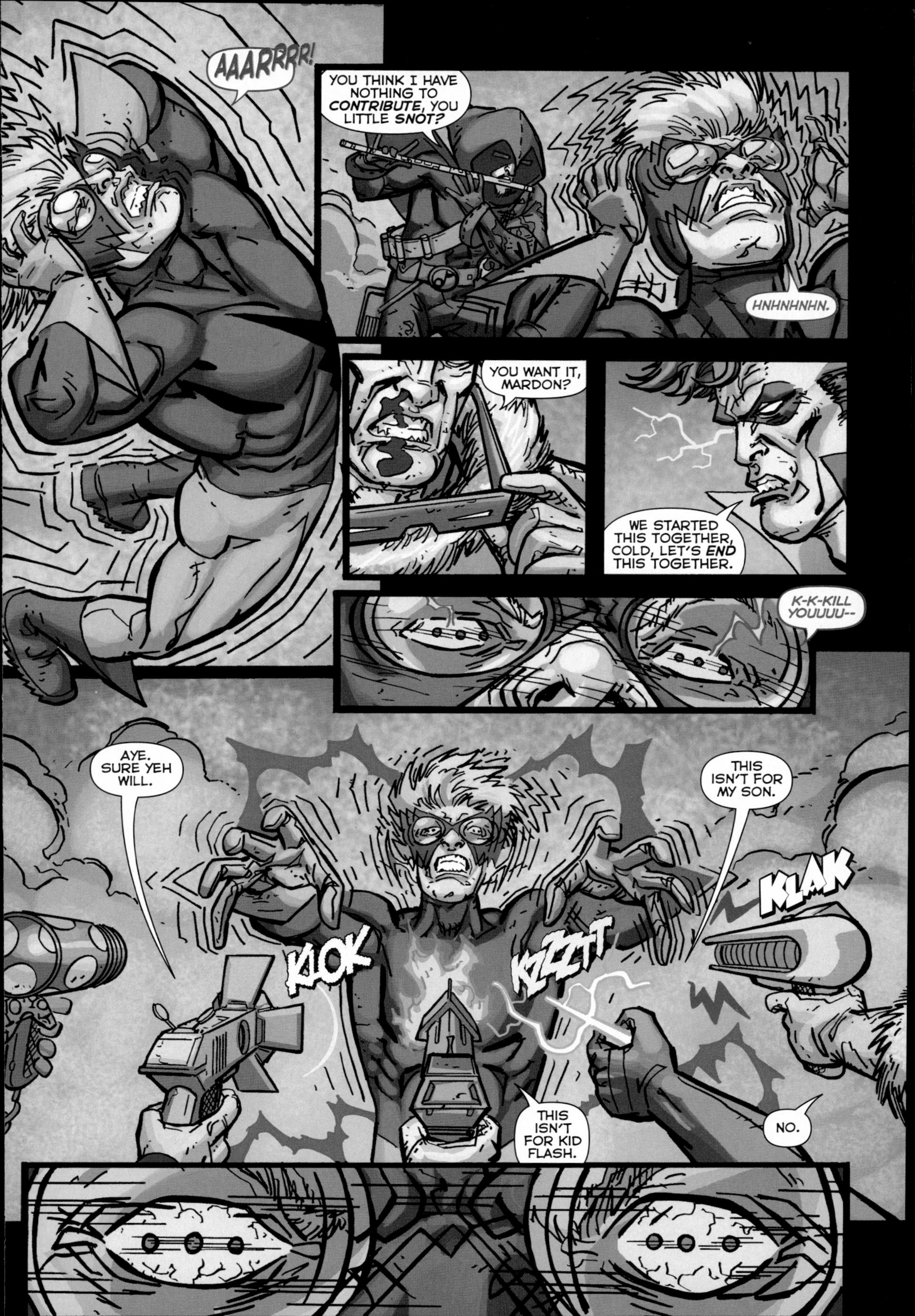
AAARRRR!
YOU THINK I HAVE NOTHING TO *CONTRIBUTE*, YOU LITTLE *SNOT?*
HNHNHNHN.
YOU WANT IT, MARDON?
WE STARTED THIS TOGETHER, COLD, LET'S *END* THIS TOGETHER.
K-K-KILL YOUUUU--
AYE. SURE YEH WILL.
THIS ISN'T FOR MY SON.
KLAK
KLOK
KZZZZTT
THIS ISN'T FOR KID FLASH.
NO.

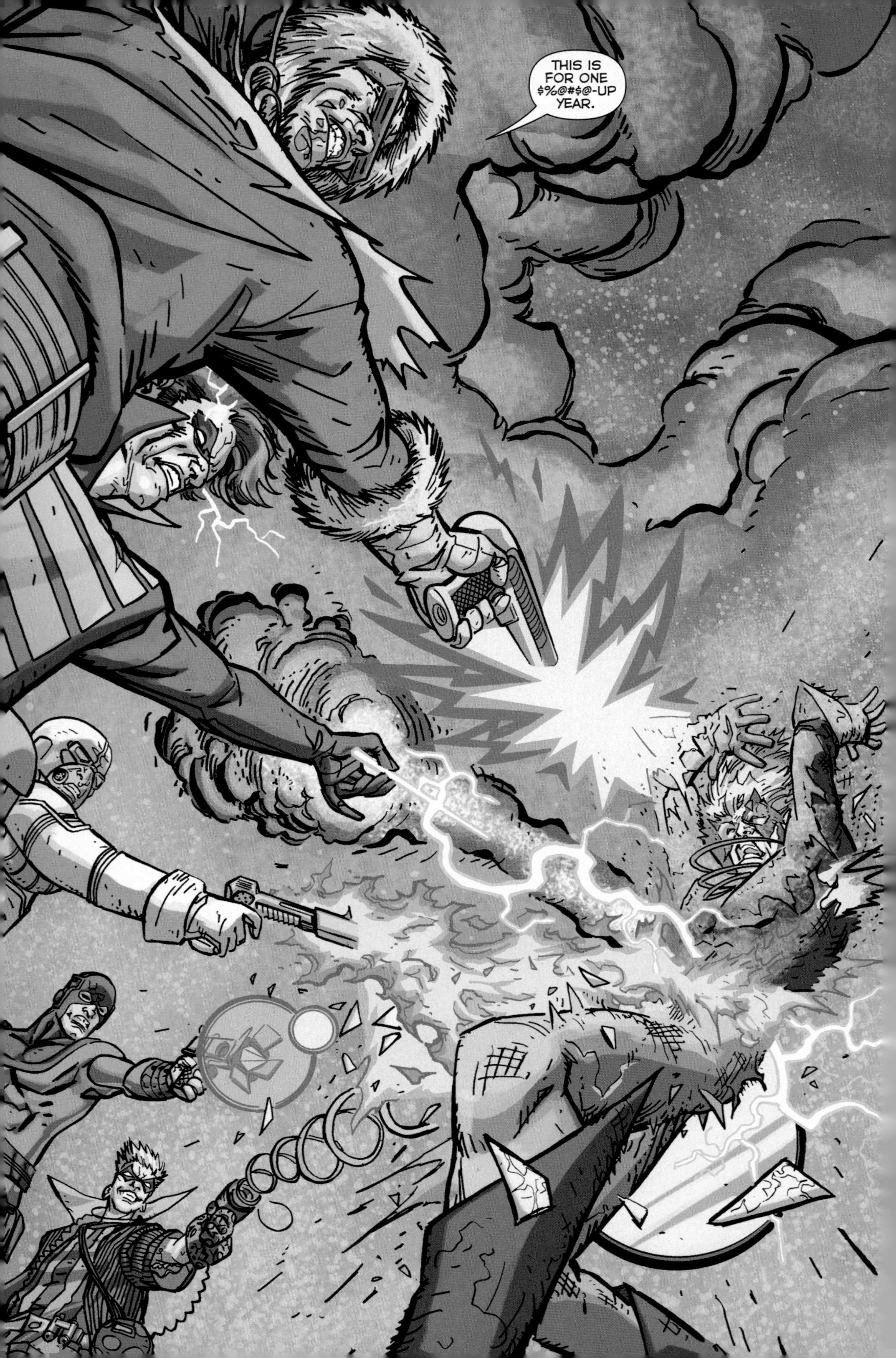
THIS IS FOR ONE $%@#$@-UP YEAR.

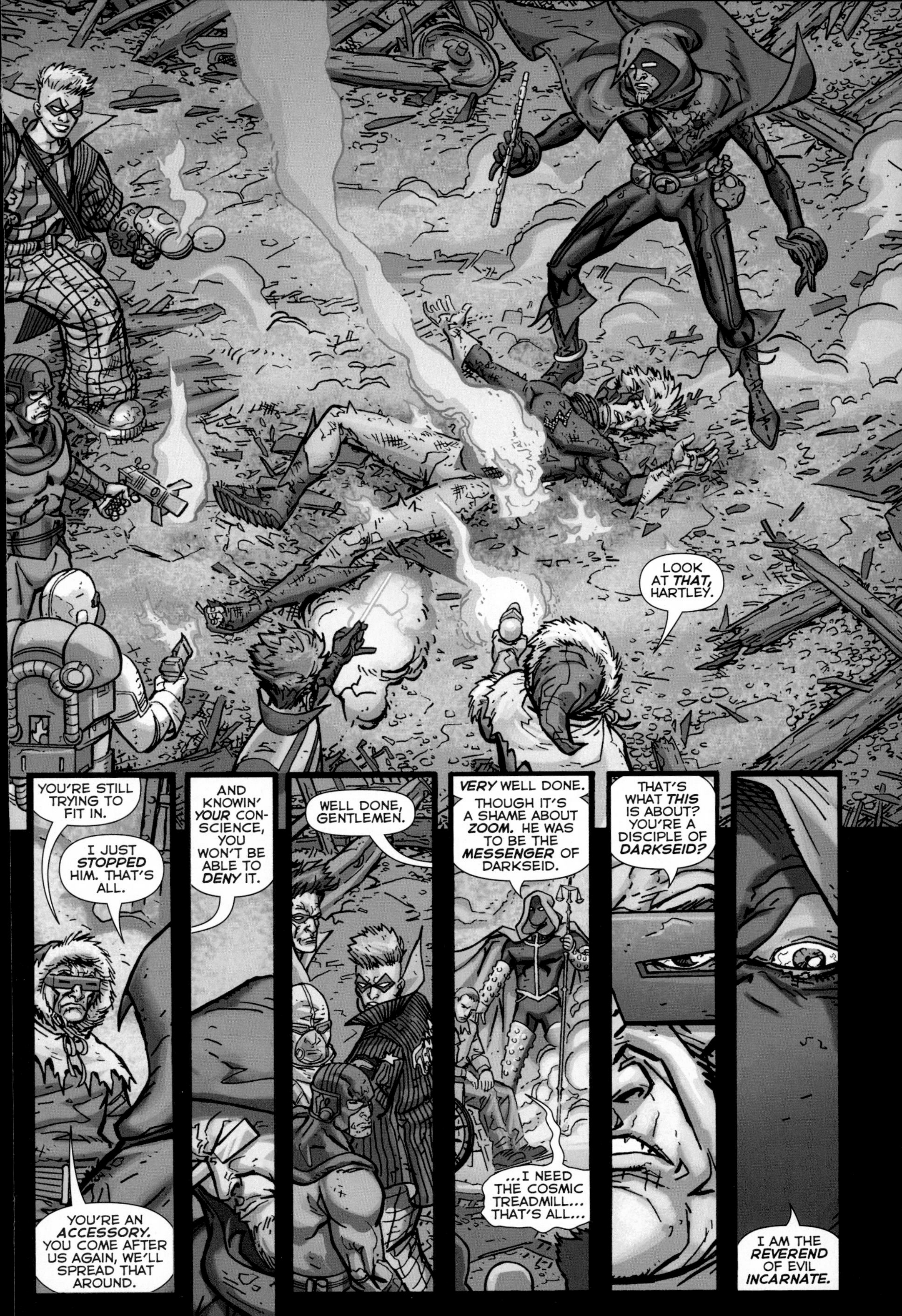
LOOK AT *THAT,* HARTLEY.
YOU'RE STILL TRYING TO FIT IN.
I JUST *STOPPED* HIM. THAT'S ALL.
YOU'RE AN *ACCESSORY.* YOU COME AFTER US AGAIN, WE'LL SPREAD THAT AROUND.
AND KNOWIN' *YOUR* CONSCIENCE, YOU WON'T BE ABLE TO *DENY* IT.
WELL DONE, GENTLEMEN.
VERY WELL DONE.
THOUGH IT'S A SHAME ABOUT *ZOOM.* HE WAS TO BE THE *MESSENGER* OF DARKSEID.
...I NEED THE COSMIC TREADMILL... THAT'S ALL...
THAT'S WHAT *THIS* IS ABOUT? YOU'RE A DISCIPLE OF *DARKSEID?*
I AM THE *REVEREND* OF EVIL *INCARNATE.*

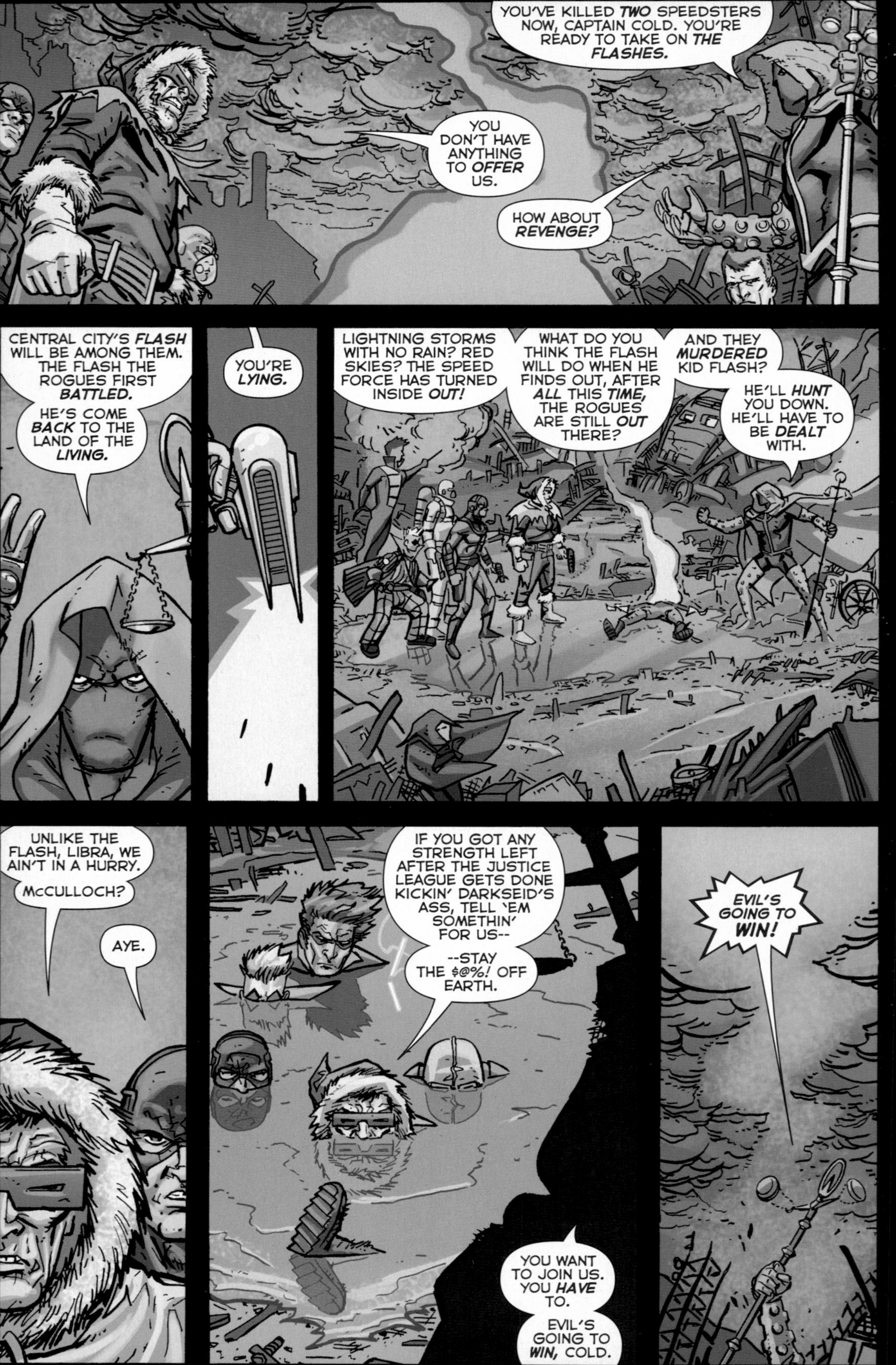
YOU'VE KILLED TWO SPEEDSTERS NOW, CAPTAIN COLD. YOU'RE READY TO TAKE ON THE FLASHES.
YOU DON'T HAVE ANYTHING TO OFFER US.
HOW ABOUT REVENGE?
CENTRAL CITY'S FLASH WILL BE AMONG THEM. THE FLASH THE ROGUES FIRST BATTLED.
HE'S COME BACK TO THE LAND OF THE LIVING.
YOU'RE LYING.
LIGHTNING STORMS WITH NO RAIN? RED SKIES? THE SPEED FORCE HAS TURNED INSIDE OUT!
WHAT DO YOU THINK THE FLASH WILL DO WHEN HE FINDS OUT, AFTER ALL THIS TIME, THE ROGUES ARE STILL OUT THERE?
AND THEY MURDERED KID FLASH?
HE'LL HUNT YOU DOWN. HE'LL HAVE TO BE DEALT WITH.
UNLIKE THE FLASH, LIBRA, WE AIN'T IN A HURRY.
McCULLOCH?
AYE.
IF YOU GOT ANY STRENGTH LEFT AFTER THE JUSTICE LEAGUE GETS DONE KICKIN' DARKSEID'S ASS, TELL 'EM SOMETHIN' FOR US--
--STAY THE $@%! OFF EARTH.
YOU WANT TO JOIN US. YOU HAVE TO.
EVIL'S GOING TO WIN, COLD.
EVIL'S GOING TO WIN!

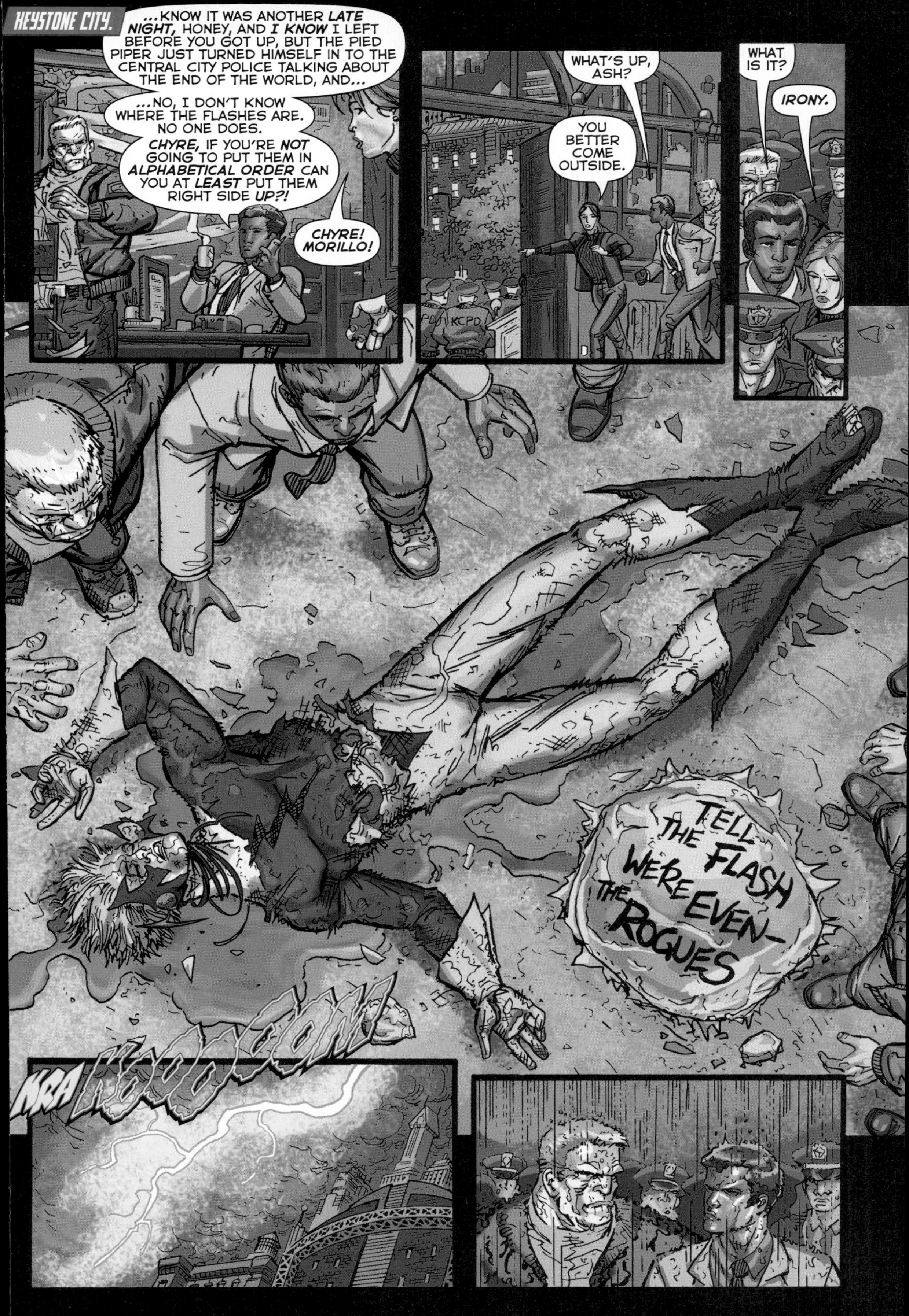
KEYSTONE CITY.
...KNOW IT WAS ANOTHER LATE NIGHT, HONEY, AND I KNOW I LEFT BEFORE YOU GOT UP, BUT THE PIED PIPER JUST TURNED HIMSELF IN TO THE CENTRAL CITY POLICE TALKING ABOUT THE END OF THE WORLD, AND...
...NO, I DON'T KNOW WHERE THE FLASHES ARE. NO ONE DOES.
CHYRE, IF YOU'RE NOT GOING TO PUT THEM IN ALPHABETICAL ORDER CAN YOU AT LEAST PUT THEM RIGHT SIDE UP?!
CHYRE! MORILLO!
WHAT'S UP, ASH?
YOU BETTER COME OUTSIDE.
WHAT IS IT?
IRONY.
KCPD
TELL THE FLASH WE'RE EVEN— THE ROGUES
KRA KOOOOOM

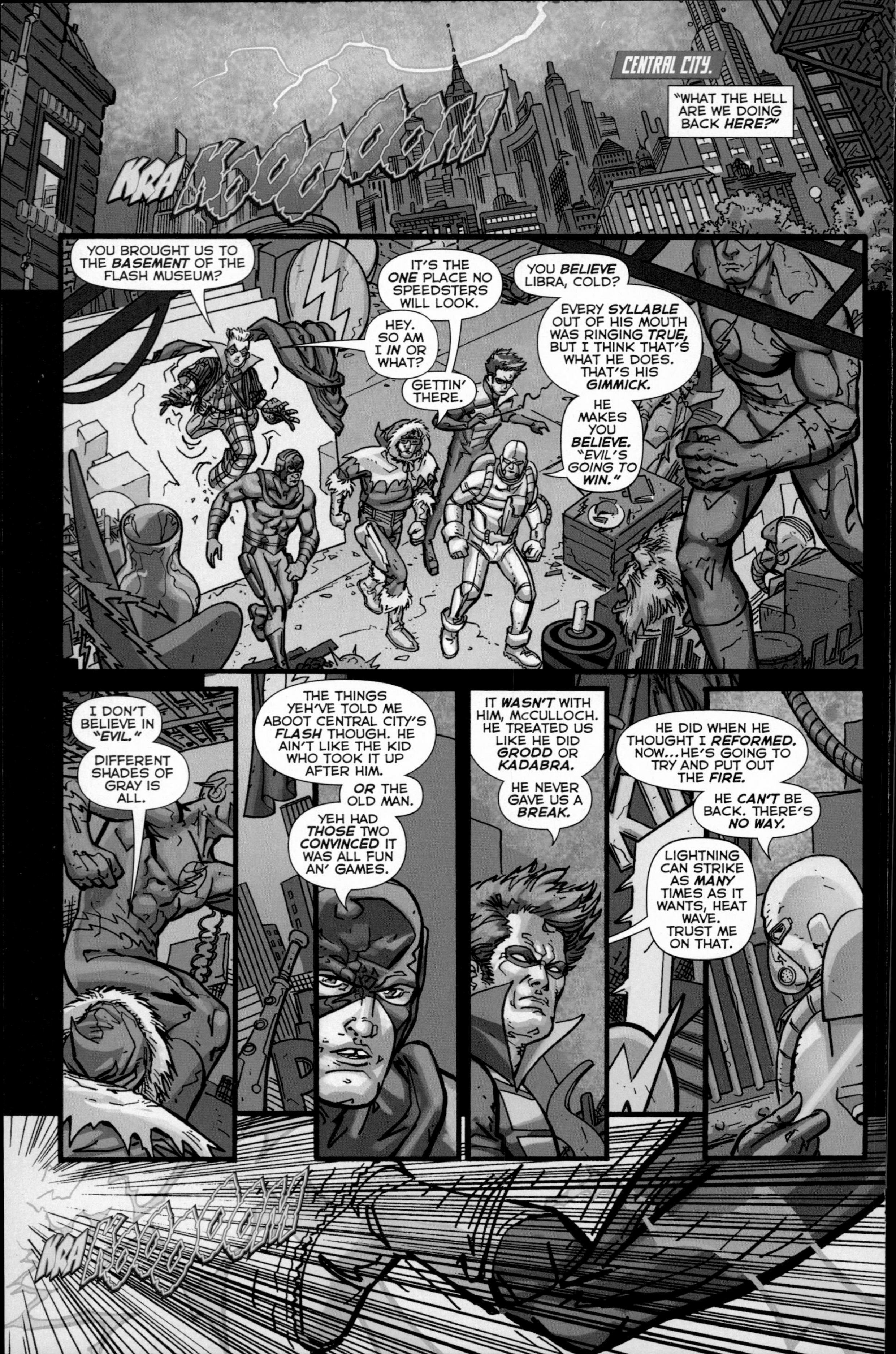
CENTRAL CITY.
"WHAT THE HELL ARE WE DOING BACK HERE?"
KRA KOOOOOM
YOU BROUGHT US TO THE BASEMENT OF THE FLASH MUSEUM?
IT'S THE ONE PLACE NO SPEEDSTERS WILL LOOK.
HEY. SO AM I IN OR WHAT?
GETTIN' THERE.
YOU BELIEVE LIBRA, COLD?
EVERY SYLLABLE OUT OF HIS MOUTH WAS RINGING TRUE, BUT I THINK THAT'S WHAT HE DOES. THAT'S HIS GIMMICK.
HE MAKES YOU BELIEVE. "EVIL'S GOING TO WIN."
I DON'T BELIEVE IN "EVIL."
DIFFERENT SHADES OF GRAY IS ALL.
THE THINGS YEH'VE TOLD ME ABOOT CENTRAL CITY'S FLASH THOUGH. HE AIN'T LIKE THE KID WHO TOOK IT UP AFTER HIM.
OR THE OLD MAN.
YEH HAD THOSE TWO CONVINCED IT WAS ALL FUN AN' GAMES.
IT WASN'T WITH HIM, McCULLOCH. HE TREATED US LIKE HE DID GRODD OR KADABRA.
HE NEVER GAVE US A BREAK.
HE DID WHEN HE THOUGHT I REFORMED. NOW... HE'S GOING TO TRY AND PUT OUT THE FIRE.
HE CAN'T BE BACK. THERE'S NO WAY.
LIGHTNING CAN STRIKE AS MANY TIMES AS IT WANTS, HEAT WAVE. TRUST ME ON THAT.
KRA KOOOOOM

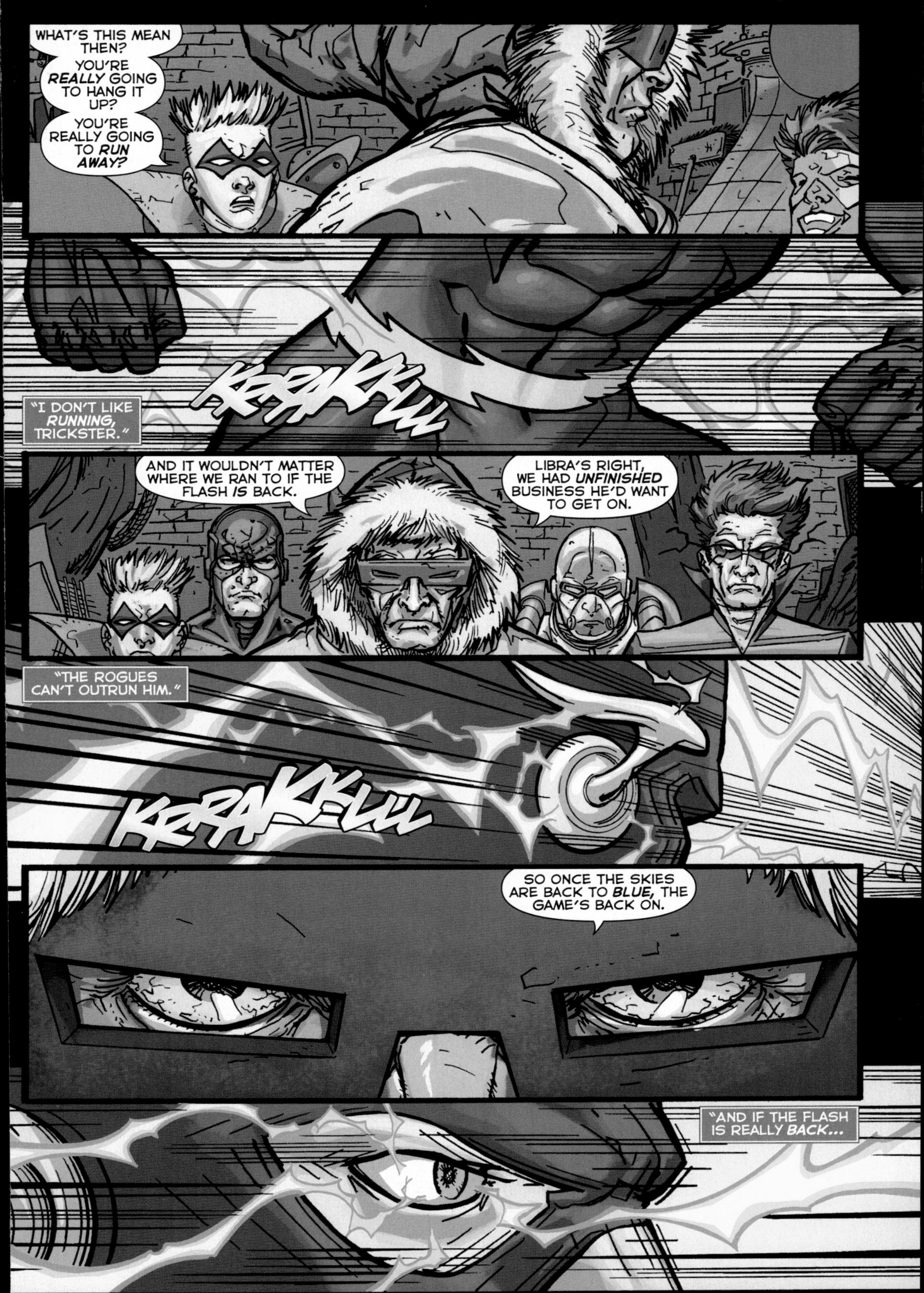

WHAT'S THIS MEAN THEN?
YOU'RE REALLY GOING TO HANG IT UP?
YOU'RE REALLY GOING TO RUN AWAY?
KRRAKKLLL
"I DON'T LIKE RUNNING, TRICKSTER."
AND IT WOULDN'T MATTER WHERE WE RAN TO IF THE FLASH IS BACK.
LIBRA'S RIGHT, WE HAD UNFINISHED BUSINESS HE'D WANT TO GET ON.
"THE ROGUES CAN'T OUTRUN HIM."
KRRAKKLLL
SO ONCE THE SKIES ARE BACK TO BLUE, THE GAME'S BACK ON.
"AND IF THE FLASH IS REALLY BACK...

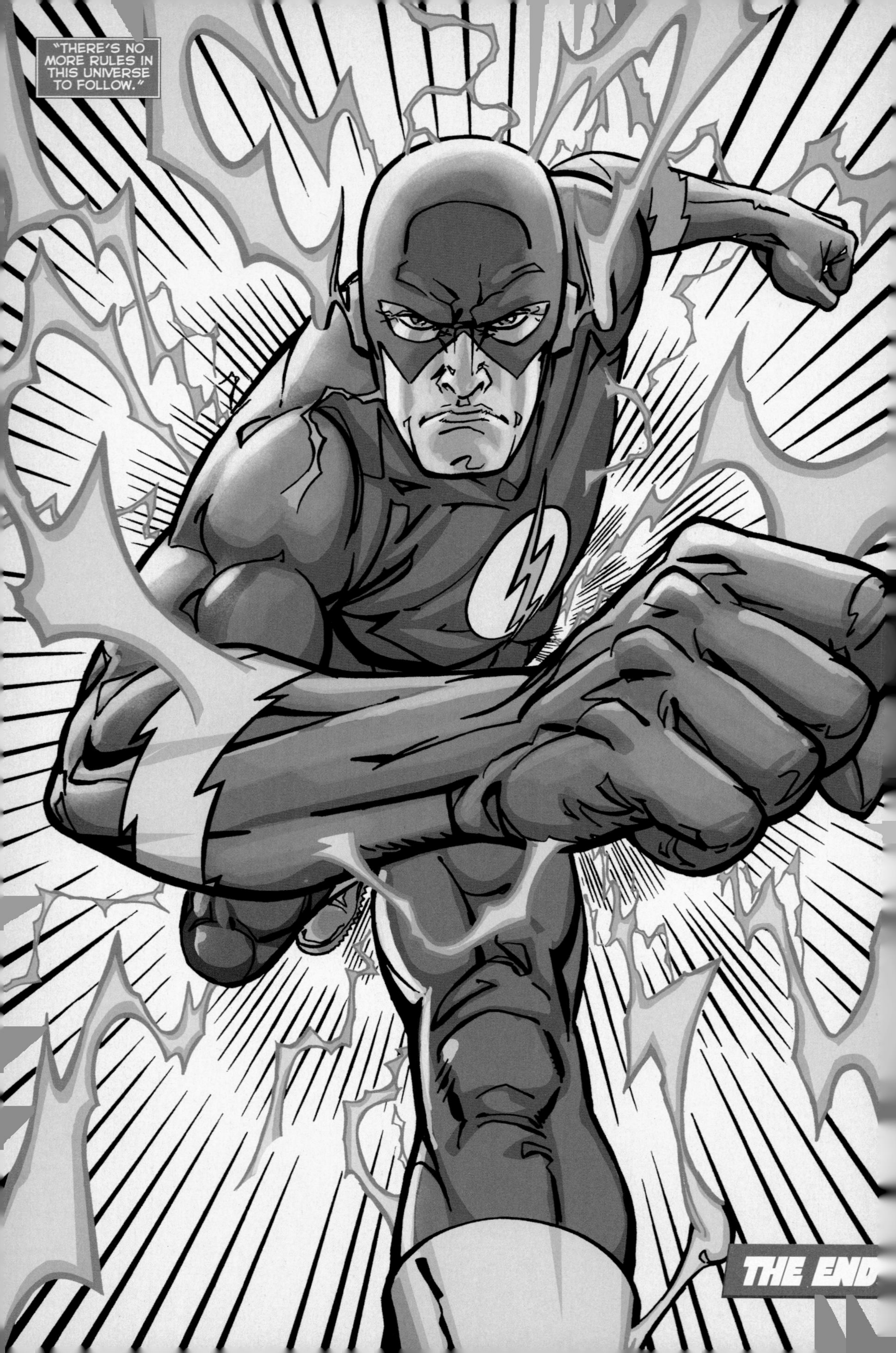
"THERE'S NO MORE RULES IN THIS UNIVERSE TO FOLLOW."
THE END

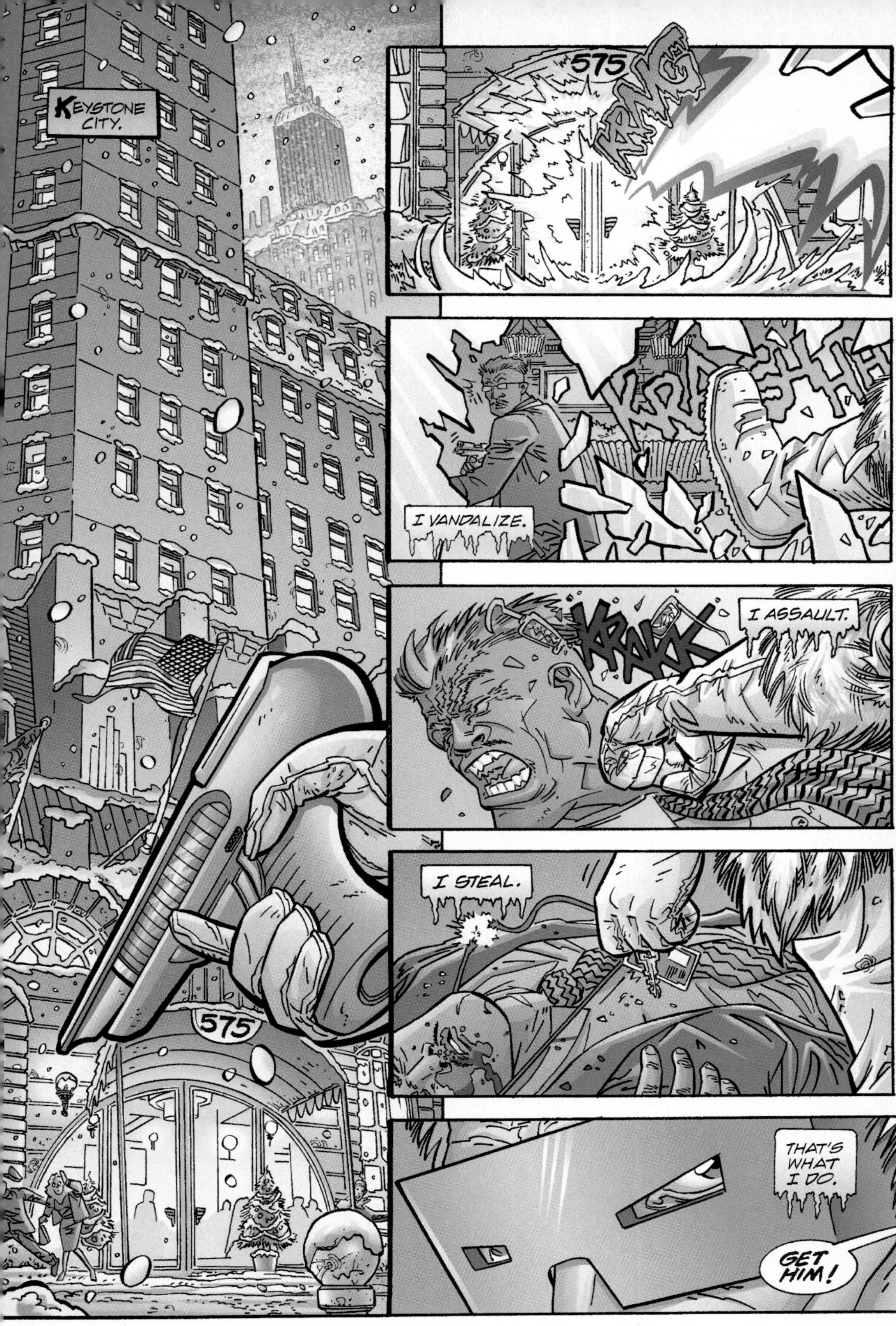

KEYSTONE CITY.
575
KRANG
575
KRASHHH
I VANDALIZE.
KRAKK
I ASSAULT.
I STEAL.
THAT'S WHAT I DO.
GET HIM!

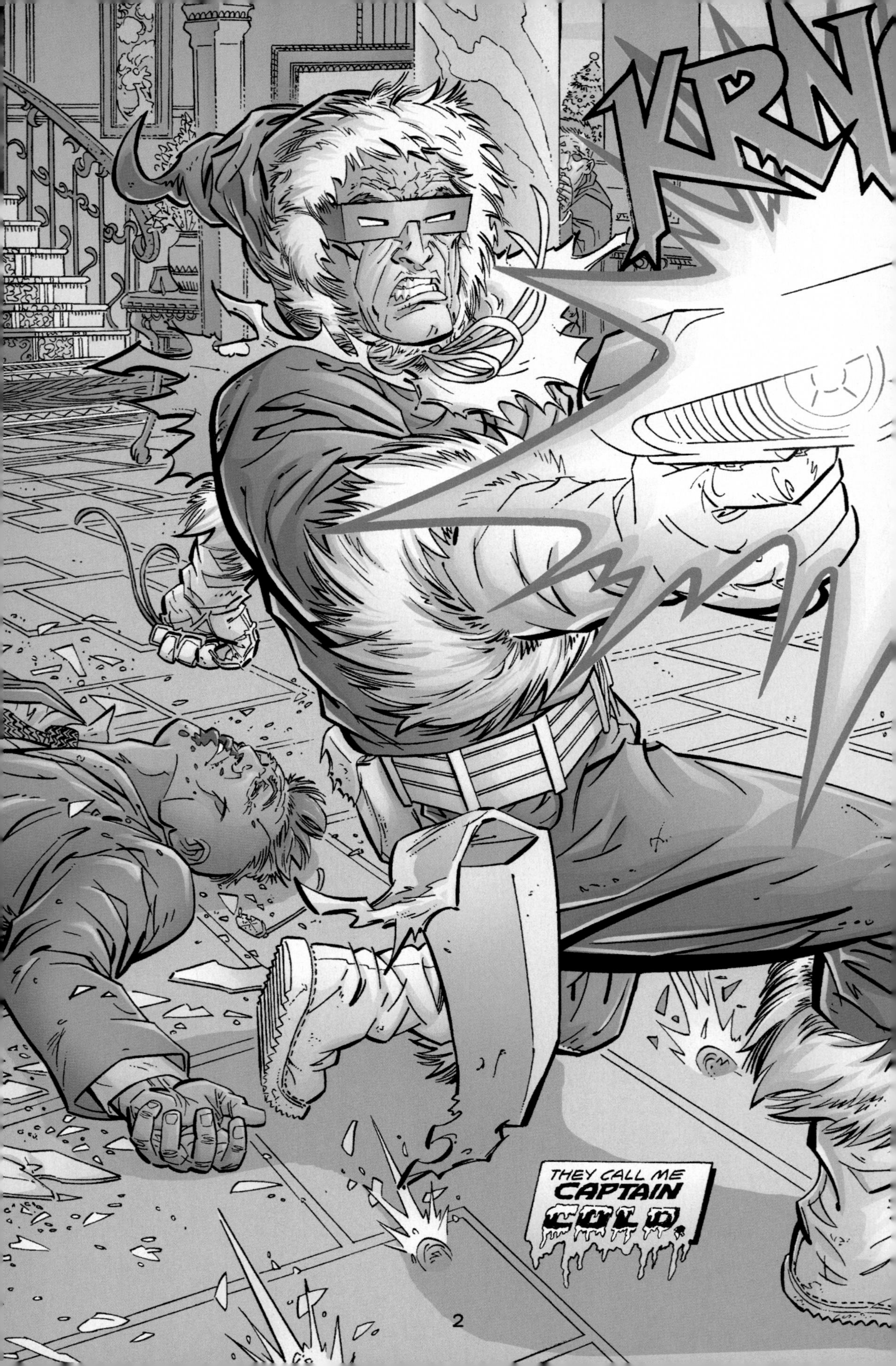
KRN
THEY CALL ME CAPTAIN COLD.

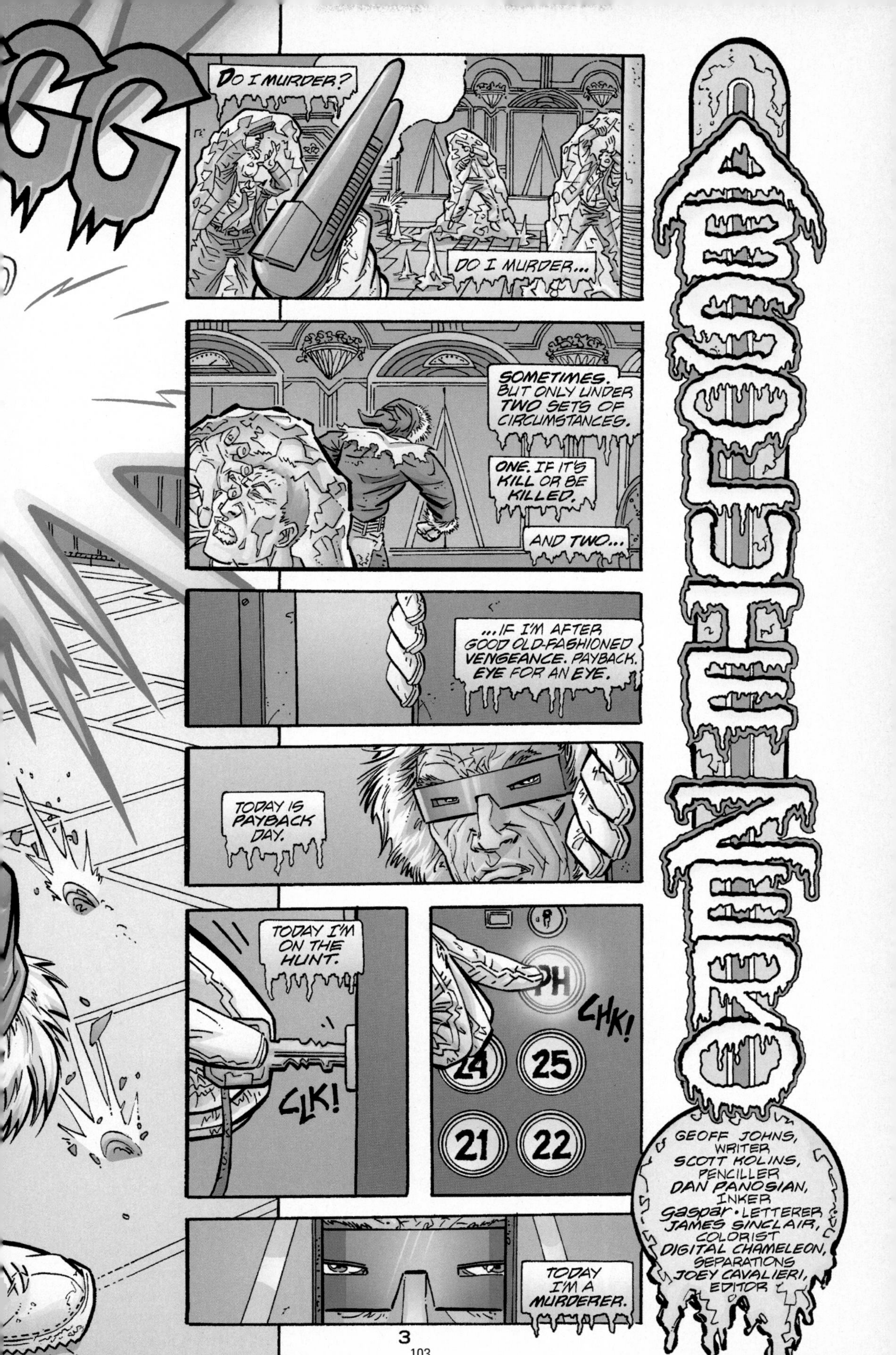
DO I MURDER?
DO I MURDER...
SOMETIMES. BUT ONLY UNDER TWO SETS OF CIRCUMSTANCES.
ONE. IF IT'S KILL OR BE KILLED.
AND TWO...
...IF I'M AFTER GOOD OLD-FASHIONED VENGEANCE. PAYBACK. EYE FOR AN EYE.
TODAY IS PAYBACK DAY.
TODAY I'M ON THE HUNT.
CLK!
PH
CHK!
24
25
21
22
TODAY I'M A MURDERER.
ABSOLUTE ZERO
GEOFF JOHNS, WRITER
SCOTT KOLINS, PENCILLER
DAN PANOSIAN, INKER
Gaspar • LETTERER
JAMES SINCLAIR, COLORIST
DIGITAL CHAMELEON, SEPARATIONS
JOEY CAVALIERI, EDITOR

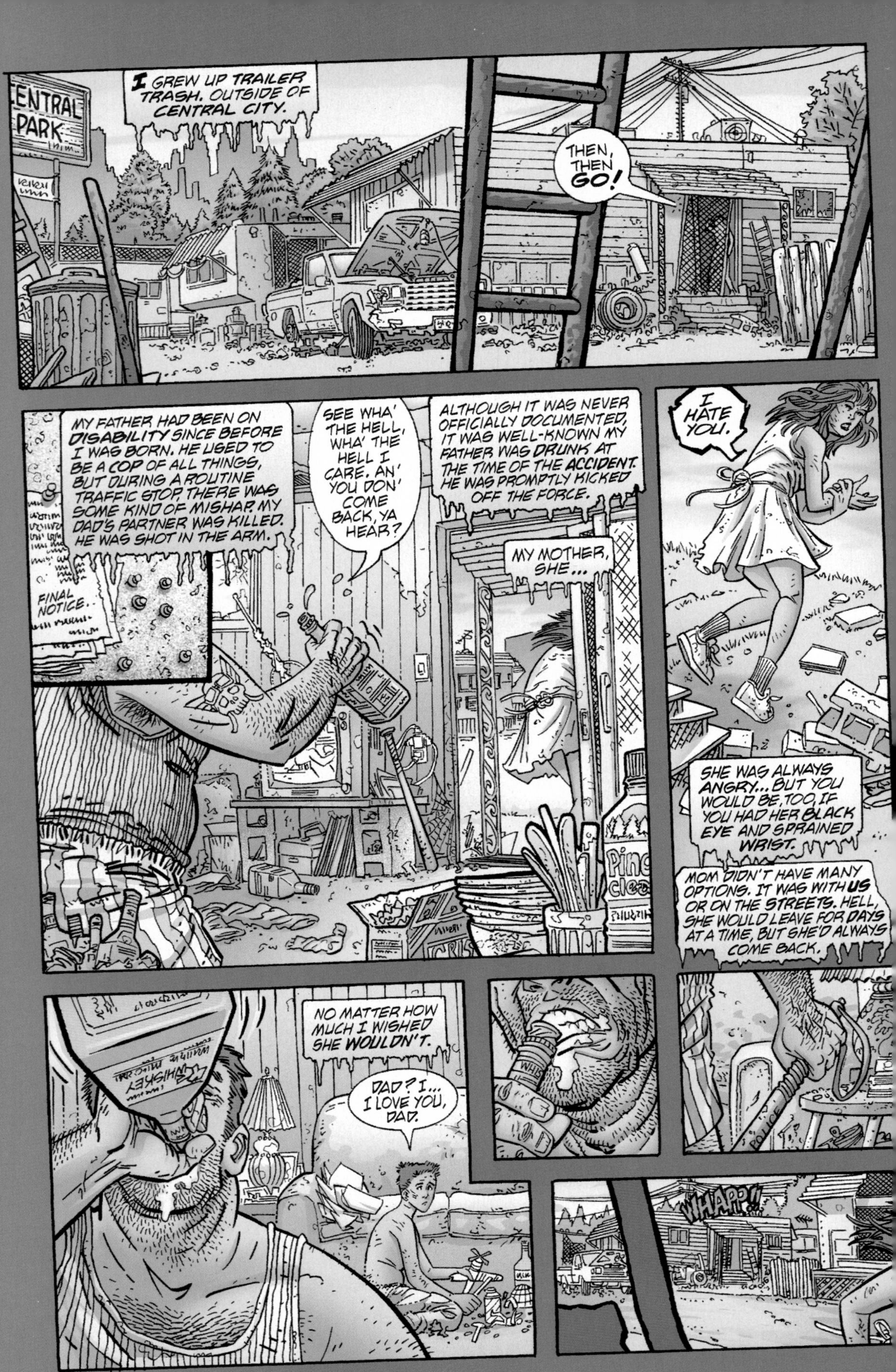

CENTRAL PARK
I GREW UP TRAILER TRASH. OUTSIDE OF CENTRAL CITY.
THEN, THEN GO!
MY FATHER HAD BEEN ON DISABILITY SINCE BEFORE I WAS BORN. HE USED TO BE A COP OF ALL THINGS, BUT DURING A ROUTINE TRAFFIC STOP THERE WAS SOME KIND OF MISHAP. MY DAD'S PARTNER WAS KILLED. HE WAS SHOT IN THE ARM.
FINAL NOTICE
SEE WHA' THE HELL, WHA' THE HELL I CARE. AN' YOU DON' COME BACK, YA HEAR?
ALTHOUGH IT WAS NEVER OFFICIALLY DOCUMENTED, IT WAS WELL-KNOWN MY FATHER WAS DRUNK AT THE TIME OF THE ACCIDENT. HE WAS PROMPTLY KICKED OFF THE FORCE.
MY MOTHER, SHE...
I HATE YOU.
SHE WAS ALWAYS ANGRY... BUT YOU WOULD BE, TOO, IF YOU HAD HER BLACK EYE AND SPRAINED WRIST.
MOM DIDN'T HAVE MANY OPTIONS. IT WAS WITH US OR ON THE STREETS. HELL, SHE WOULD LEAVE FOR DAYS AT A TIME, BUT SHE'D ALWAYS COME BACK.
NO MATTER HOW MUCH I WISHED SHE WOULDN'T.
WHISKEY
DAD? I... I LOVE YOU, DAD.
POLICE
WHAPP!!

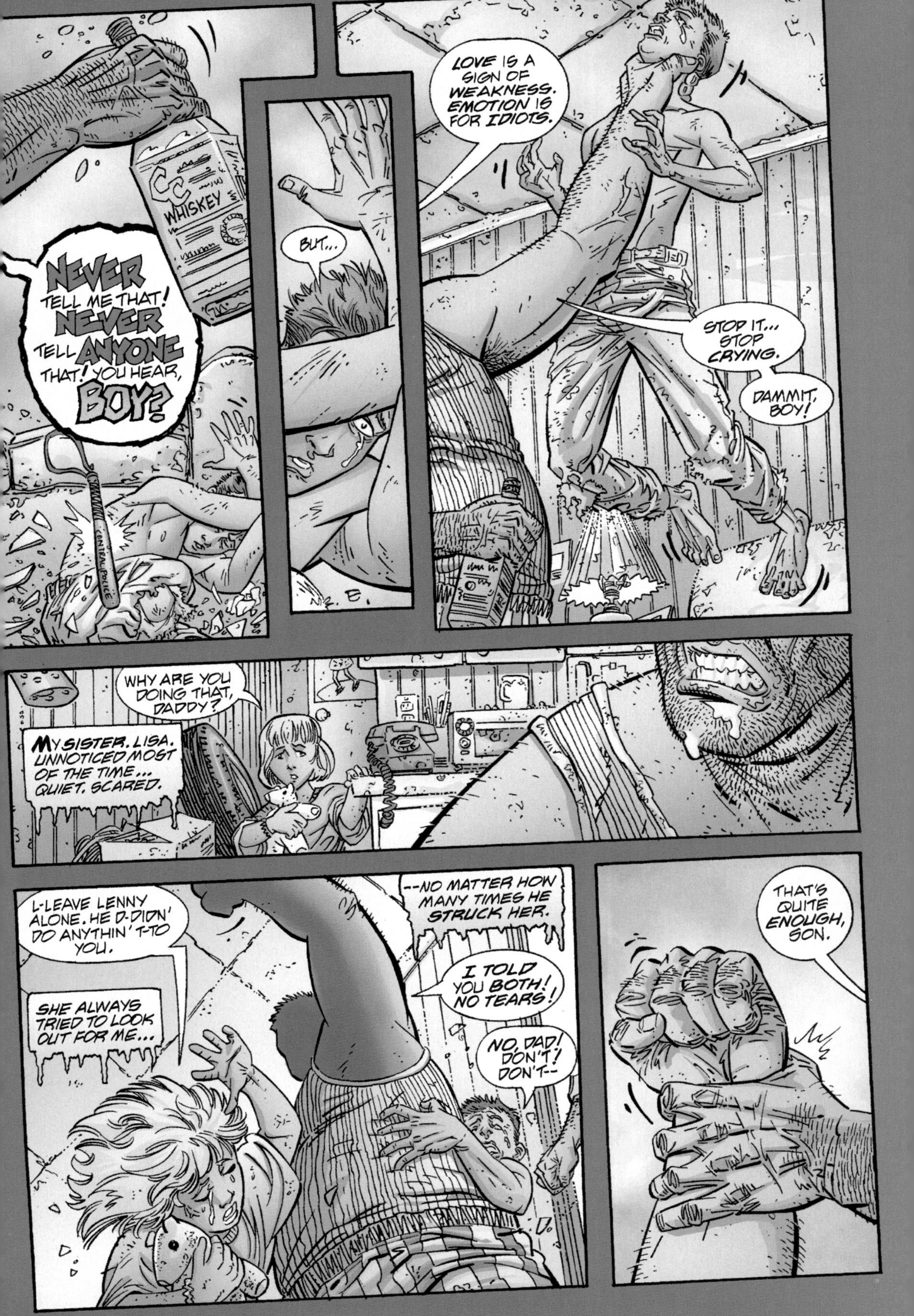
NEVER TELL ME THAT! NEVER TELL ANYONE THAT! YOU HEAR, BOY?
WHISKEY
CENTRAL POLICE
BUT...
LOVE IS A SIGN OF WEAKNESS. EMOTION IS FOR IDIOTS.
STOP IT... STOP CRYING.
DAMMIT, BOY!
WHY ARE YOU DOING THAT, DADDY?
MY SISTER. LISA. UNNOTICED MOST OF THE TIME... QUIET. SCARED.
L-LEAVE LENNY ALONE. HE D-DIDN' DO ANYTHIN' T-TO YOU.
SHE ALWAYS TRIED TO LOOK OUT FOR ME...
--NO MATTER HOW MANY TIMES HE STRUCK HER.
I TOLD YOU BOTH! NO TEARS!
NO, DAD! DON'T! DON'T--
THAT'S QUITE ENOUGH, SON.

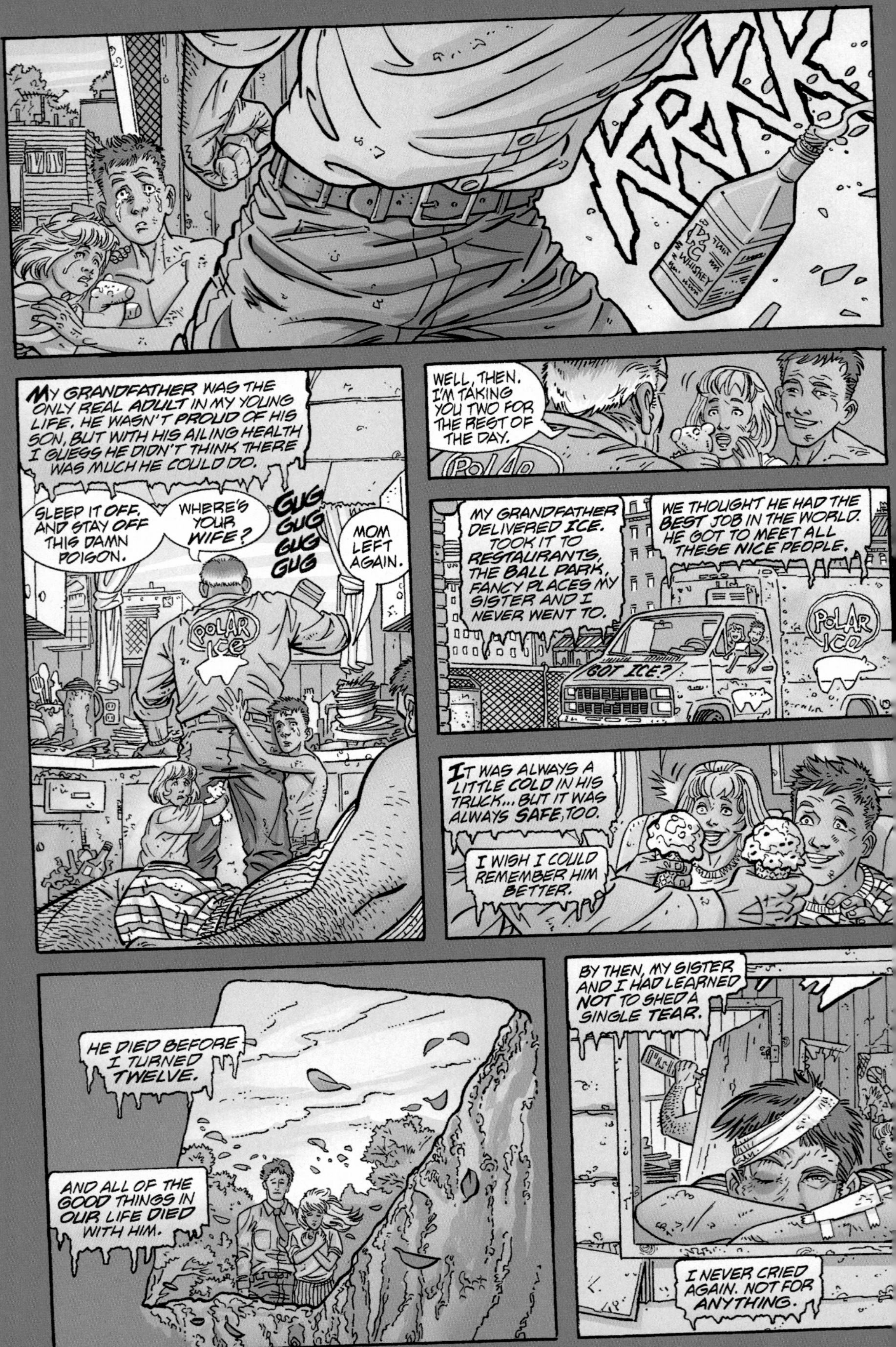
KRAKK
MY GRANDFATHER WAS THE ONLY REAL ADULT IN MY YOUNG LIFE. HE WASN'T PROUD OF HIS SON, BUT WITH HIS AILING HEALTH I GUESS HE DIDN'T THINK THERE WAS MUCH HE COULD DO.
SLEEP IT OFF. AND STAY OFF THIS DAMN POISON.
WHERE'S YOUR WIFE?
GUG GUG GUG GUG
MOM LEFT AGAIN.
POLAR ICE
WELL, THEN. I'M TAKING YOU TWO FOR THE REST OF THE DAY.
MY GRANDFATHER DELIVERED ICE. TOOK IT TO RESTAURANTS, THE BALL PARK, FANCY PLACES MY SISTER AND I NEVER WENT TO.
WE THOUGHT HE HAD THE BEST JOB IN THE WORLD. HE GOT TO MEET ALL THESE NICE PEOPLE.
GOT ICE?
POLAR ICE
IT WAS ALWAYS A LITTLE COLD IN HIS TRUCK... BUT IT WAS ALWAYS SAFE, TOO.
I WISH I COULD REMEMBER HIM BETTER.
HE DIED BEFORE I TURNED TWELVE.
AND ALL OF THE GOOD THINGS IN OUR LIFE DIED WITH HIM.
BY THEN, MY SISTER AND I HAD LEARNED NOT TO SHED A SINGLE TEAR.
I NEVER CRIED AGAIN. NOT FOR ANYTHING.

NGG!

PH

24 25

NOT EVEN WHEN SHE DIED.

BBRATT!

NOTHING LIKE A LITTLE *COLD FIELD* TO SLOW THINGS *DOWN*, eh?

KRNGGG

AAAAA!

TSSSH

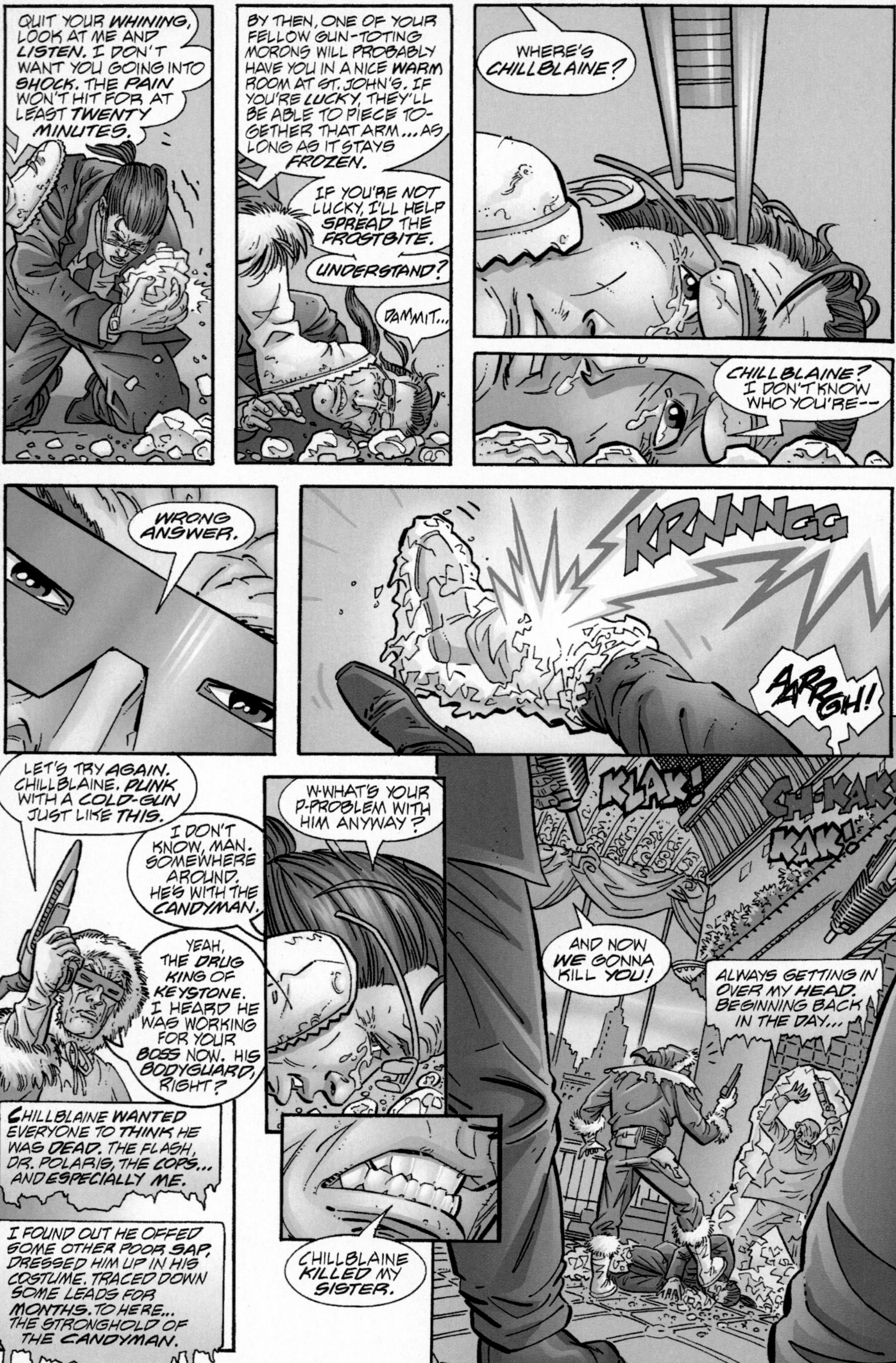
QUIT YOUR WHINING, LOOK AT ME AND LISTEN. I DON'T WANT YOU GOING INTO SHOCK. THE PAIN WON'T HIT FOR AT LEAST TWENTY MINUTES.
BY THEN, ONE OF YOUR FELLOW GUN-TOTING MORONS WILL PROBABLY HAVE YOU IN A NICE WARM ROOM AT ST. JOHN'S. IF YOU'RE LUCKY, THEY'LL BE ABLE TO PIECE TOGETHER THAT ARM... AS LONG AS IT STAYS FROZEN.
IF YOU'RE NOT LUCKY, I'LL HELP SPREAD THE FROSTBITE.
UNDERSTAND?
DAMMIT...
WHERE'S CHILLBLAINE?
CHILLBLAINE? I DON'T KNOW WHO YOU'RE--
WRONG ANSWER.
KRNNNGG
AARRGH!
LET'S TRY AGAIN. CHILLBLAINE. PUNK WITH A COLD-GUN JUST LIKE THIS.
I DON'T KNOW, MAN. SOMEWHERE AROUND. HE'S WITH THE CANDYMAN.
YEAH, THE DRUG KING OF KEYSTONE. I HEARD HE WAS WORKING FOR YOUR BOSS NOW. HIS BODYGUARD, RIGHT?
W-WHAT'S YOUR P-PROBLEM WITH HIM ANYWAY?
CHILLBLAINE KILLED MY SISTER.
CHILLBLAINE WANTED EVERYONE TO THINK HE WAS DEAD. THE FLASH, DR. POLARIS, THE COPS... AND ESPECIALLY ME.
I FOUND OUT HE OFFED SOME OTHER POOR SAP, DRESSED HIM UP IN HIS COSTUME. TRACED DOWN SOME LEADS FOR MONTHS. TO HERE... THE STRONGHOLD OF THE CANDYMAN.
KLAK!
CH-KAK!
KAK!
AND NOW WE GONNA KILL YOU!
ALWAYS GETTING IN OVER MY HEAD. BEGINNING BACK IN THE DAY...

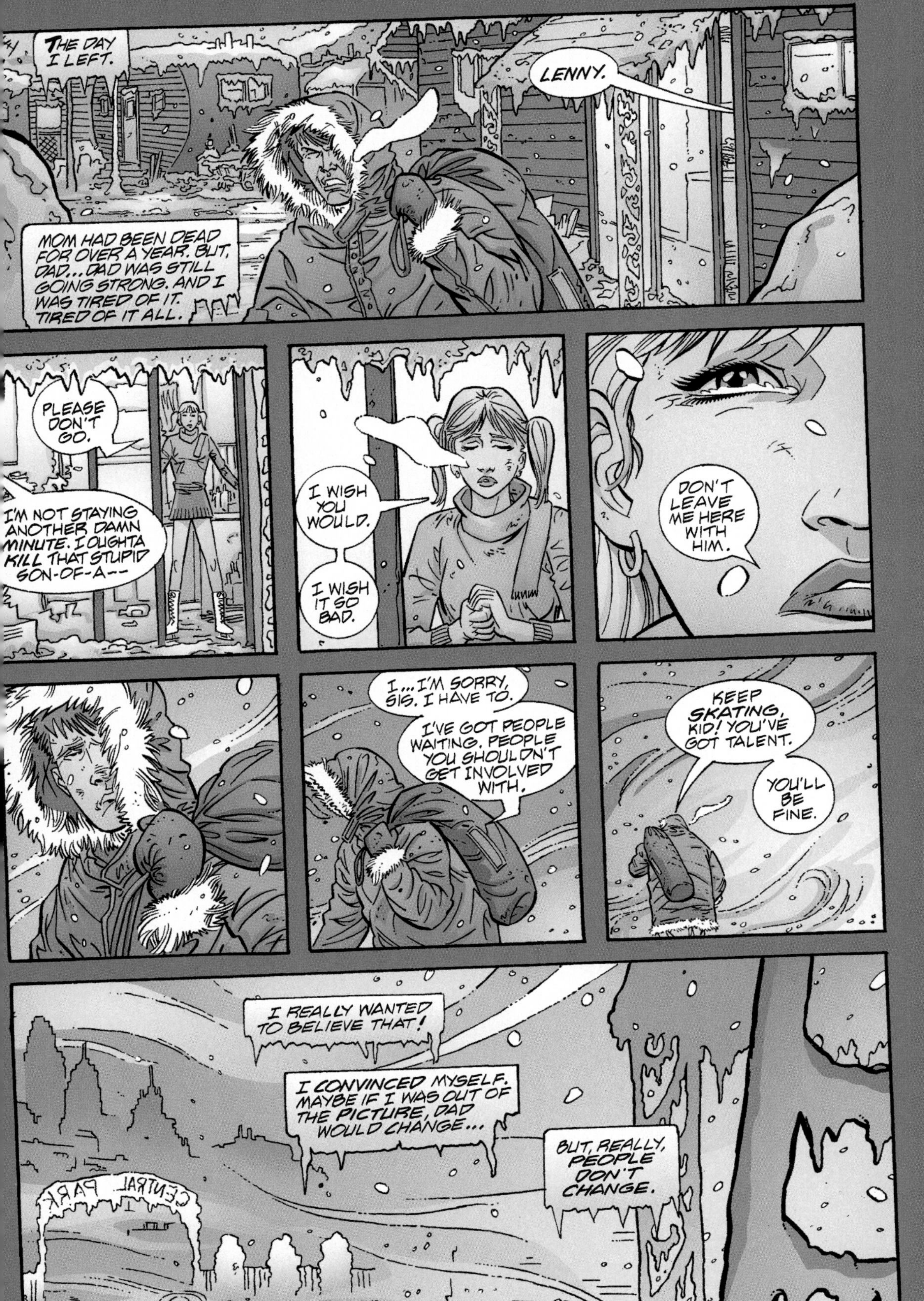
THE DAY I LEFT.
LENNY.
MOM HAD BEEN DEAD FOR OVER A YEAR. BUT, DAD... DAD WAS STILL GOING STRONG. AND I WAS TIRED OF IT. TIRED OF IT ALL.
PLEASE DON'T GO.
I'M NOT STAYING ANOTHER DAMN MINUTE. I OUGHTA KILL THAT STUPID SON-OF-A--
I WISH YOU WOULD.
I WISH IT SO BAD.
DON'T LEAVE ME HERE WITH HIM.
I... I'M SORRY, SIS. I HAVE TO.
I'VE GOT PEOPLE WAITING. PEOPLE YOU SHOULDN'T GET INVOLVED WITH.
KEEP SKATING, KID! YOU'VE GOT TALENT.
YOU'LL BE FINE.
I REALLY WANTED TO BELIEVE THAT!
I CONVINCED MYSELF. MAYBE IF I WAS OUT OF THE PICTURE, DAD WOULD CHANGE...
BUT, REALLY, PEOPLE DON'T CHANGE.
CENTRAL PARK

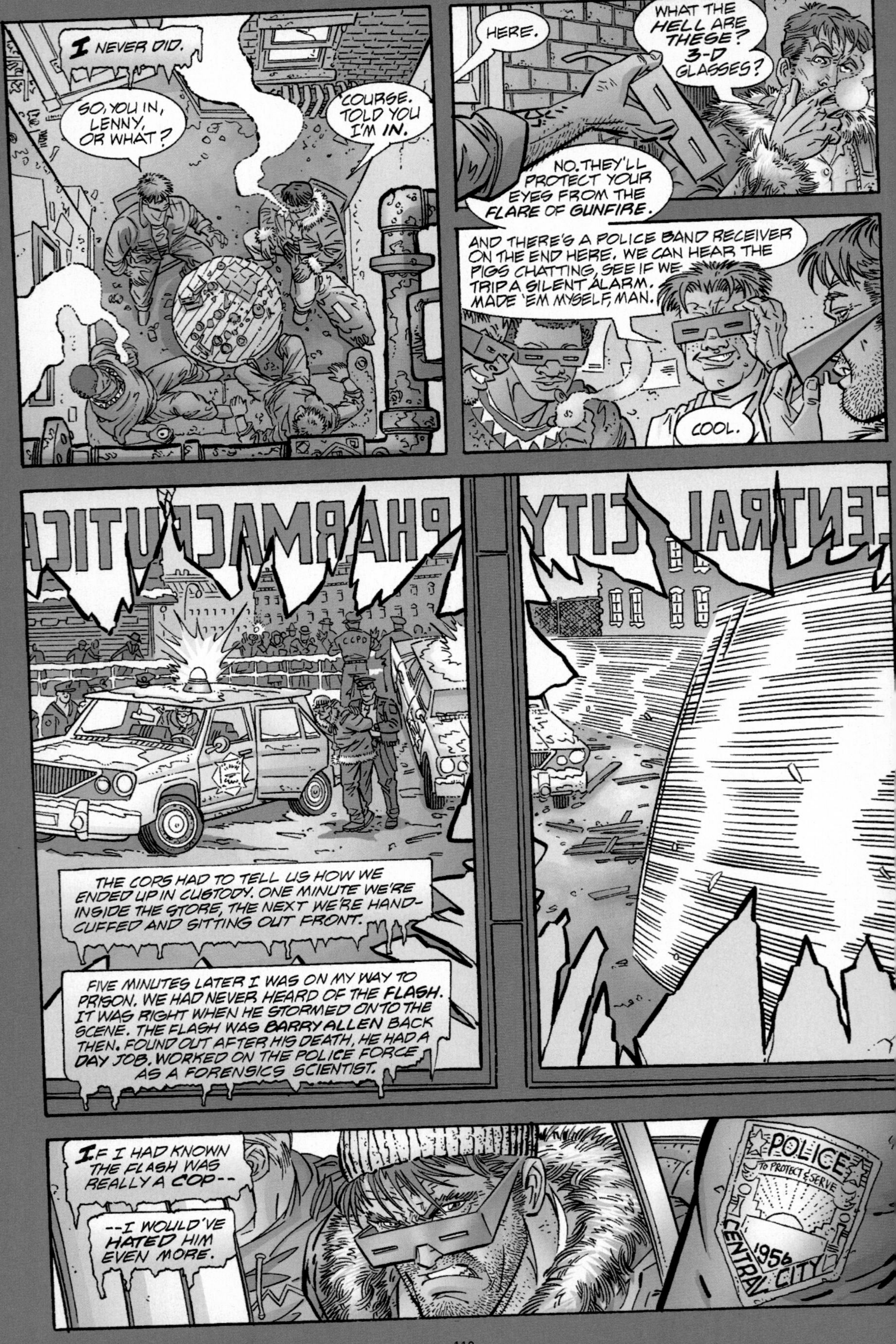
I NEVER DID.
SO, YOU IN, LENNY, OR WHAT?
COURSE. TOLD YOU I'M IN.
HERE.
WHAT THE HELL ARE THESE? 3-D GLASSES?
NO. THEY'LL PROTECT YOUR EYES FROM THE FLARE OF GUNFIRE.
AND THERE'S A POLICE BAND RECEIVER ON THE END HERE. WE CAN HEAR THE PIGS CHATTING, SEE IF WE TRIP A SILENT ALARM. MADE 'EM MYSELF, MAN.
COOL.
PHARMACEUTICA
CENTRAL CITY
CCPD
THE COPS HAD TO TELL US HOW WE ENDED UP IN CUSTODY. ONE MINUTE WE'RE INSIDE THE STORE, THE NEXT WE'RE HAND-CUFFED AND SITTING OUT FRONT.
FIVE MINUTES LATER I WAS ON MY WAY TO PRISON. WE HAD NEVER HEARD OF THE FLASH. IT WAS RIGHT WHEN HE STORMED ONTO THE SCENE. THE FLASH WAS BARRY ALLEN BACK THEN. FOUND OUT AFTER HIS DEATH, HE HAD A DAY JOB. WORKED ON THE POLICE FORCE AS A FORENSICS SCIENTIST.
IF I HAD KNOWN THE FLASH WAS REALLY A COP--
--I WOULD'VE HATED HIM EVEN MORE.
POLICE
TO PROTECT & SERVE
CENTRAL 1956 CITY

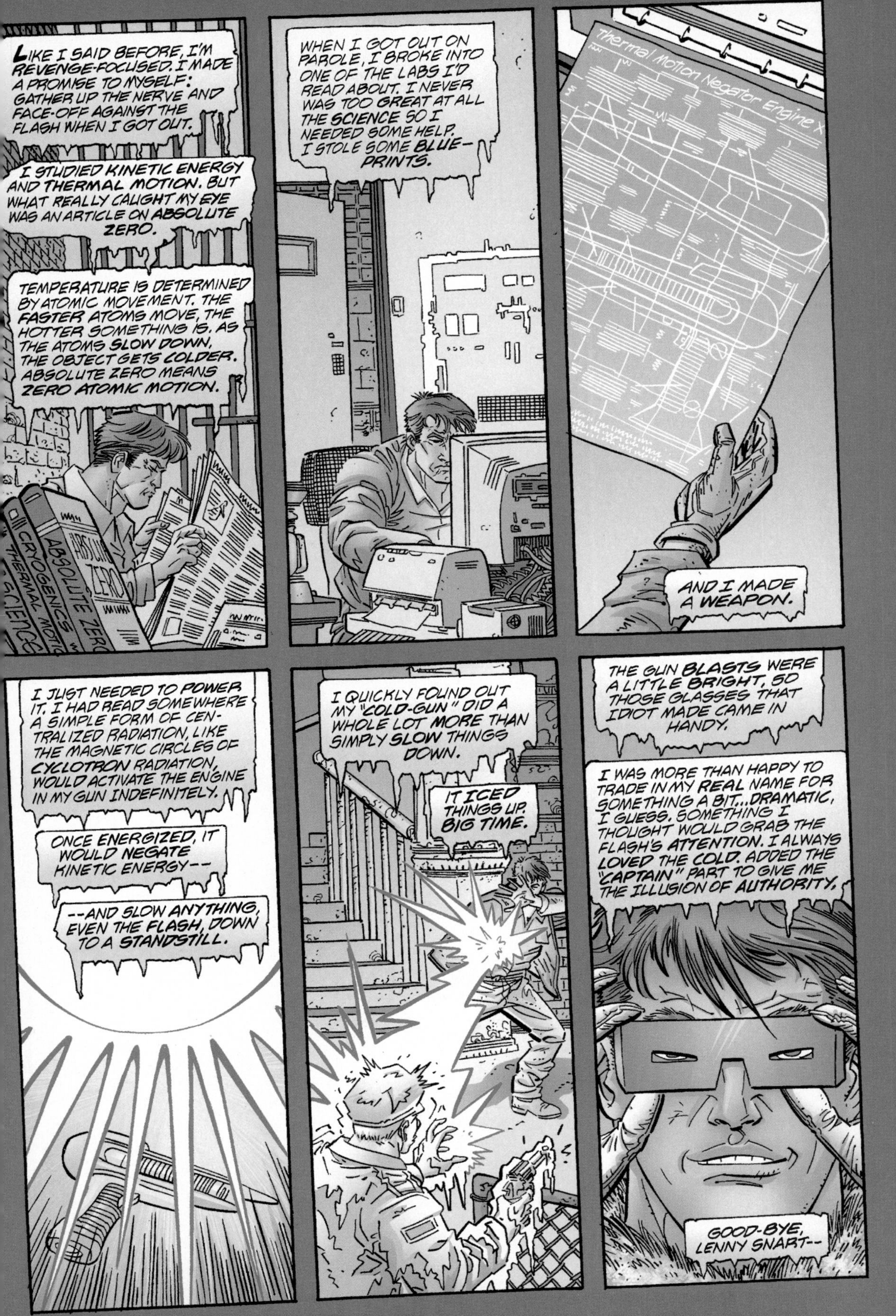
LIKE I SAID BEFORE, I'M REVENGE-FOCUSED. I MADE A PROMISE TO MYSELF: GATHER UP THE NERVE AND FACE-OFF AGAINST THE FLASH WHEN I GOT OUT.
I STUDIED KINETIC ENERGY AND THERMAL MOTION. BUT WHAT REALLY CAUGHT MY EYE WAS AN ARTICLE ON ABSOLUTE ZERO.
TEMPERATURE IS DETERMINED BY ATOMIC MOVEMENT. THE FASTER ATOMS MOVE, THE HOTTER SOMETHING IS. AS THE ATOMS SLOW DOWN, THE OBJECT GETS COLDER. ABSOLUTE ZERO MEANS ZERO ATOMIC MOTION.
ABSOLUTE ZERO
CRYOGENICS
WHEN I GOT OUT ON PAROLE, I BROKE INTO ONE OF THE LABS I'D READ ABOUT. I NEVER WAS TOO GREAT AT ALL THE SCIENCE SO I NEEDED SOME HELP. I STOLE SOME BLUE-PRINTS.
Thermal Motion Negator Engine X
AND I MADE A WEAPON.
I JUST NEEDED TO POWER IT. I HAD READ SOMEWHERE A SIMPLE FORM OF CEN-TRALIZED RADIATION, LIKE THE MAGNETIC CIRCLES OF CYCLOTRON RADIATION, WOULD ACTIVATE THE ENGINE IN MY GUN INDEFINITELY.
ONCE ENERGIZED, IT WOULD NEGATE KINETIC ENERGY--
--AND SLOW ANYTHING, EVEN THE FLASH, DOWN TO A STANDSTILL.
I QUICKLY FOUND OUT MY "COLD-GUN" DID A WHOLE LOT MORE THAN SIMPLY SLOW THINGS DOWN.
IT ICED THINGS UP. BIG TIME.
THE GUN BLASTS WERE A LITTLE BRIGHT, SO THOSE GLASSES THAT IDIOT MADE CAME IN HANDY.
I WAS MORE THAN HAPPY TO TRADE IN MY REAL NAME FOR SOMETHING A BIT...DRAMATIC, I GUESS. SOMETHING I THOUGHT WOULD GRAB THE FLASH'S ATTENTION. I ALWAYS LOVED THE COLD. ADDED THE "CAPTAIN" PART TO GIVE ME THE ILLUSION OF AUTHORITY.
GOOD-BYE, LENNY SNART--

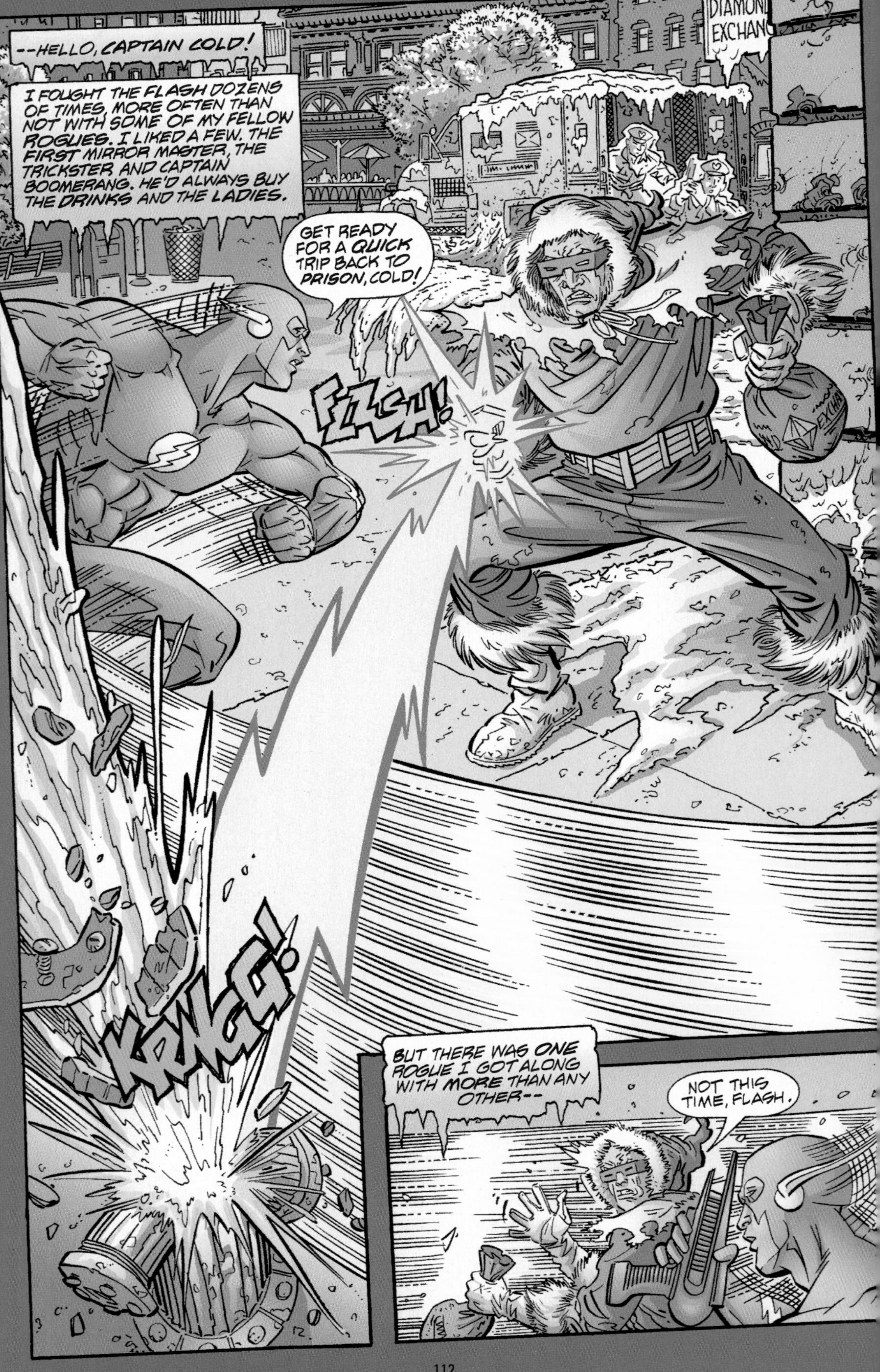
--HELLO, CAPTAIN COLD!
I FOUGHT THE FLASH DOZENS OF TIMES, MORE OFTEN THAN NOT WITH SOME OF MY FELLOW ROGUES. I LIKED A FEW. THE FIRST MIRROR MASTER, THE TRICKSTER AND CAPTAIN BOOMERANG. HE'D ALWAYS BUY THE DRINKS AND THE LADIES.
DIAMOND EXCHANG
GET READY FOR A QUICK TRIP BACK TO PRISON, COLD!
FZZSH!
KRAGG!
BUT THERE WAS ONE ROGUE I GOT ALONG WITH MORE THAN ANY OTHER--
NOT THIS TIME, FLASH.

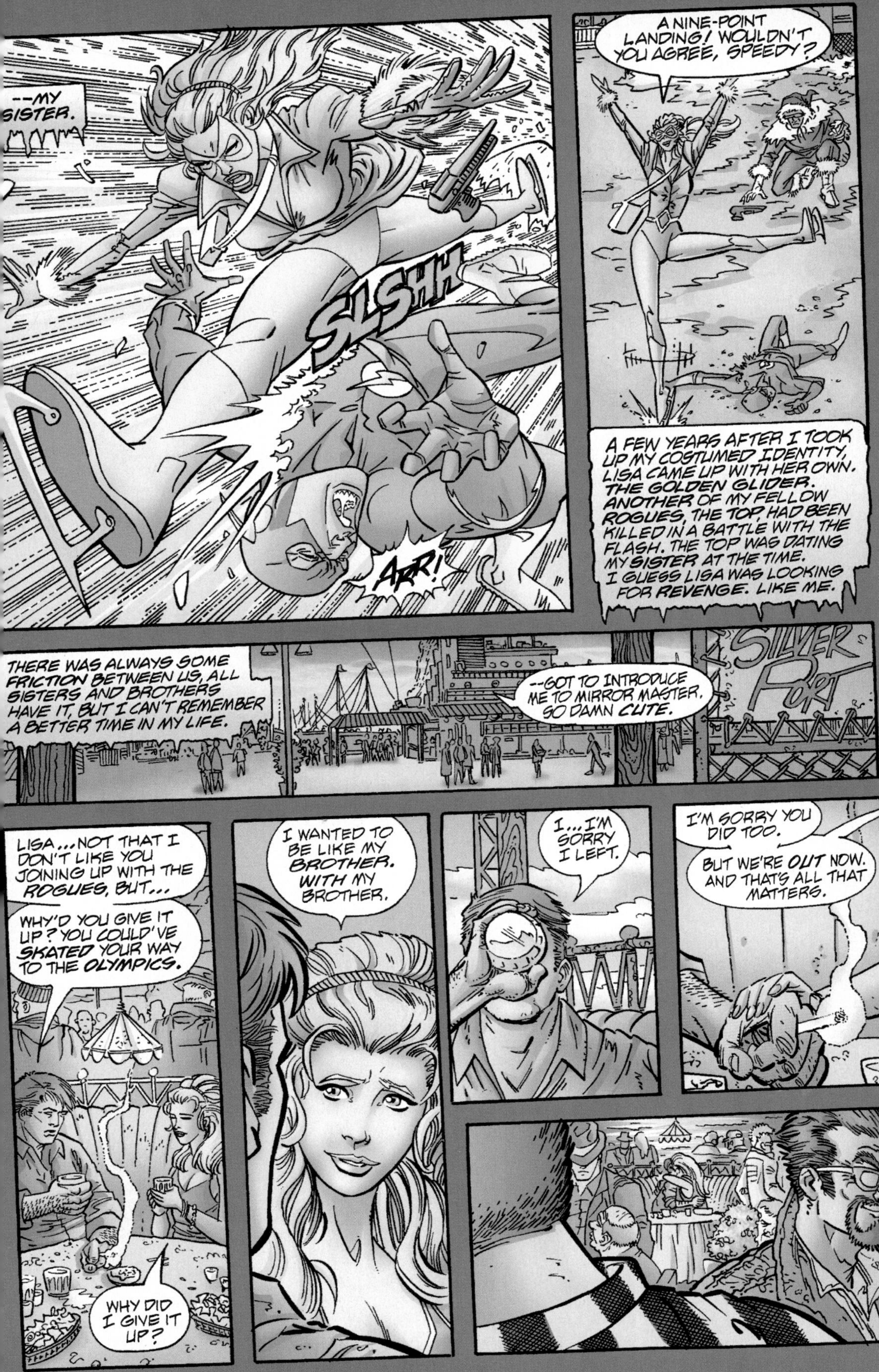
--MY SISTER.
SLSHH
ARR!
A NINE-POINT LANDING! WOULDN'T YOU AGREE, SPEEDY?
A FEW YEARS AFTER I TOOK UP MY COSTUMED IDENTITY, LISA CAME UP WITH HER OWN. THE GOLDEN GLIDER. ANOTHER OF MY FELLOW ROGUES, THE TOP, HAD BEEN KILLED IN A BATTLE WITH THE FLASH. THE TOP WAS DATING MY SISTER AT THE TIME. I GUESS LISA WAS LOOKING FOR REVENGE. LIKE ME.
THERE WAS ALWAYS SOME FRICTION BETWEEN US, ALL SISTERS AND BROTHERS HAVE IT, BUT I CAN'T REMEMBER A BETTER TIME IN MY LIFE.
--GOT TO INTRODUCE ME TO MIRROR MASTER. SO DAMN CUTE.
SILVER PORT
LISA... NOT THAT I DON'T LIKE YOU JOINING UP WITH THE ROGUES, BUT...
WHY'D YOU GIVE IT UP? YOU COULD'VE SKATED YOUR WAY TO THE OLYMPICS.
WHY DID I GIVE IT UP?
I WANTED TO BE LIKE MY BROTHER. WITH MY BROTHER.
I... I'M SORRY I LEFT.
I'M SORRY YOU DID TOO.
BUT WE'RE OUT NOW. AND THAT'S ALL THAT MATTERS.

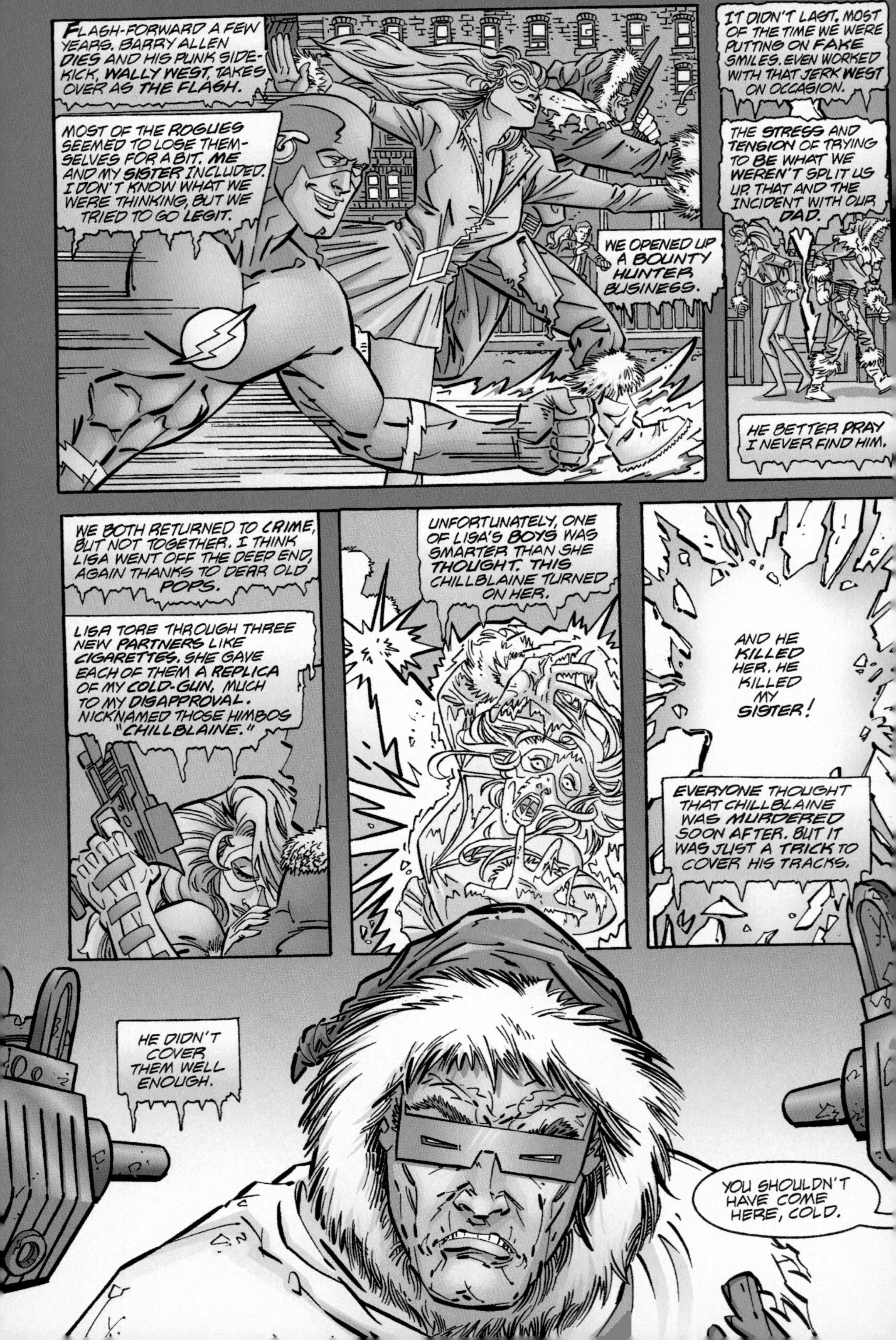
FLASH-FORWARD A FEW YEARS. BARRY ALLEN DIES AND HIS PUNK SIDE-KICK, WALLY WEST, TAKES OVER AS THE FLASH.
MOST OF THE ROGUES SEEMED TO LOSE THEM-SELVES FOR A BIT. ME AND MY SISTER INCLUDED. I DON'T KNOW WHAT WE WERE THINKING, BUT WE TRIED TO GO LEGIT.
WE OPENED UP A BOUNTY HUNTER BUSINESS.
IT DIDN'T LAST. MOST OF THE TIME WE WERE PUTTING ON FAKE SMILES. EVEN WORKED WITH THAT JERK WEST ON OCCASION.
THE STRESS AND TENSION OF TRYING TO BE WHAT WE WEREN'T SPLIT US UP. THAT AND THE INCIDENT WITH OUR DAD.
HE BETTER PRAY I NEVER FIND HIM.
WE BOTH RETURNED TO CRIME, BUT NOT TOGETHER. I THINK LISA WENT OFF THE DEEP END, AGAIN THANKS TO DEAR OLD POPS.
LISA TORE THROUGH THREE NEW PARTNERS LIKE CIGARETTES. SHE GAVE EACH OF THEM A REPLICA OF MY COLD-GUN, MUCH TO MY DISAPPROVAL. NICKNAMED THOSE HIMBOS "CHILLBLAINE."
UNFORTUNATELY, ONE OF LISA'S BOYS WAS SMARTER THAN SHE THOUGHT. THIS CHILLBLAINE TURNED ON HER.
AND HE KILLED HER. HE KILLED MY SISTER!
EVERYONE THOUGHT THAT CHILLBLAINE WAS MURDERED SOON AFTER. BUT IT WAS JUST A TRICK TO COVER HIS TRACKS.
HE DIDN'T COVER THEM WELL ENOUGH.
YOU SHOULDN'T HAVE COME HERE, COLD.

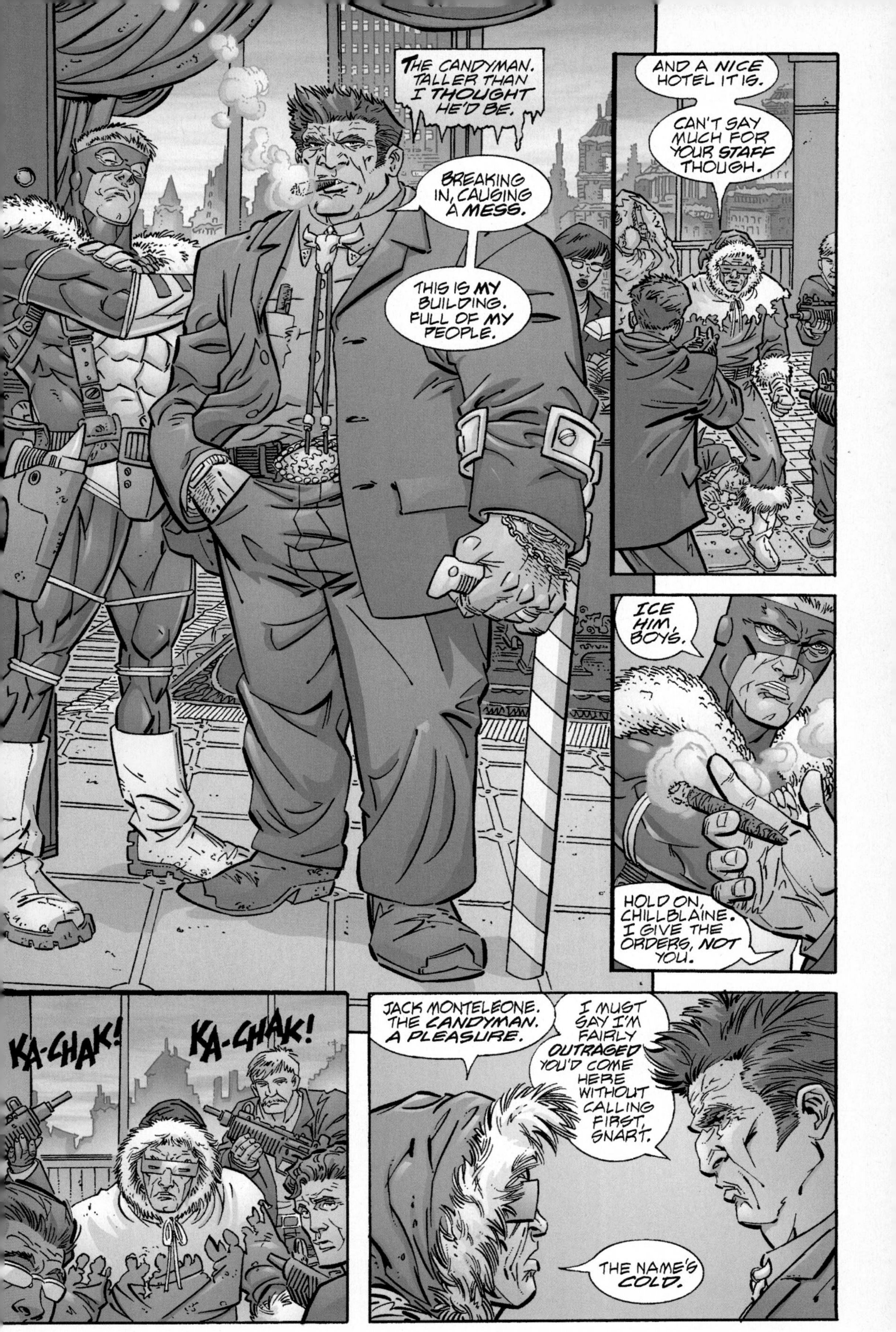
THE CANDYMAN. TALLER THAN I THOUGHT HE'D BE.
BREAKING IN, CAUSING A MESS.
THIS IS MY BUILDING. FULL OF MY PEOPLE.
AND A NICE HOTEL IT IS.
CAN'T SAY MUCH FOR YOUR STAFF THOUGH.
ICE HIM, BOYS.
HOLD ON, CHILLBLAINE. I GIVE THE ORDERS, NOT YOU.
KA-CHAK!
KA-CHAK!
JACK MONTELEONE. THE CANDYMAN. A PLEASURE.
I MUST SAY I'M FAIRLY OUTRAGED YOU'D COME HERE WITHOUT CALLING FIRST, SNART.
THE NAME'S COLD.

I KNOW WHAT YOUR *HANDLE* IS, FRIEND.

YOUR REPUTATION PRECEDES YOU, "CAPTAIN COLD."

YOU'VE CAUSED ME QUITE A BIT OF *TROUBLE* TODAY. NOT TO MENTION YOUR LITTLE *SCUFFLE* WITH MY *BROTHER, JOEY,* A FEW WEEKS BACK.*

THE *TWERP!*

EDITOR'S NOTE:
* JOEY MONTELEONE A.K.A. TAR PIT! SEE THE FLASH #174.

KID'S GOT A *LITTLE* WEIGHT PROBLEM.

YOU LISTEN TO *ME,* COLD. YOU *DO* REALIZE THAT MY ENTIRE *ORGANIZATION* IS UNDER THE PROTECTION OF THE *NETWORK!* THAT INCLUDES YOU *ROGUES.*

BLACKSMITH GAVE ME HER *WORD.*

THE ROGUES *DON'T* INTERFERE WITH ME OR MY PEOPLE.

I DON'T TAKE ORDERS FROM *ANYBODY,* PAL. I'M THE *ROGUE* AMONG *ROGUES*--

--SO DON'T THINK YOU'RE *SAFE* FROM ME BECAUSE OF A *HANDSHAKE* WITH THAT *WITCH.* THE *NETWORK* IS GOOD FOR *BUSINESS,* BUT I'M NOT HERE ON BUSINESS.

THIS IS *PERSONAL.*

DO I NEED TO *REMIND* YOU, YOU'RE IN A HOTEL FILLED WITH OVER *TWO HUNDRED* ARMED MEN. MY *ARMY.* YOU'VE GOT A *DOZEN* AUTOMATICS STARING AT YOU.

YOU'RE IN NO POSITION TO *THREATEN* ANYONE.

IT MIGHT *LOOK* THAT WAY, "*JACK,*" BUT I *PROMISE* YOU... I'LL TAKE THESE *IDIOTS* OUT BEFORE THEY CAN *BLINK.* DID YOU *FORGET* I'M USED TO TANGLING WITH SOMEONE THAT MOVES AT THE SPEED OF *LIGHT?*

THEN I'LL COME AFTER *YOU.* SHOVE THIS GUN DOWN YOUR *THROAT* AND *FREEZE* YOU FROM THE *INSIDE* OUT.

IT CAN TAKE UP TO *FIFTEEN* MINUTES TO FINISH YOU OFF, BUT I'VE GOT THE TIME.

THINK I'M *BLUFFING?* TELL THEM TO *SHOOT.*

WHAT DO YOU WANT?

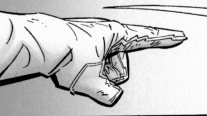

HIM.

JUST *HIM.*

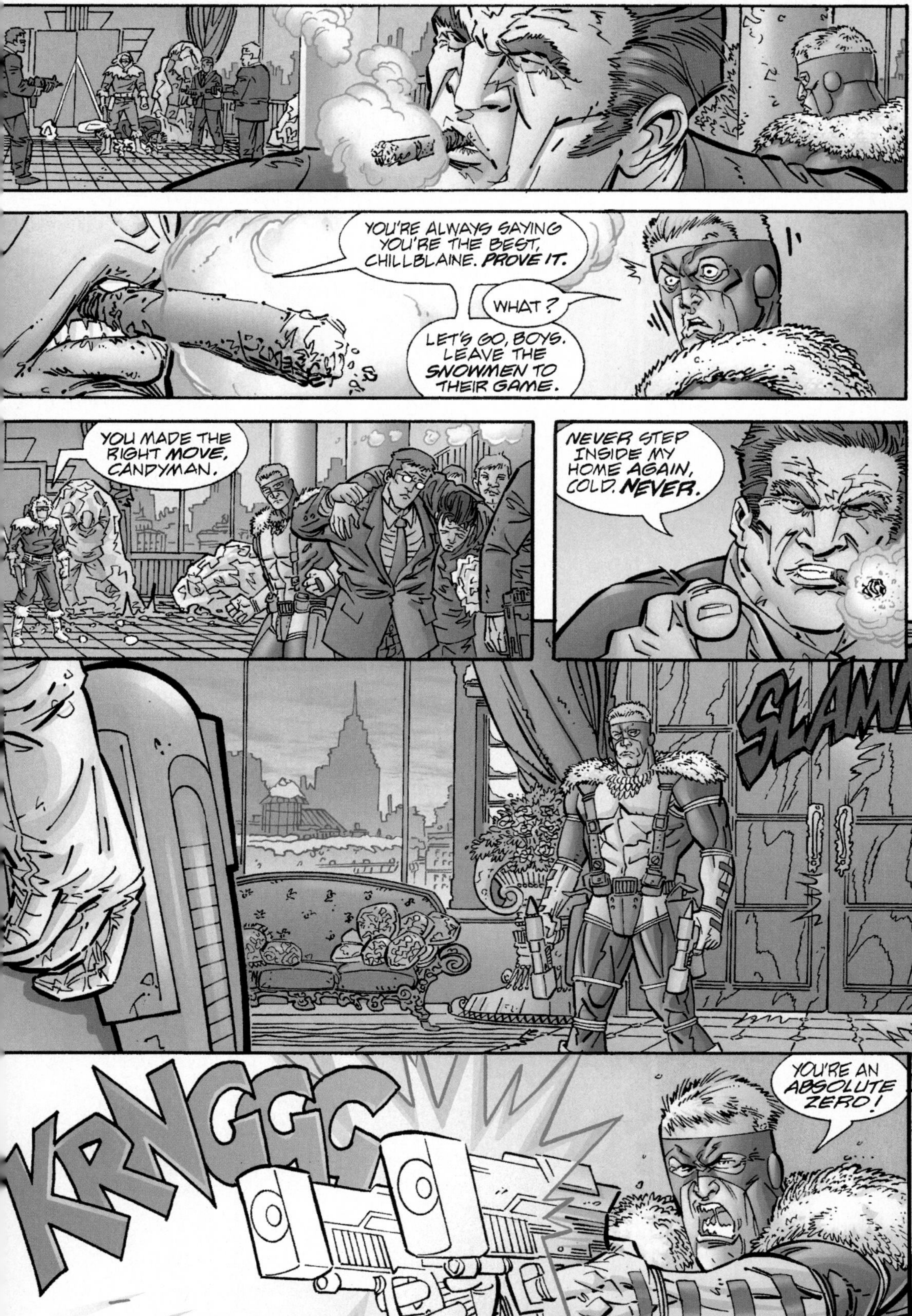
YOU'RE ALWAYS SAYING YOU'RE THE BEST, CHILLBLAINE. PROVE IT.
WHAT?
LET'S GO, BOYS. LEAVE THE SNOWMEN TO THEIR GAME.
YOU MADE THE RIGHT MOVE, CANDYMAN.
NEVER STEP INSIDE MY HOME AGAIN, COLD. NEVER.
SLAMM!
KRNGGC
YOU'RE AN ABSOLUTE ZERO!

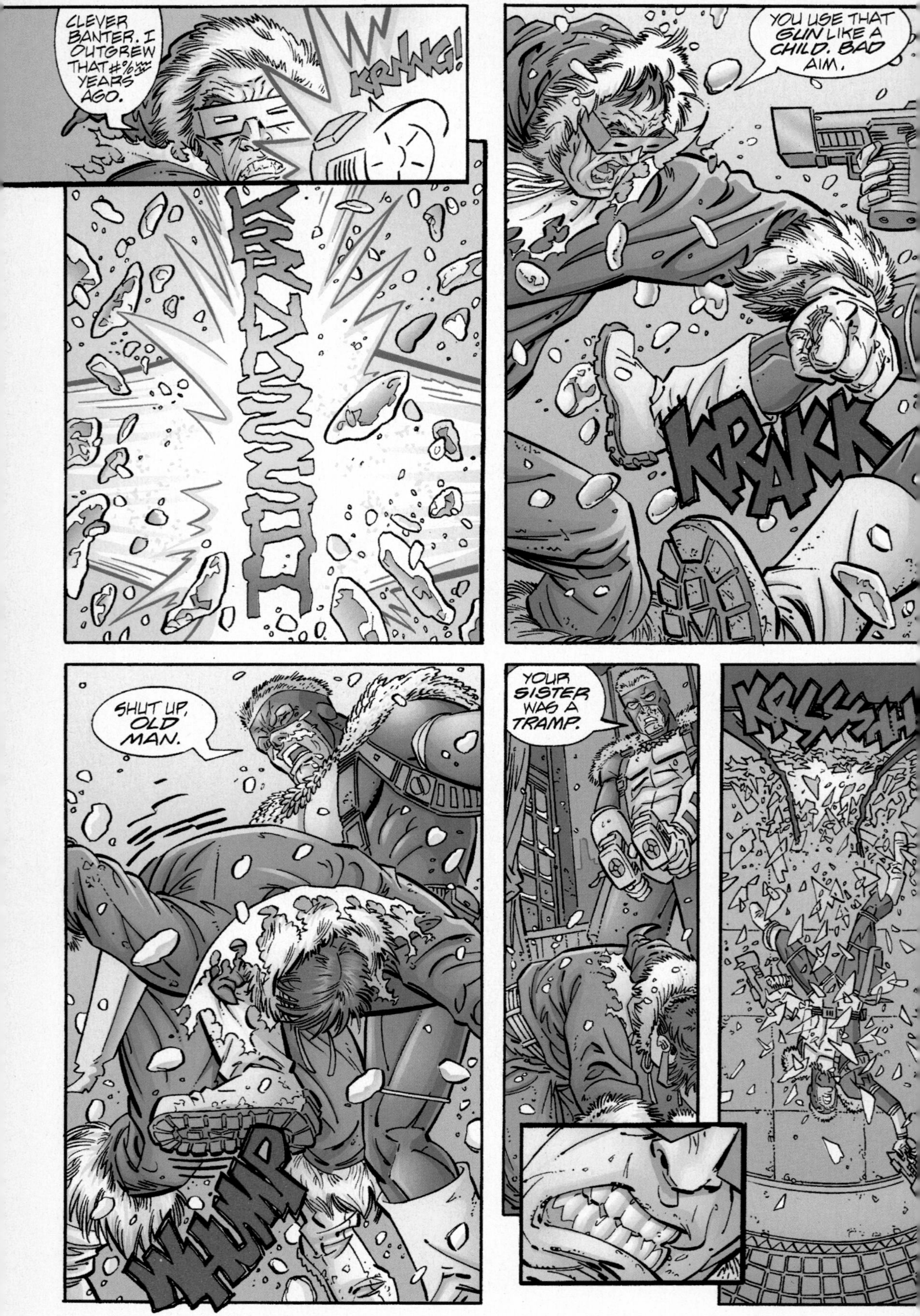
CLEVER BANTER. I OUTGREW THAT #%! YEARS AGO.
KRANG!
KRASSSH
YOU USE THAT GUN LIKE A CHILD. BAD AIM.
KRAKK
SHUT UP, OLD MAN.
WHUMP
YOUR SISTER WAS A TRAMP.

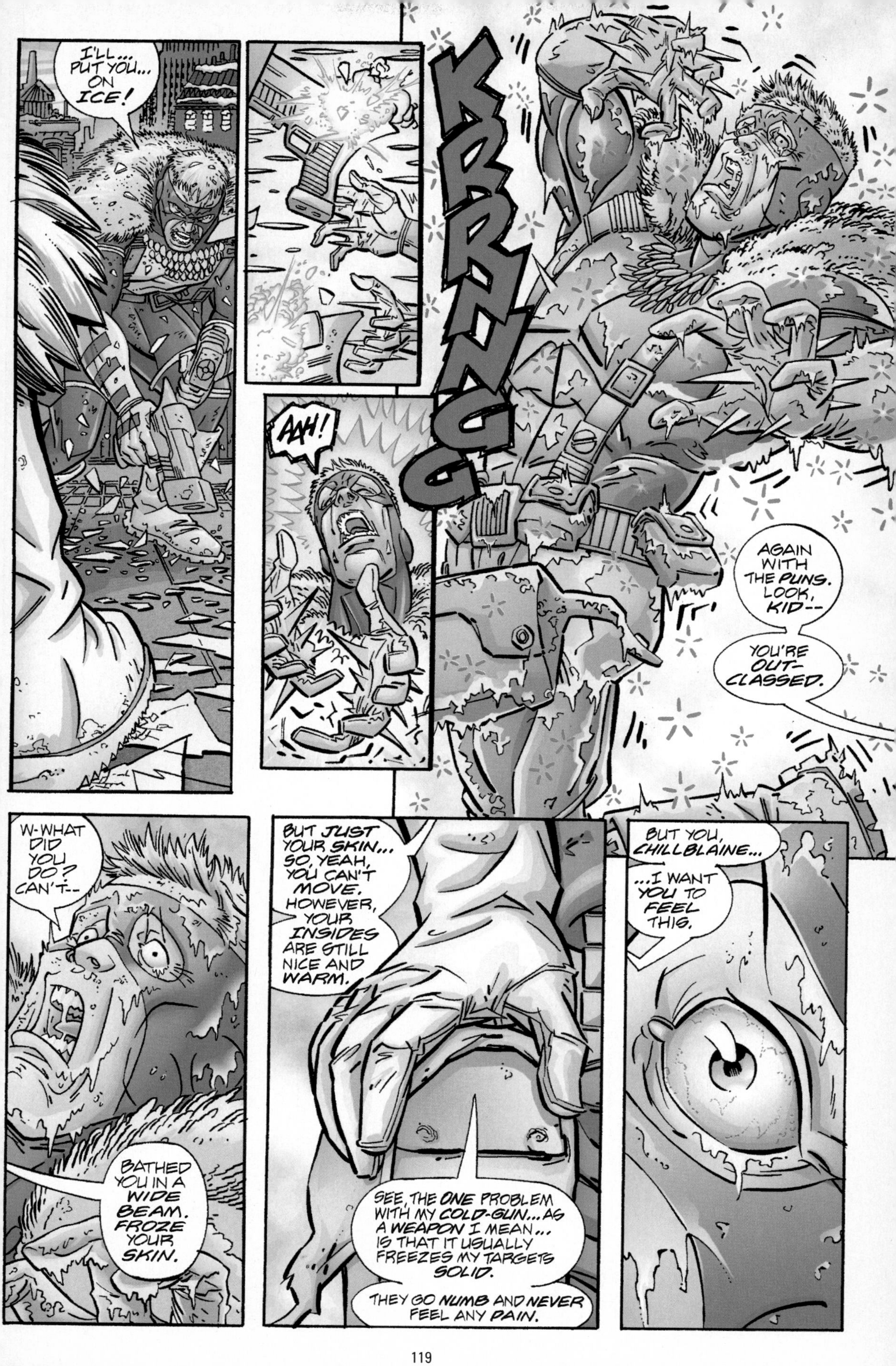

I'LL... PUT YOU... ON ICE!
AAH!
KRRANG
AGAIN WITH THE PUNS. LOOK, KID--
YOU'RE OUT-CLASSED.
W-WHAT DID YOU DO? CAN'T--
BATHED YOU IN A WIDE BEAM. FROZE YOUR SKIN.
BUT JUST YOUR SKIN... SO, YEAH, YOU CAN'T MOVE. HOWEVER, YOUR INSIDES ARE STILL NICE AND WARM.
SEE, THE ONE PROBLEM WITH MY COLD-GUN... AS A WEAPON I MEAN... IS THAT IT USUALLY FREEZES MY TARGETS SOLID.
THEY GO NUMB AND NEVER FEEL ANY PAIN.
BUT YOU, CHILLBLAINE...
...I WANT YOU TO FEEL THIS.

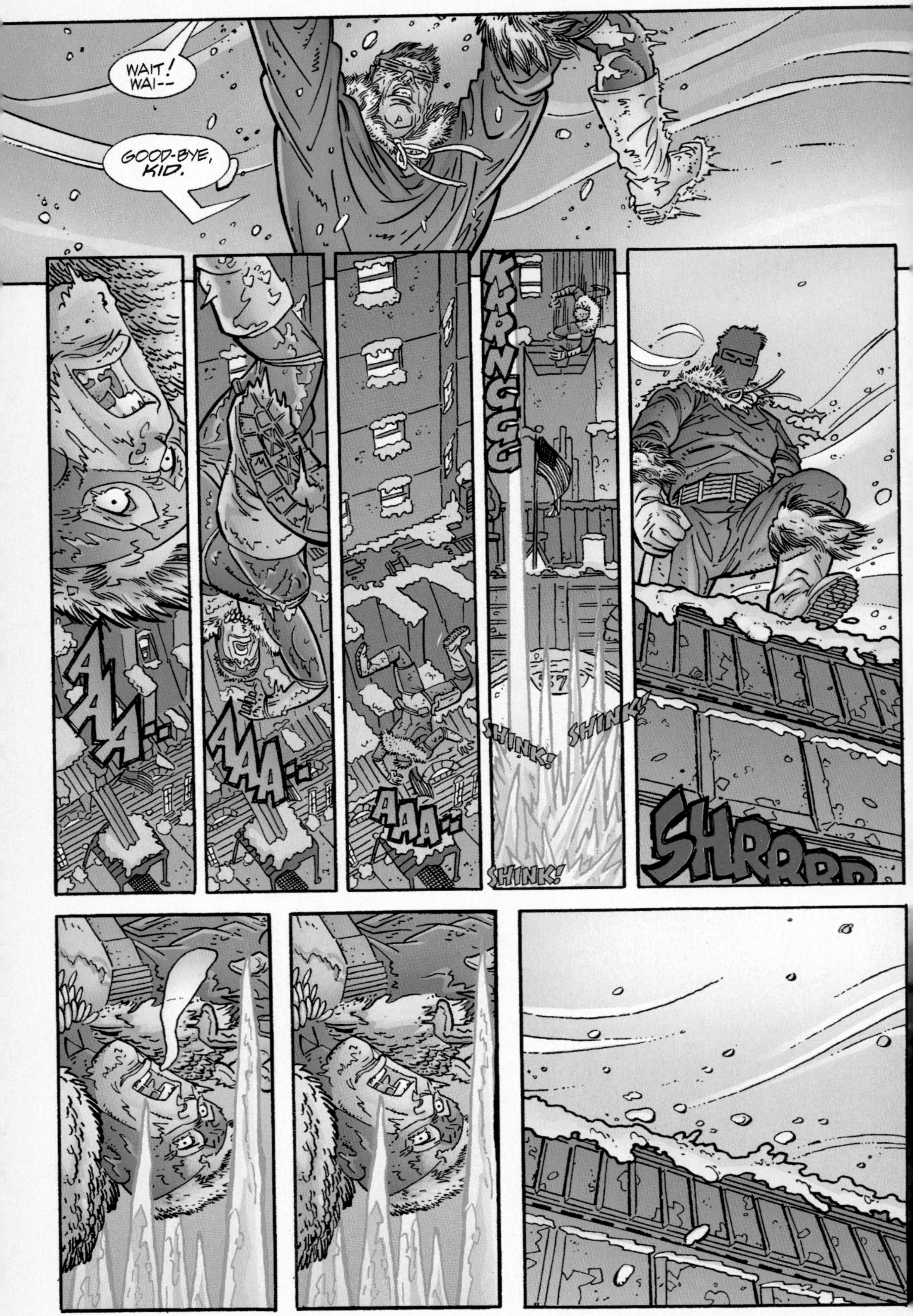
WAIT! WAI--
GOOD-BYE, KID.
AAA--
AAAA--
AAA--
KRRNGGG
SHINK!
SHINK!
SHINK!
SHRRRR

LENNY!? YOU THERE?

NOK! NOK!

JUST A SEC...

ANGIE. WHAT ARE YOU--?

615

IT'S WEDNESDAY, LENNY. ELEVEN. OUR USUAL "DATE."

NOT... NOT TONIGHT.

BUT, HONEY. I TURNED DOWN OTHER WORK FOR--

HERE, COME BACK NEXT WEEK.

YOU SURE YOU DON'T WANT... ANYTHING?

YEAH. SEE YOU LATER, OKAY?

YOUR MONEY. I'LL SEE YOU WEDNESDAY, SWEETIE.

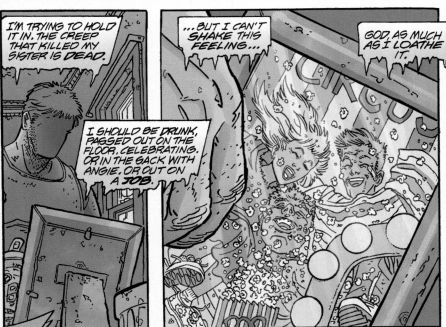

I'M TRYING TO HOLD IT IN. THE CREEP THAT KILLED MY SISTER IS DEAD.

...BUT I CAN'T SHAKE THIS FEELING...

GOD, AS MUCH AS I LOATHE IT.

I SHOULD BE DRUNK, PASSED OUT ON THE FLOOR. CELEBRATING. OR IN THE SACK WITH ANGIE. OR OUT ON A JOB.

AS MUCH AS I HATE IT--

121

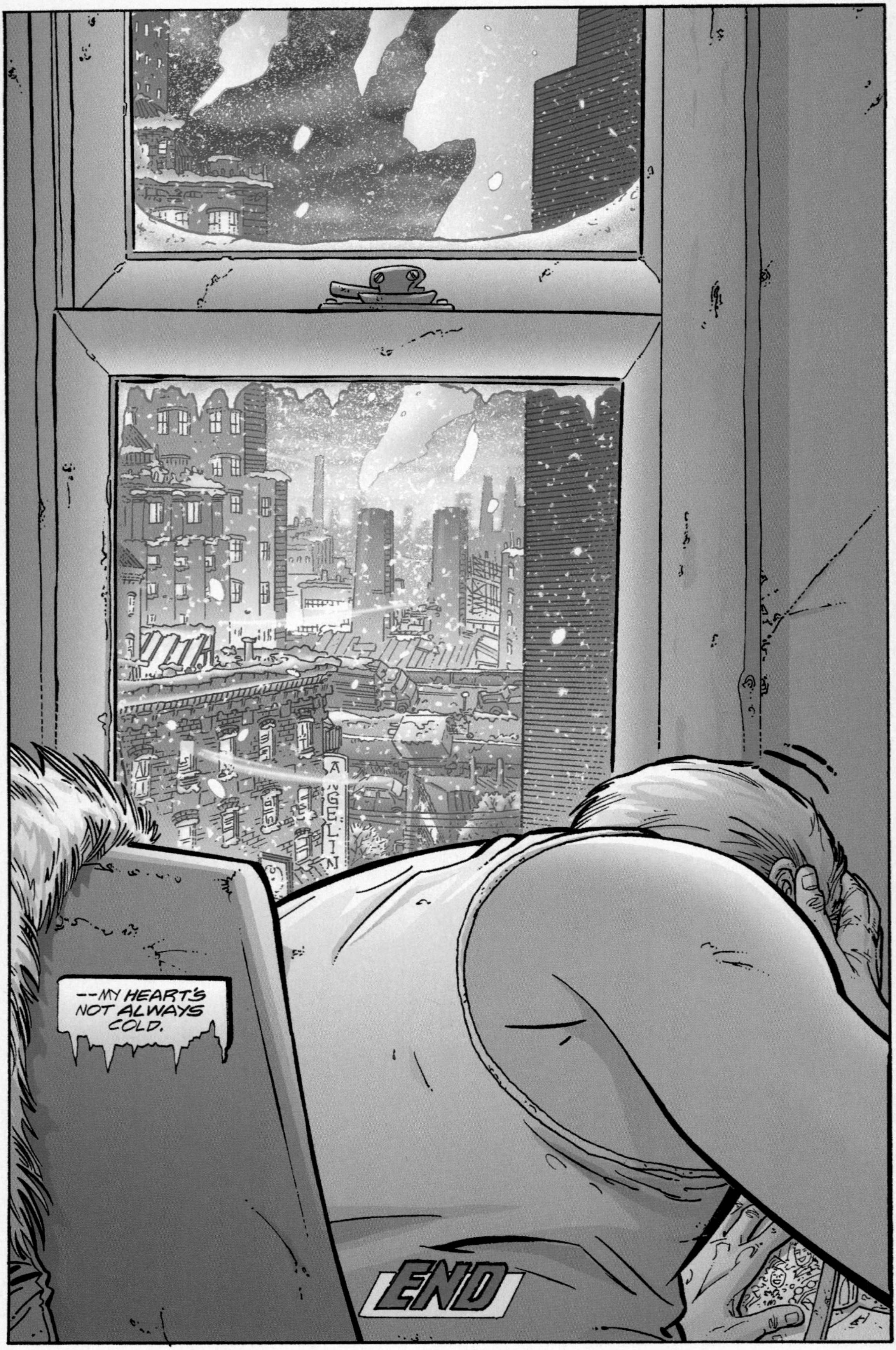
--MY HEART'S NOT ALWAYS COLD.
END

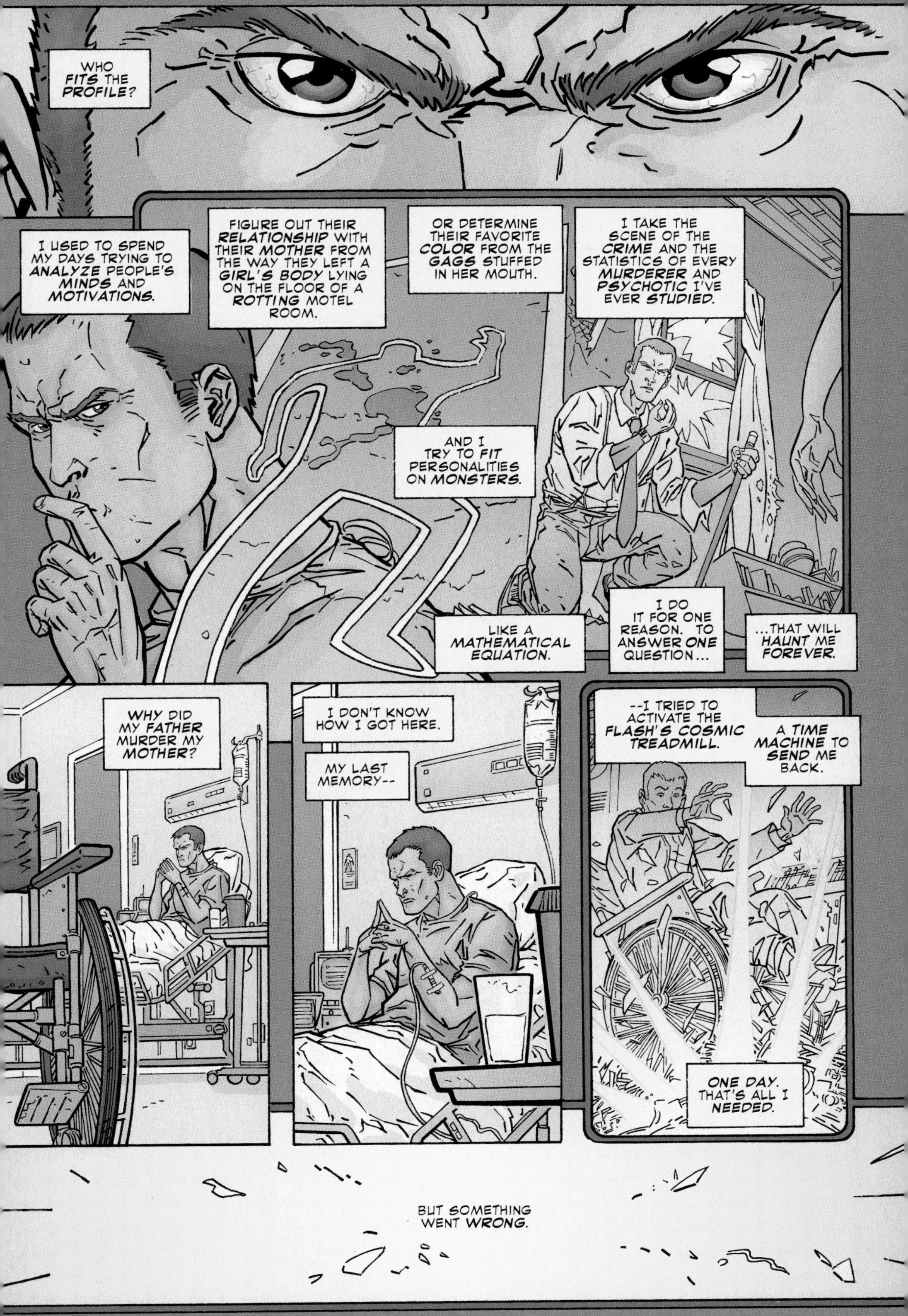
WHO FITS THE PROFILE?
I USED TO SPEND MY DAYS TRYING TO ANALYZE PEOPLE'S MINDS AND MOTIVATIONS.
FIGURE OUT THEIR RELATIONSHIP WITH THEIR MOTHER FROM THE WAY THEY LEFT A GIRL'S BODY LYING ON THE FLOOR OF A ROTTING MOTEL ROOM.
OR DETERMINE THEIR FAVORITE COLOR FROM THE GAGS STUFFED IN HER MOUTH.
I TAKE THE SCENE OF THE CRIME AND THE STATISTICS OF EVERY MURDERER AND PSYCHOTIC I'VE EVER STUDIED.
AND I TRY TO FIT PERSONALITIES ON MONSTERS.
LIKE A MATHEMATICAL EQUATION.
I DO IT FOR ONE REASON. TO ANSWER ONE QUESTION...
...THAT WILL HAUNT ME FOREVER.
WHY DID MY FATHER MURDER MY MOTHER?
I DON'T KNOW HOW I GOT HERE.
MY LAST MEMORY--
--I TRIED TO ACTIVATE THE FLASH'S COSMIC TREADMILL.
A TIME MACHINE TO SEND ME BACK.
ONE DAY. THAT'S ALL I NEEDED.
BUT SOMETHING WENT WRONG.

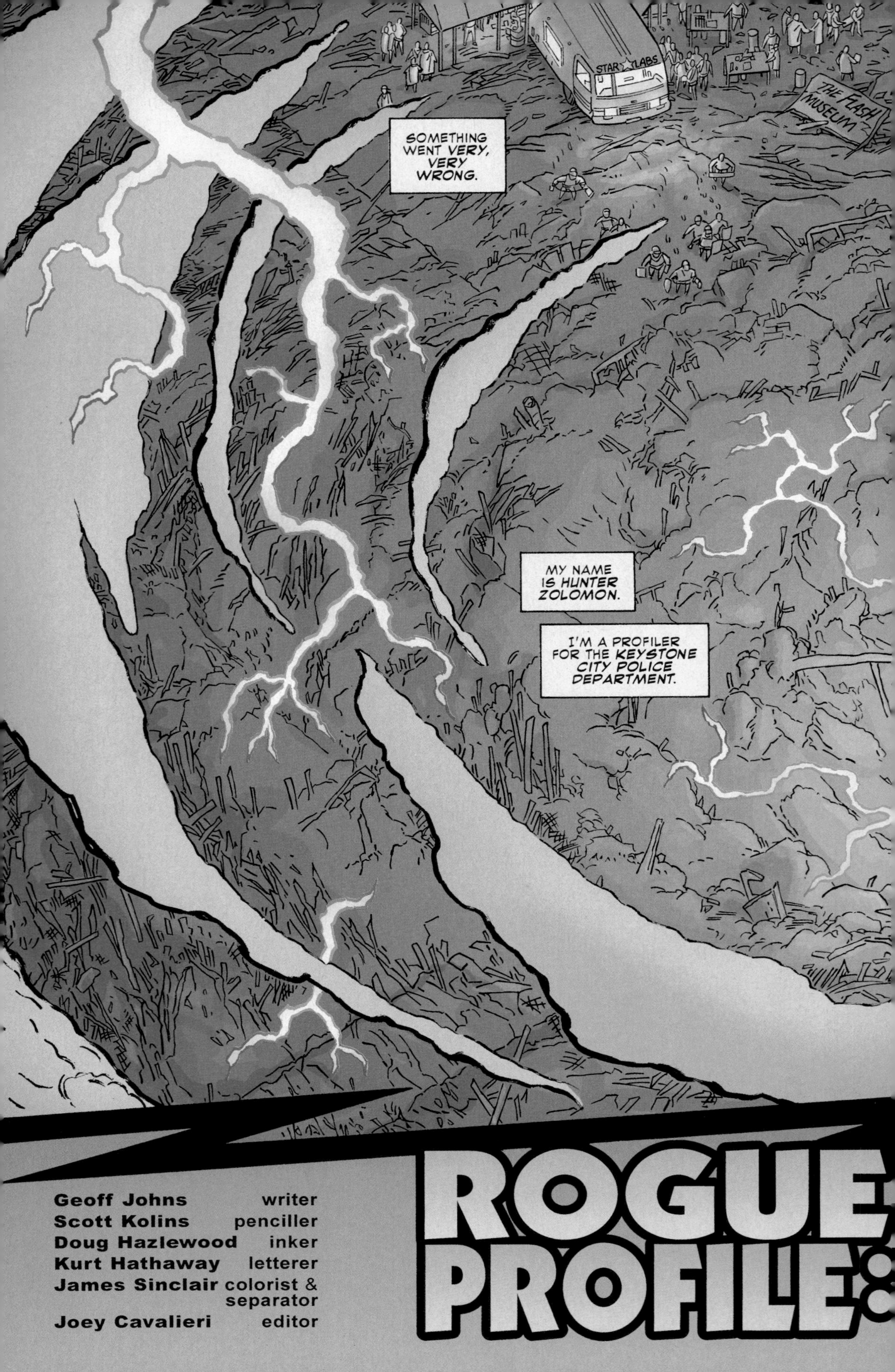
STAR LABS
THE FLASH MUSEUM
SOMETHING WENT VERY, VERY WRONG.
MY NAME IS HUNTER ZOLOMON.
I'M A PROFILER FOR THE KEYSTONE CITY POLICE DEPARTMENT.

ROGUE PROFILE:

Geoff Johns writer
Scott Kolins penciller
Doug Hazlewood inker
Kurt Hathaway letterer
James Sinclair colorist & separator
Joey Cavalieri editor

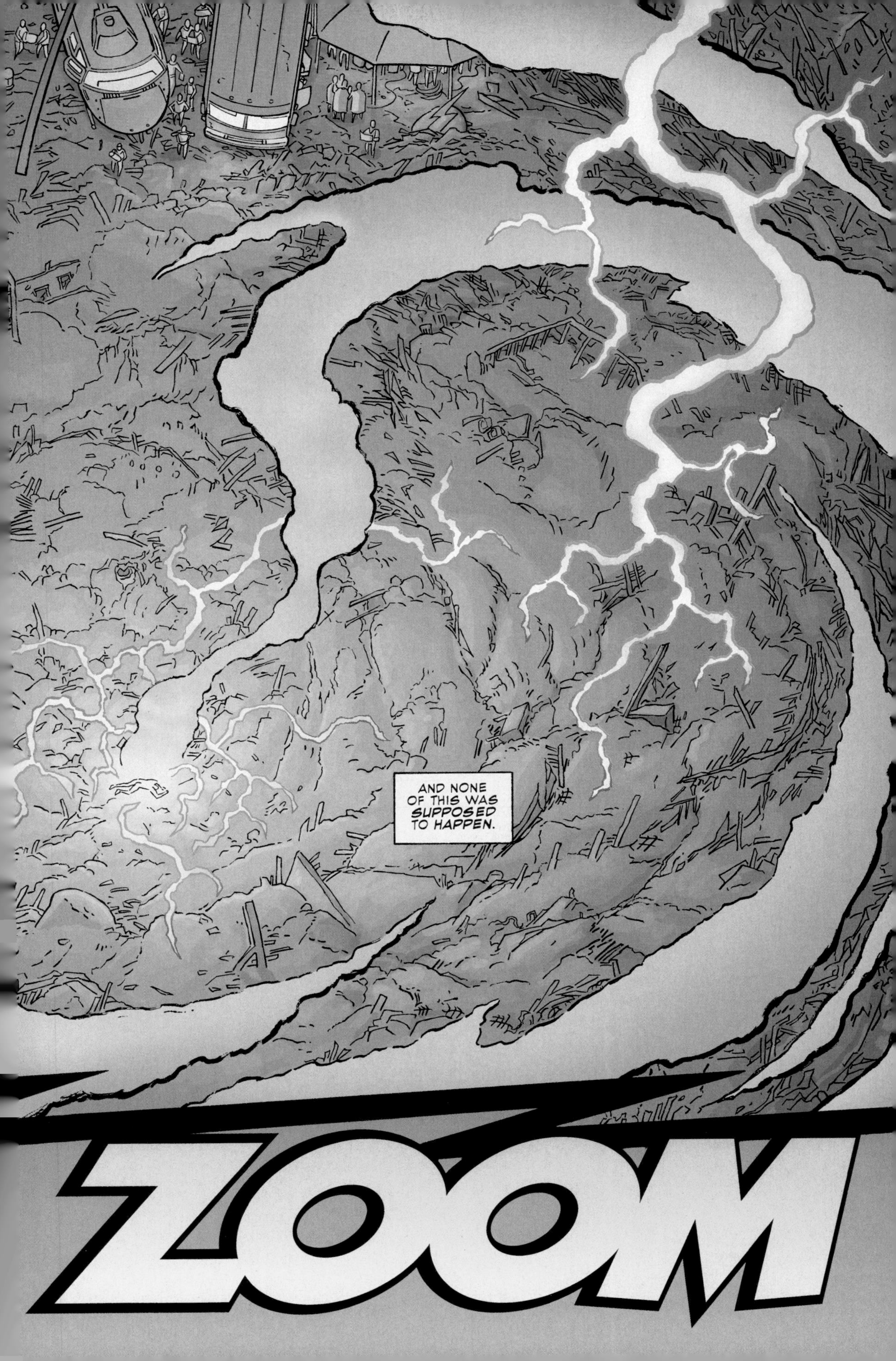
AND NONE OF THIS WAS SUPPOSED TO HAPPEN.
ZOOM

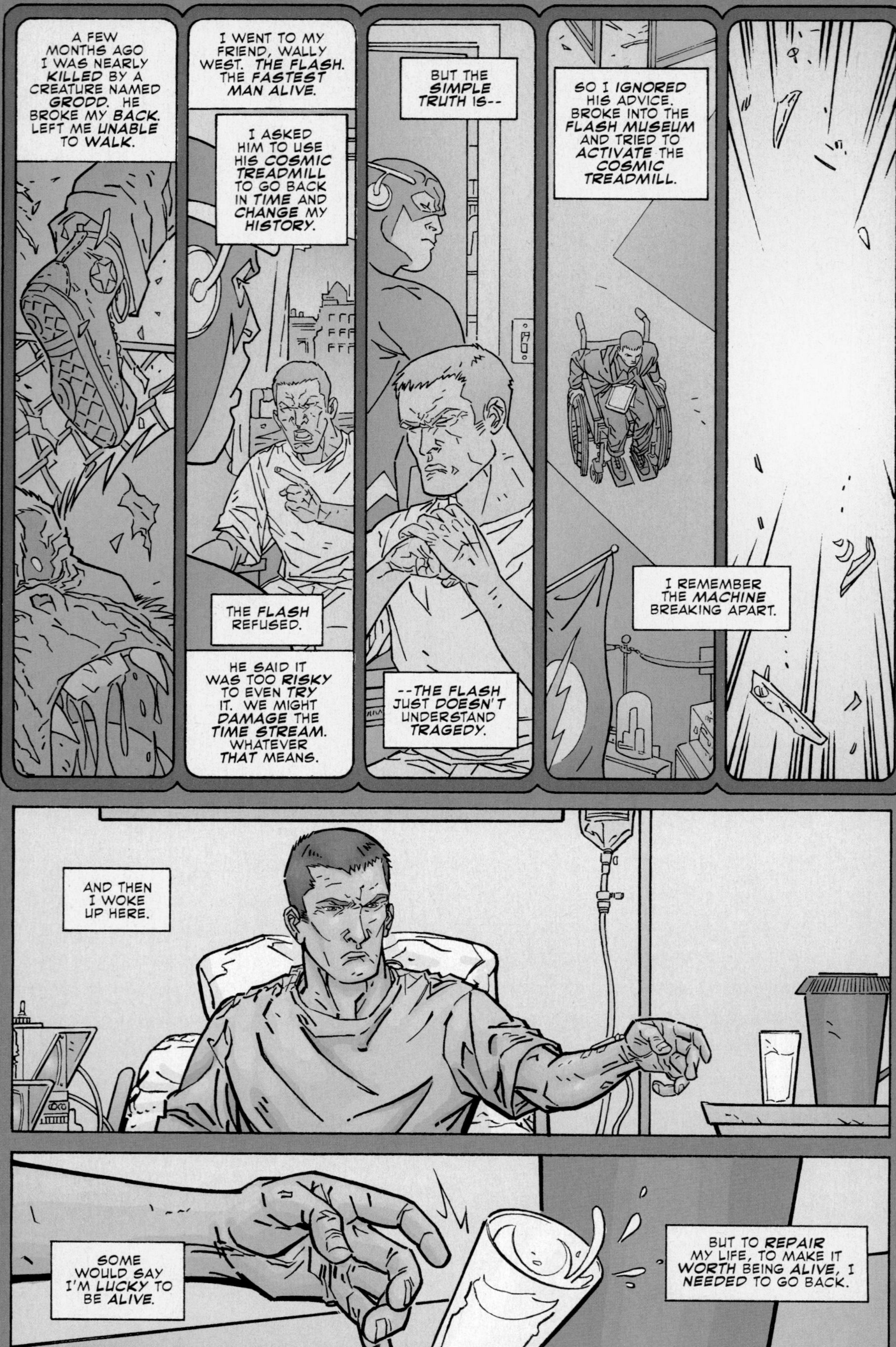
A FEW MONTHS AGO I WAS NEARLY KILLED BY A CREATURE NAMED GRODD. HE BROKE MY BACK. LEFT ME UNABLE TO WALK.
I WENT TO MY FRIEND, WALLY WEST. THE FLASH. THE FASTEST MAN ALIVE.
I ASKED HIM TO USE HIS COSMIC TREADMILL TO GO BACK IN TIME AND CHANGE MY HISTORY.
THE FLASH REFUSED.
HE SAID IT WAS TOO RISKY TO EVEN TRY IT. WE MIGHT DAMAGE THE TIME STREAM. WHATEVER THAT MEANS.
BUT THE SIMPLE TRUTH IS--
--THE FLASH JUST DOESN'T UNDERSTAND TRAGEDY.
SO I IGNORED HIS ADVICE. BROKE INTO THE FLASH MUSEUM AND TRIED TO ACTIVATE THE COSMIC TREADMILL.
I REMEMBER THE MACHINE BREAKING APART.
AND THEN I WOKE UP HERE.
SOME WOULD SAY I'M LUCKY TO BE ALIVE.
BUT TO REPAIR MY LIFE, TO MAKE IT WORTH BEING ALIVE, I NEEDED TO GO BACK.

BACK IN TIME...

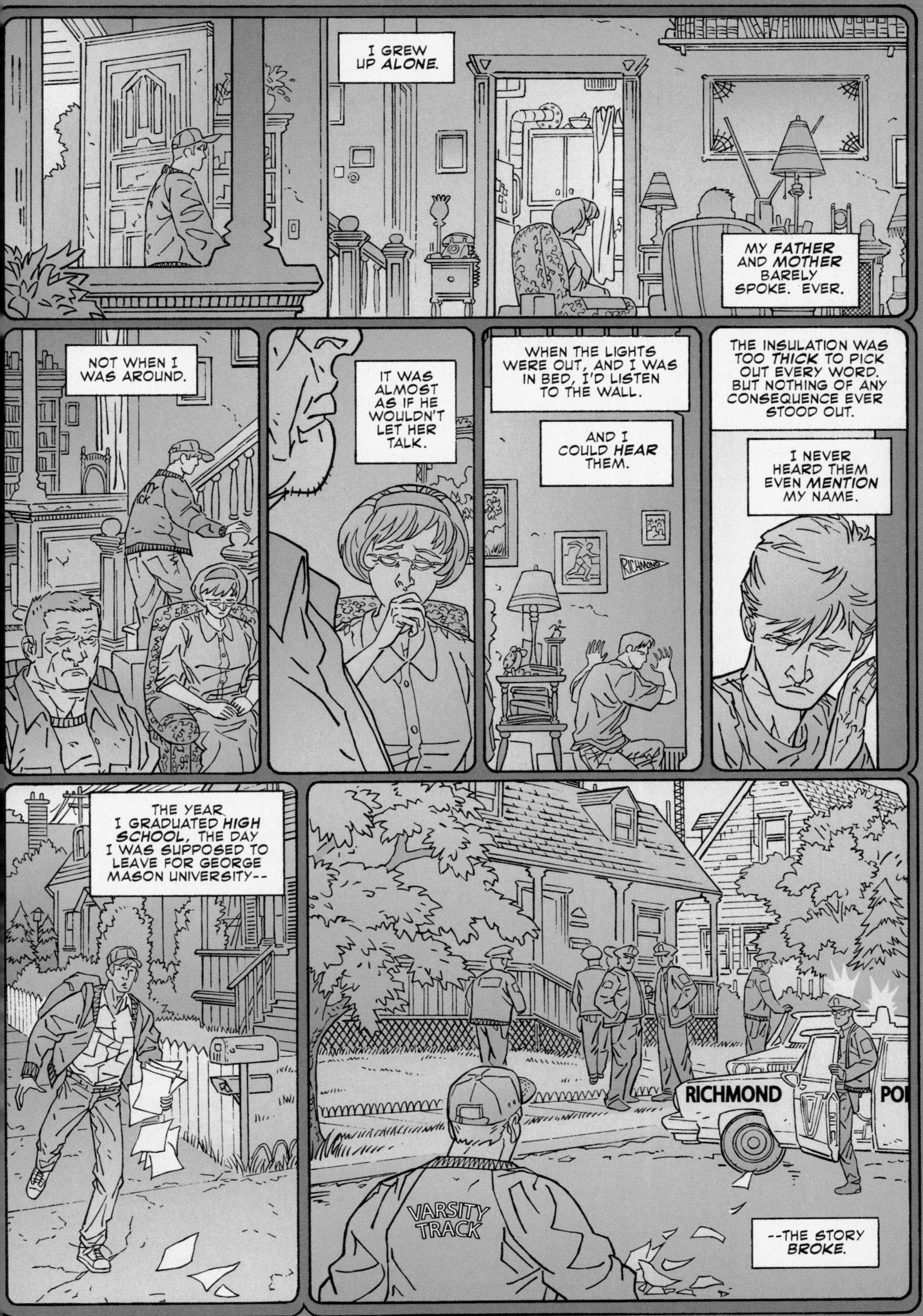
I GREW UP ALONE.
MY FATHER AND MOTHER BARELY SPOKE. EVER.
NOT WHEN I WAS AROUND.
IT WAS ALMOST AS IF HE WOULDN'T LET HER TALK.
WHEN THE LIGHTS WERE OUT, AND I WAS IN BED, I'D LISTEN TO THE WALL.
AND I COULD HEAR THEM.
RICHMOND
THE INSULATION WAS TOO THICK TO PICK OUT EVERY WORD. BUT NOTHING OF ANY CONSEQUENCE EVER STOOD OUT.
I NEVER HEARD THEM EVEN MENTION MY NAME.
THE YEAR I GRADUATED HIGH SCHOOL, THE DAY I WAS SUPPOSED TO LEAVE FOR GEORGE MASON UNIVERSITY--
RICHMOND PO
VARSITY TRACK
--THE STORY BROKE.

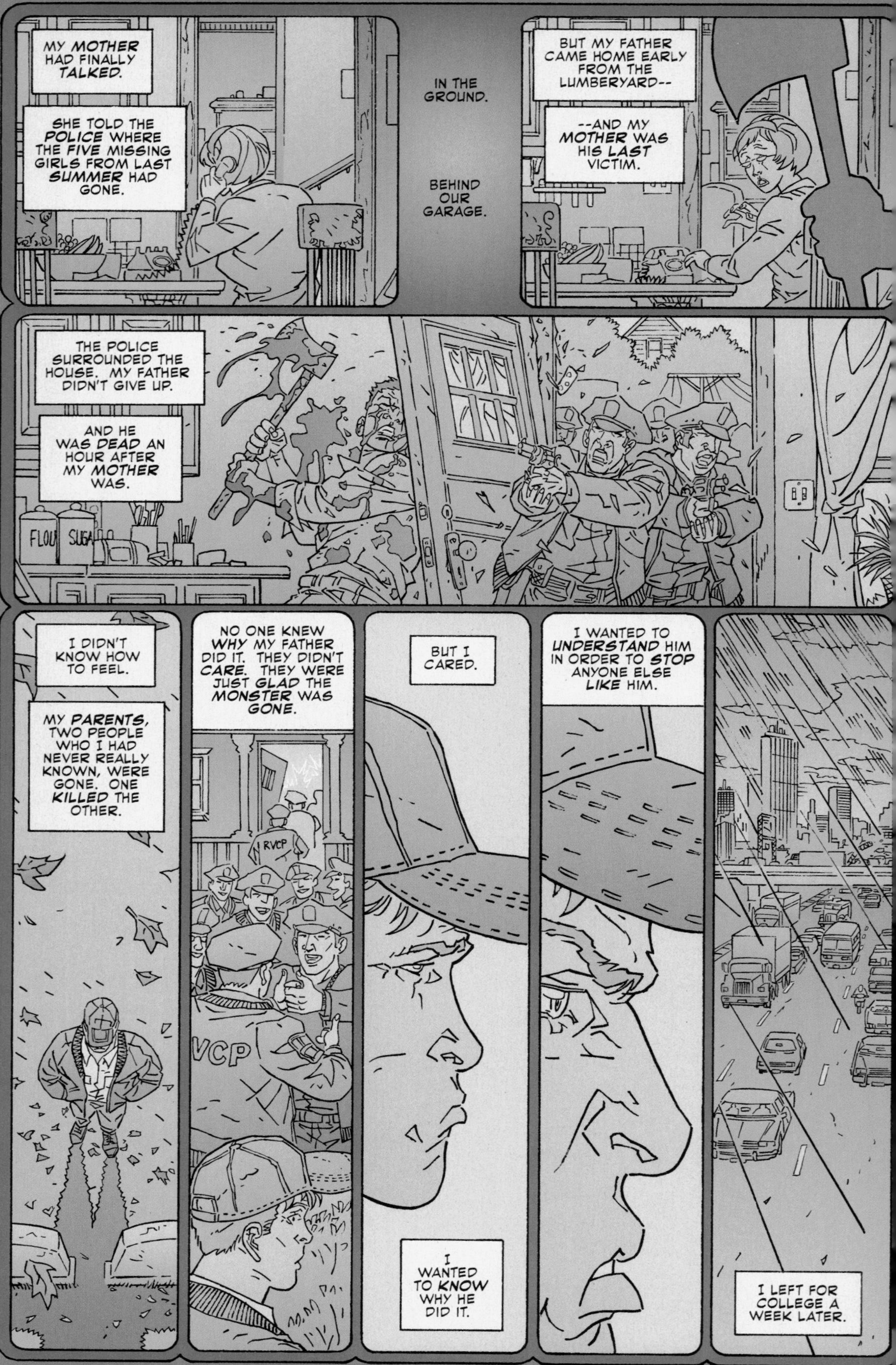
MY MOTHER HAD FINALLY TALKED.
SHE TOLD THE POLICE WHERE THE FIVE MISSING GIRLS FROM LAST SUMMER HAD GONE.
IN THE GROUND.
BEHIND OUR GARAGE.
BUT MY FATHER CAME HOME EARLY FROM THE LUMBERYARD--
--AND MY MOTHER WAS HIS LAST VICTIM.
THE POLICE SURROUNDED THE HOUSE. MY FATHER DIDN'T GIVE UP.
AND HE WAS DEAD AN HOUR AFTER MY MOTHER WAS.
FLOU
SUGA
I DIDN'T KNOW HOW TO FEEL.
MY PARENTS, TWO PEOPLE WHO I HAD NEVER REALLY KNOWN, WERE GONE. ONE KILLED THE OTHER.
NO ONE KNEW WHY MY FATHER DID IT. THEY DIDN'T CARE. THEY WERE JUST GLAD THE MONSTER WAS GONE.
RVCP
VCP
BUT I CARED.
I WANTED TO KNOW WHY HE DID IT.
I WANTED TO UNDERSTAND HIM IN ORDER TO STOP ANYONE ELSE LIKE HIM.
I LEFT FOR COLLEGE A WEEK LATER.

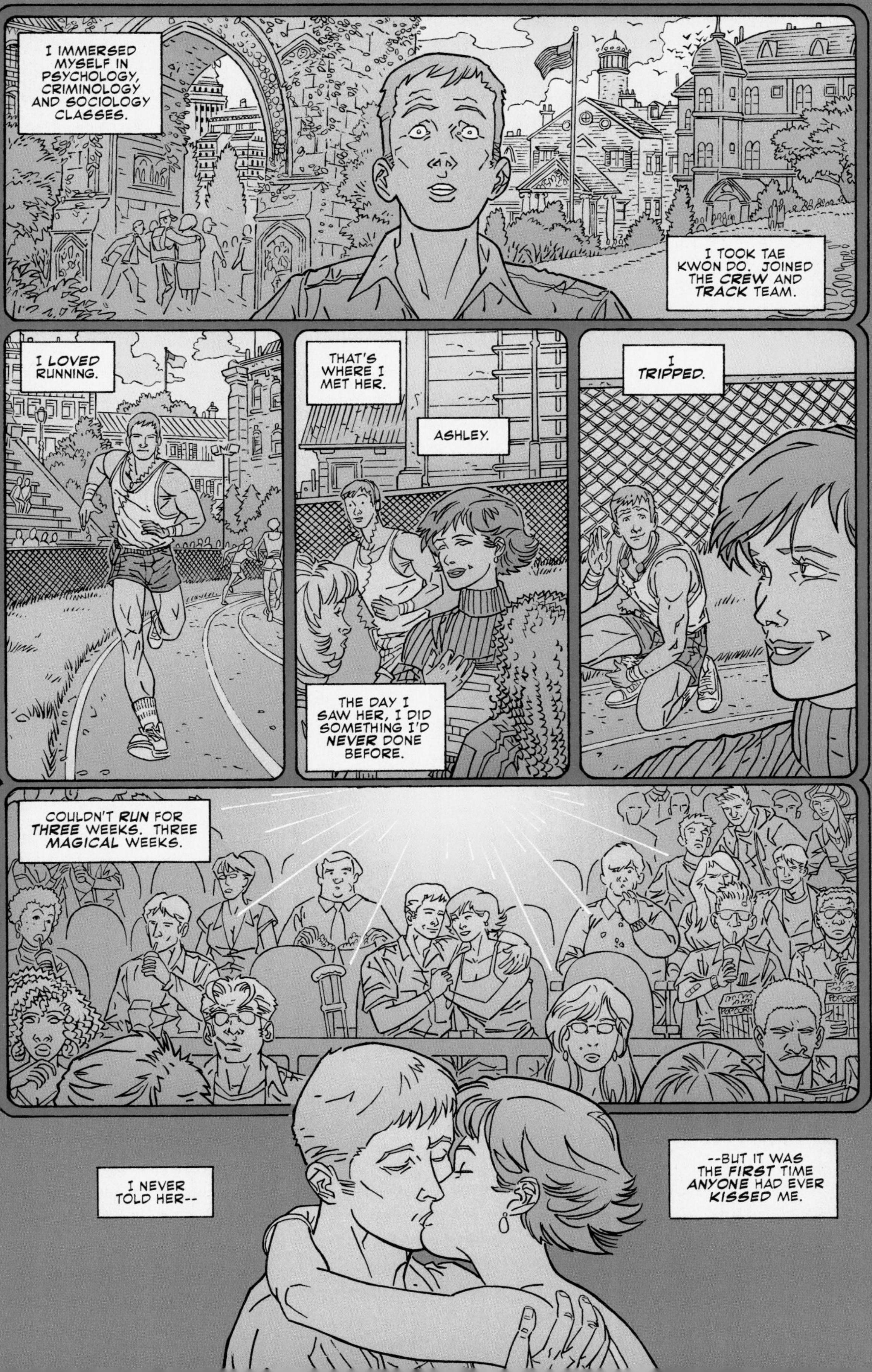
I IMMERSED MYSELF IN PSYCHOLOGY, CRIMINOLOGY AND SOCIOLOGY CLASSES.
I TOOK TAE KWON DO. JOINED THE CREW AND TRACK TEAM.
I LOVED RUNNING.
THAT'S WHERE I MET HER.
ASHLEY.
THE DAY I SAW HER, I DID SOMETHING I'D NEVER DONE BEFORE.
I TRIPPED.
COULDN'T RUN FOR THREE WEEKS. THREE MAGICAL WEEKS.
POPCORN
I NEVER TOLD HER--
--BUT IT WAS THE FIRST TIME ANYONE HAD EVER KISSED ME.

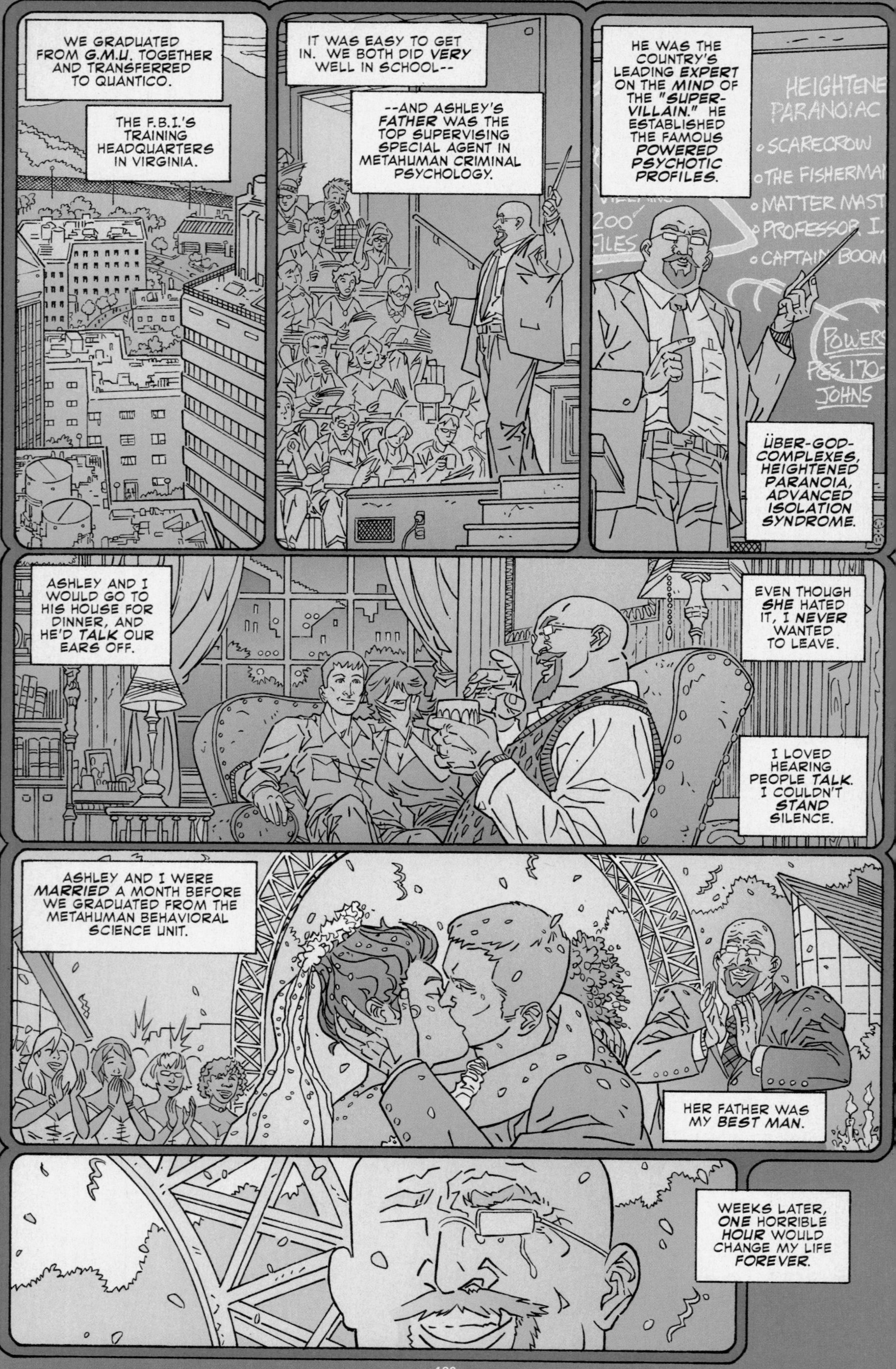

WE GRADUATED FROM G.M.U. TOGETHER AND TRANSFERRED TO QUANTICO.
THE F.B.I.'S TRAINING HEADQUARTERS IN VIRGINIA.
IT WAS EASY TO GET IN. WE BOTH DID VERY WELL IN SCHOOL--
--AND ASHLEY'S FATHER WAS THE TOP SUPERVISING SPECIAL AGENT IN METAHUMAN CRIMINAL PSYCHOLOGY.
HE WAS THE COUNTRY'S LEADING EXPERT ON THE MIND OF THE "SUPER-VILLAIN." HE ESTABLISHED THE FAMOUS POWERED PSYCHOTIC PROFILES.
HEIGHTENE
PARANOIAC
SCARECROW
THE FISHERMA
MATTER MAST
PROFESSOR I.
CAPTAIN BOOM
POWERS
PGS. 170-
JOHNS
ÜBER-GOD-COMPLEXES, HEIGHTENED PARANOIA, ADVANCED ISOLATION SYNDROME.
ASHLEY AND I WOULD GO TO HIS HOUSE FOR DINNER, AND HE'D TALK OUR EARS OFF.
EVEN THOUGH SHE HATED IT, I NEVER WANTED TO LEAVE.
I LOVED HEARING PEOPLE TALK. I COULDN'T STAND SILENCE.
ASHLEY AND I WERE MARRIED A MONTH BEFORE WE GRADUATED FROM THE METAHUMAN BEHAVIORAL SCIENCE UNIT.
HER FATHER WAS MY BEST MAN.
WEEKS LATER, ONE HORRIBLE HOUR WOULD CHANGE MY LIFE FOREVER.

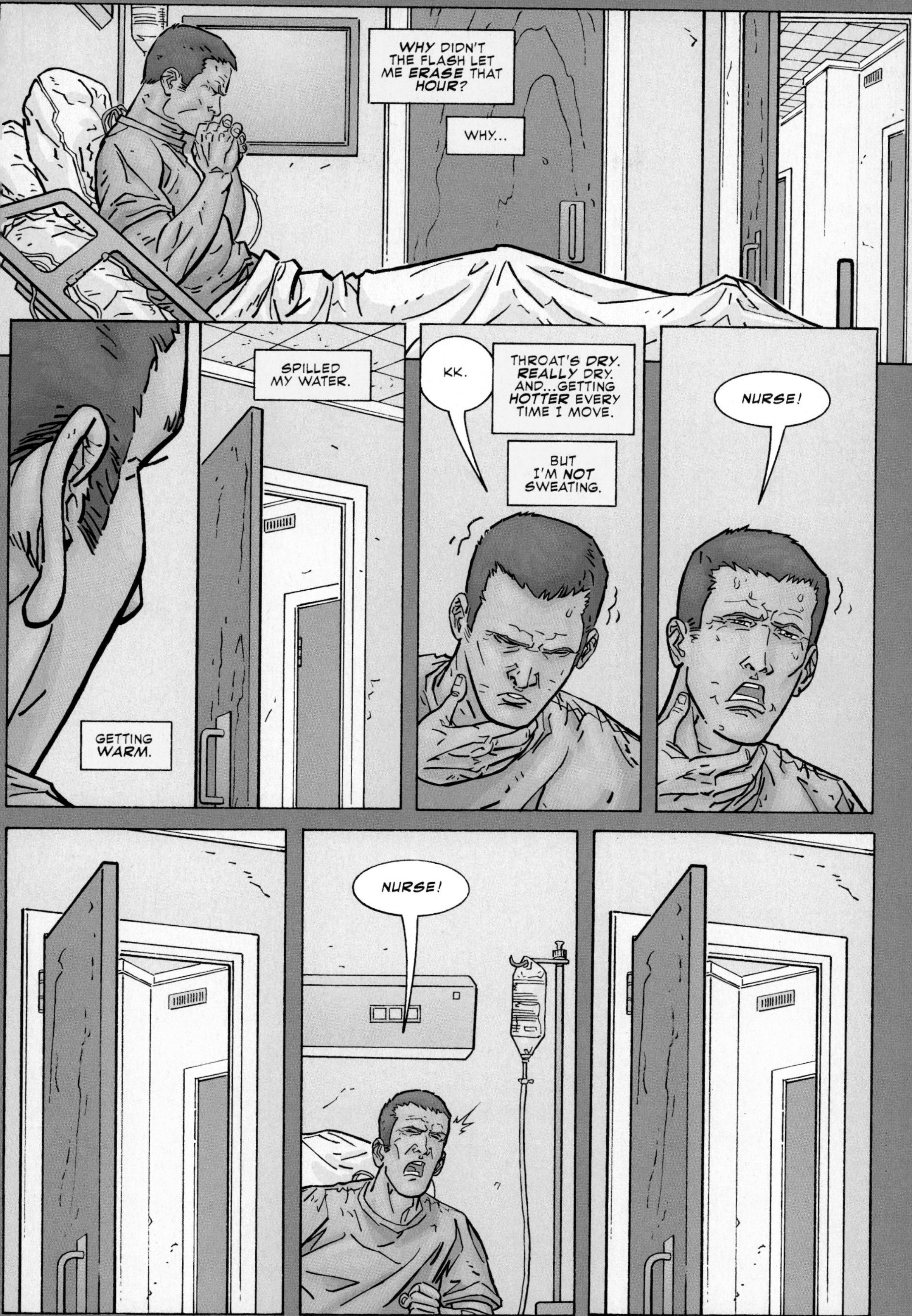
WHY DIDN'T THE FLASH LET ME ERASE THAT HOUR?
WHY...
GETTING WARM.
SPILLED MY WATER.
KK.
THROAT'S DRY. REALLY DRY. AND...GETTING HOTTER EVERY TIME I MOVE.
BUT I'M NOT SWEATING.
NURSE!
NURSE!

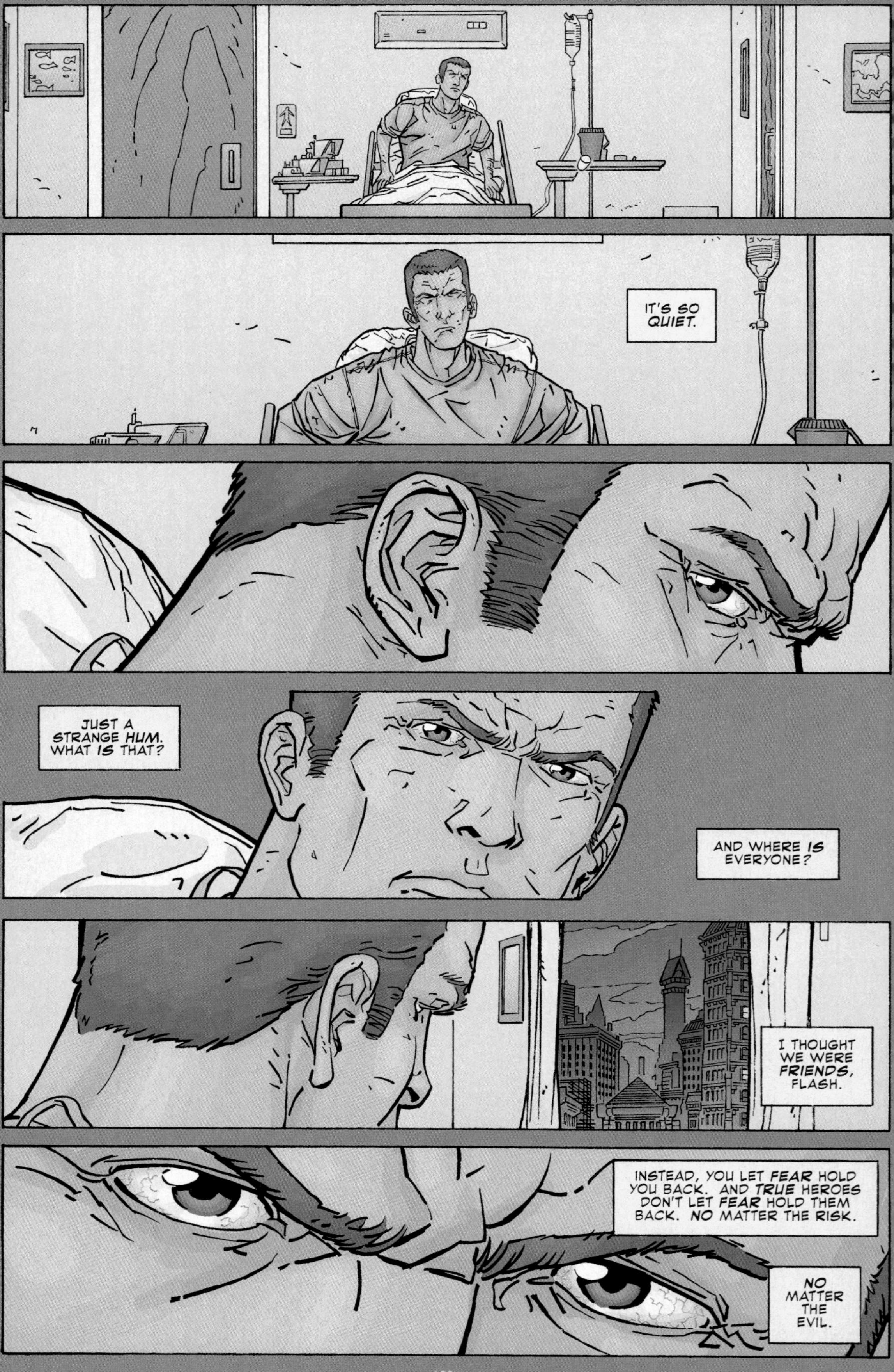
IT'S SO QUIET.
JUST A STRANGE HUM. WHAT IS THAT?
AND WHERE IS EVERYONE?
I THOUGHT WE WERE FRIENDS, FLASH.
INSTEAD, YOU LET FEAR HOLD YOU BACK. AND TRUE HEROES DON'T LET FEAR HOLD THEM BACK. NO MATTER THE RISK.
NO MATTER THE EVIL.

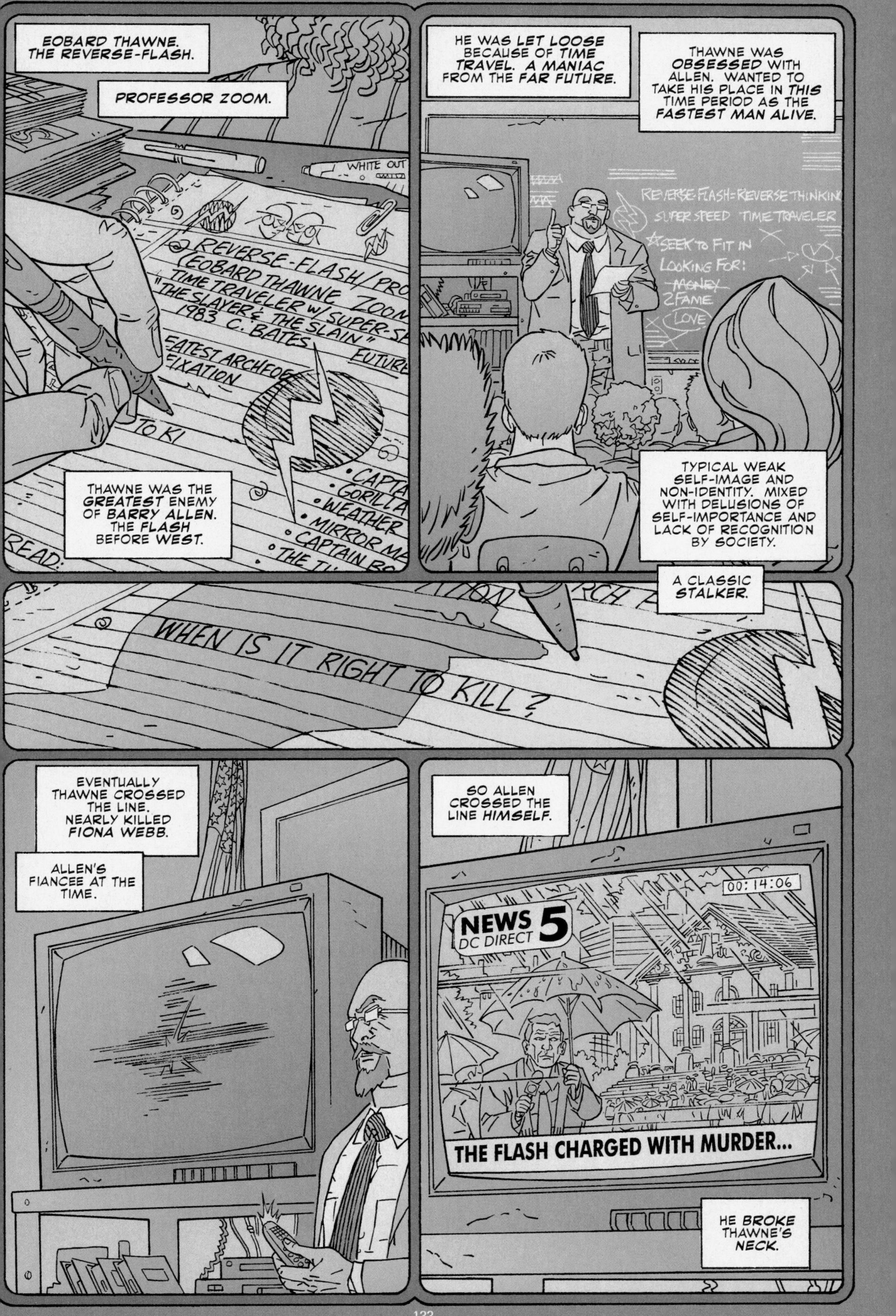
EOBARD THAWNE. THE REVERSE-FLASH.
PROFESSOR ZOOM.
WHITE OUT
REVERSE-FLASH / PRO
(EOBARD THAWNE ZOOM
TIME TRAVELER W/ SUPER-S
"THE SLAYER & THE SLAIN"
1983 C. BATES
FUTURE
FATEST ARCHFOE
FIXATION
TO KI
THAWNE WAS THE GREATEST ENEMY OF BARRY ALLEN. THE FLASH BEFORE WEST.
READ:
•CAPTA
•GORILLA
•WEATHER
•MIRROR MA
•CAPTAIN BO
•THE TI
HE WAS LET LOOSE BECAUSE OF TIME TRAVEL. A MANIAC FROM THE FAR FUTURE.
THAWNE WAS OBSESSED WITH ALLEN. WANTED TO TAKE HIS PLACE IN THIS TIME PERIOD AS THE FASTEST MAN ALIVE.
REVERSE-FLASH = REVERSE THINKING
SUPER SPEED
TIME TRAVELER
SEEK TO FIT IN
LOOKING FOR:
MONEY
2 FAME
LOVE
TYPICAL WEAK SELF-IMAGE AND NON-IDENTITY. MIXED WITH DELUSIONS OF SELF-IMPORTANCE AND LACK OF RECOGNITION BY SOCIETY.
A CLASSIC STALKER.
WHEN IS IT RIGHT TO KILL?
EVENTUALLY THAWNE CROSSED THE LINE. NEARLY KILLED FIONA WEBB.
ALLEN'S FIANCEE AT THE TIME.
SO ALLEN CROSSED THE LINE HIMSELF.
00:14:06
NEWS 5
DC DIRECT
THE FLASH CHARGED WITH MURDER...
HE BROKE THAWNE'S NECK.

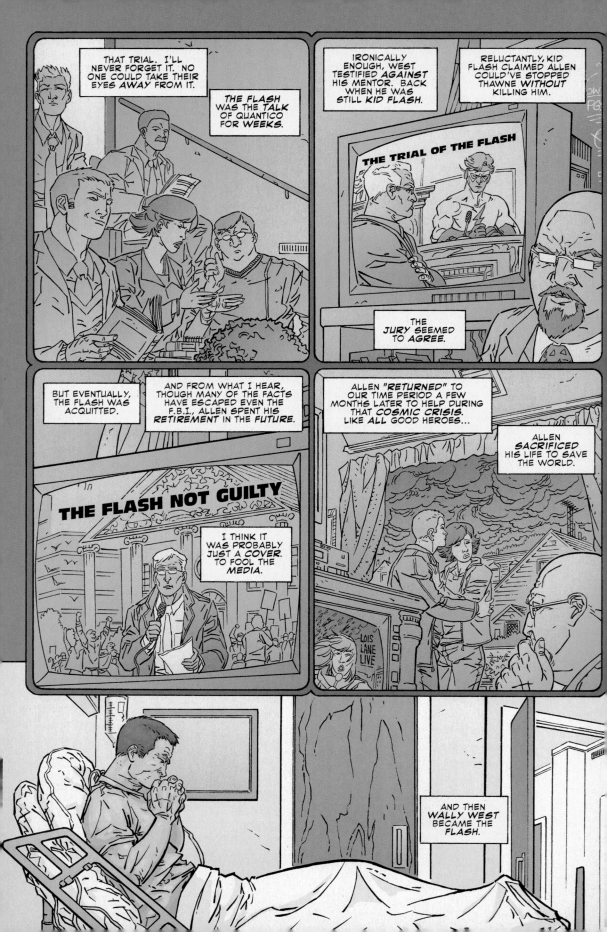

THAT TRIAL. I'LL NEVER FORGET IT. NO ONE COULD TAKE THEIR EYES *AWAY* FROM IT.

THE *FLASH* WAS THE *TALK* OF QUANTICO FOR WEEKS.

IRONICALLY ENOUGH, WEST TESTIFIED *AGAINST* HIS MENTOR. BACK WHEN HE WAS STILL *KID FLASH.*

RELUCTANTLY, KID FLASH CLAIMED ALLEN COULD'VE STOPPED THAWNE *WITHOUT* KILLING HIM.

THE TRIAL OF THE FLASH

THE *JURY* SEEMED TO *AGREE.*

BUT EVENTUALLY, THE FLASH WAS ACQUITTED.

AND FROM WHAT I HEAR, THOUGH MANY OF THE FACTS HAVE ESCAPED EVEN THE F.B.I., ALLEN SPENT HIS *RETIREMENT* IN THE *FUTURE.*

ALLEN *"RETURNED"* TO OUR TIME PERIOD A FEW MONTHS LATER TO HELP DURING THAT *COSMIC CRISIS.* LIKE *ALL* GOOD HEROES...

ALLEN *SACRIFICED* HIS LIFE TO SAVE THE WORLD.

THE FLASH NOT GUILTY

I THINK IT WAS PROBABLY JUST A *COVER.* TO FOOL THE *MEDIA.*

LOIS LANE LIVE

AND THEN WALLY WEST BECAME THE FLASH.

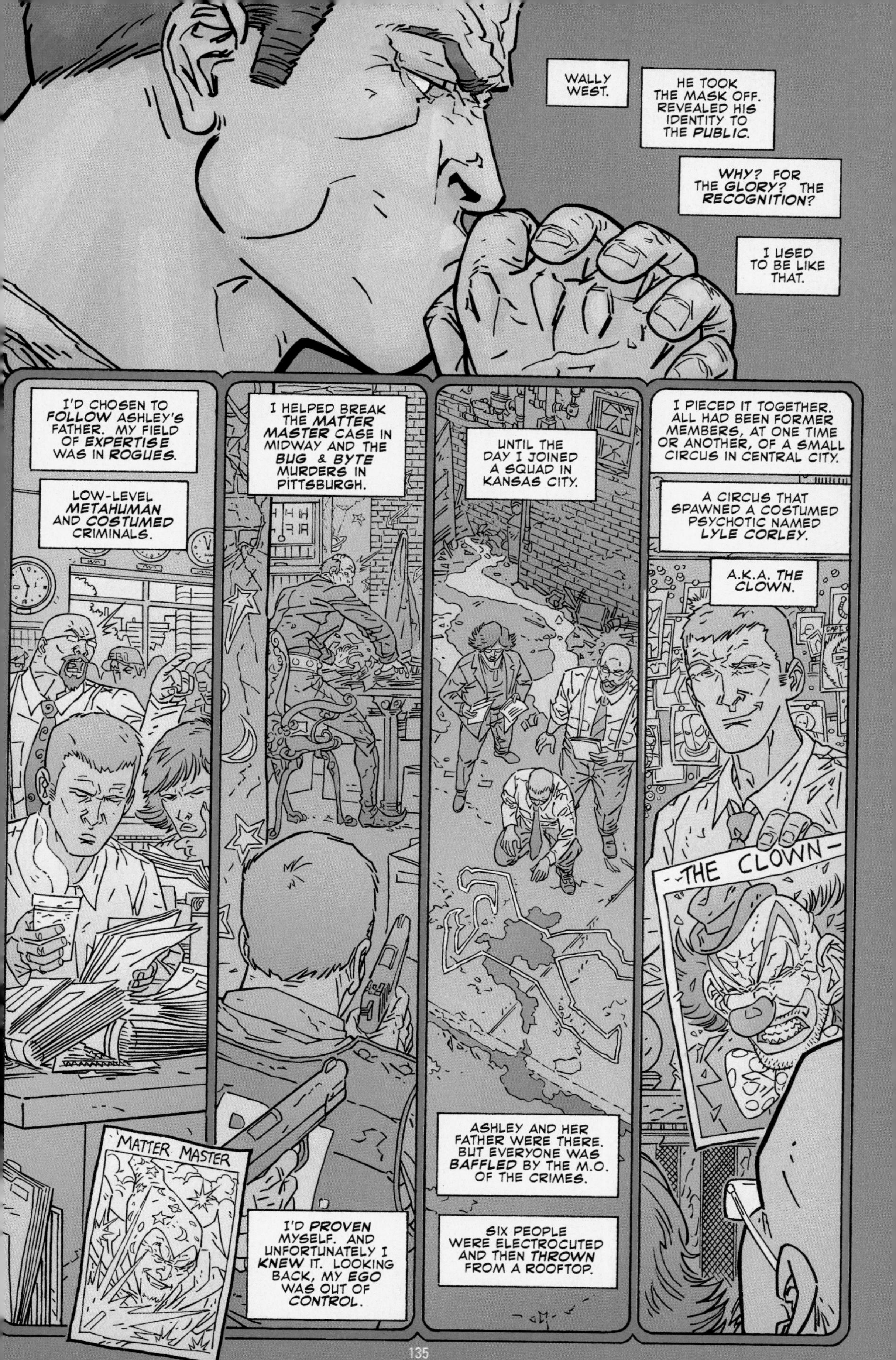

WALLY WEST.
HE TOOK THE MASK OFF. REVEALED HIS IDENTITY TO THE PUBLIC.
WHY? FOR THE GLORY? THE RECOGNITION?
I USED TO BE LIKE THAT.
I'D CHOSEN TO FOLLOW ASHLEY'S FATHER. MY FIELD OF EXPERTISE WAS IN ROGUES.
LOW-LEVEL METAHUMAN AND COSTUMED CRIMINALS.
MATTER MASTER
I HELPED BREAK THE MATTER MASTER CASE IN MIDWAY AND THE BUG & BYTE MURDERS IN PITTSBURGH.
I'D PROVEN MYSELF. AND UNFORTUNATELY I KNEW IT. LOOKING BACK, MY EGO WAS OUT OF CONTROL.
UNTIL THE DAY I JOINED A SQUAD IN KANSAS CITY.
ASHLEY AND HER FATHER WERE THERE. BUT EVERYONE WAS BAFFLED BY THE M.O. OF THE CRIMES.
SIX PEOPLE WERE ELECTROCUTED AND THEN THROWN FROM A ROOFTOP.
I PIECED IT TOGETHER. ALL HAD BEEN FORMER MEMBERS, AT ONE TIME OR ANOTHER, OF A SMALL CIRCUS IN CENTRAL CITY.
A CIRCUS THAT SPAWNED A COSTUMED PSYCHOTIC NAMED LYLE CORLEY.
A.K.A. THE CLOWN.
-THE CLOWN-

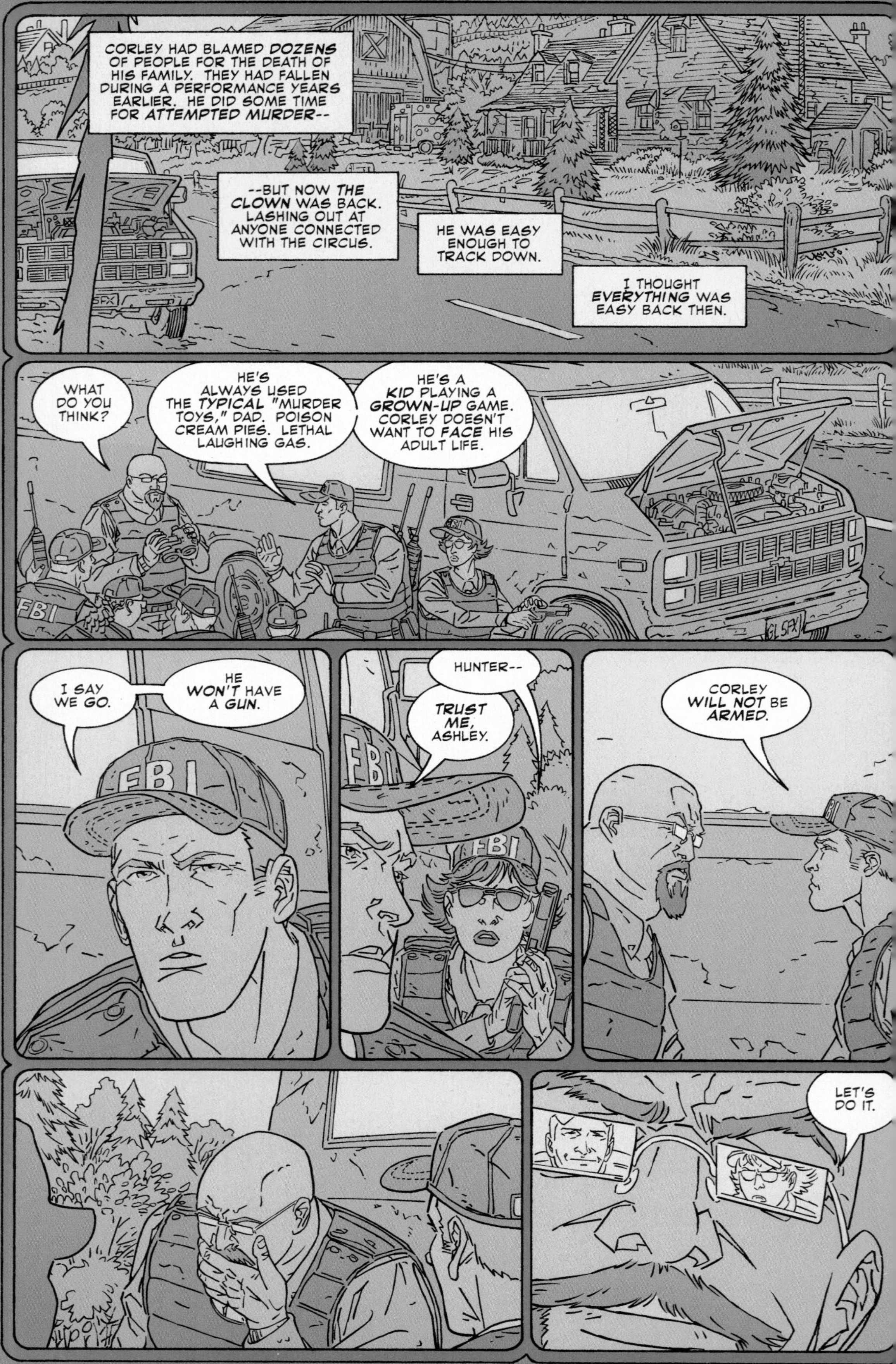
CORLEY HAD BLAMED DOZENS OF PEOPLE FOR THE DEATH OF HIS FAMILY. THEY HAD FALLEN DURING A PERFORMANCE YEARS EARLIER. HE DID SOME TIME FOR ATTEMPTED MURDER--
--BUT NOW THE CLOWN WAS BACK. LASHING OUT AT ANYONE CONNECTED WITH THE CIRCUS.
HE WAS EASY ENOUGH TO TRACK DOWN.
I THOUGHT EVERYTHING WAS EASY BACK THEN.
WHAT DO YOU THINK?
HE'S ALWAYS USED THE TYPICAL "MURDER TOYS," DAD. POISON CREAM PIES. LETHAL LAUGHING GAS.
HE'S A KID PLAYING A GROWN-UP GAME. CORLEY DOESN'T WANT TO FACE HIS ADULT LIFE.
I SAY WE GO.
HE WON'T HAVE A GUN.
HUNTER--
TRUST ME, ASHLEY.
CORLEY WILL NOT BE ARMED.
LET'S DO IT.

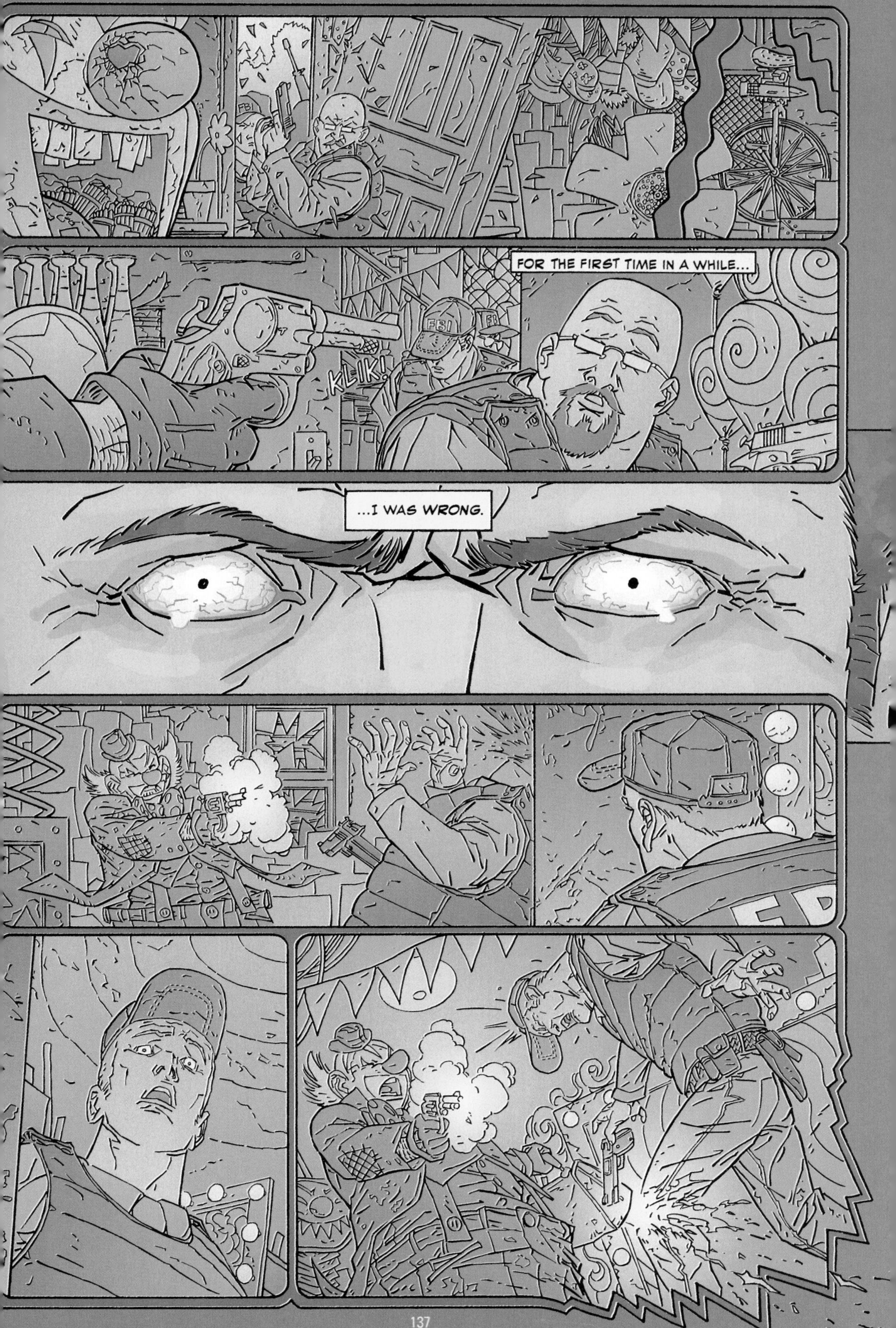
KLIK!
FOR THE FIRST TIME IN A WHILE...
...I WAS WRONG.

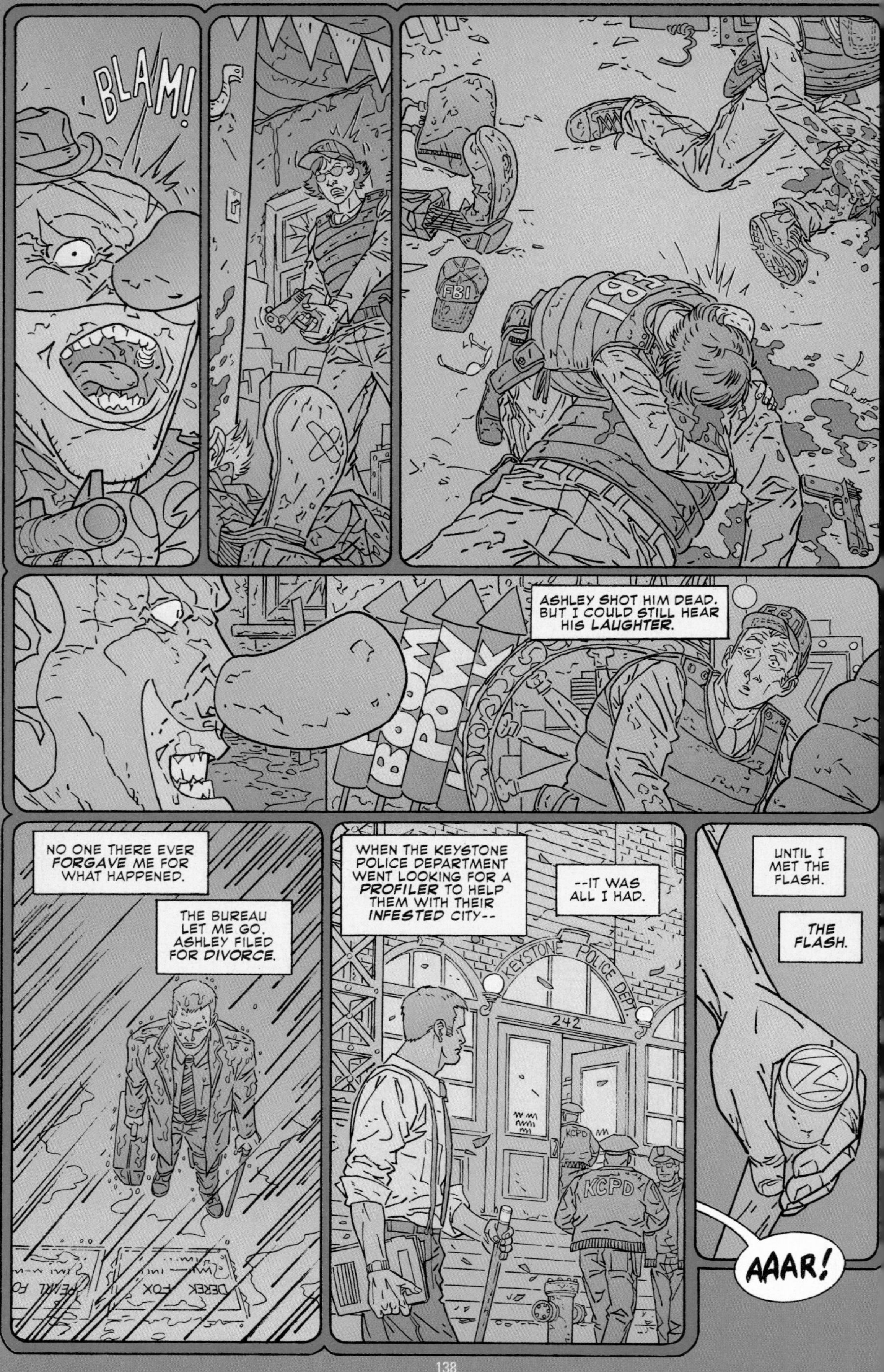
BLAM!
FBI
ASHLEY SHOT HIM DEAD. BUT I COULD STILL HEAR HIS LAUGHTER.
NO ONE THERE EVER FORGAVE ME FOR WHAT HAPPENED.
THE BUREAU LET ME GO. ASHLEY FILED FOR DIVORCE.
WHEN THE KEYSTONE POLICE DEPARTMENT WENT LOOKING FOR A PROFILER TO HELP THEM WITH THEIR INFESTED CITY--
--IT WAS ALL I HAD.
KEYSTONE POLICE DEPT.
242
KCPD
UNTIL I MET THE FLASH.
THE FLASH.
AAAR!

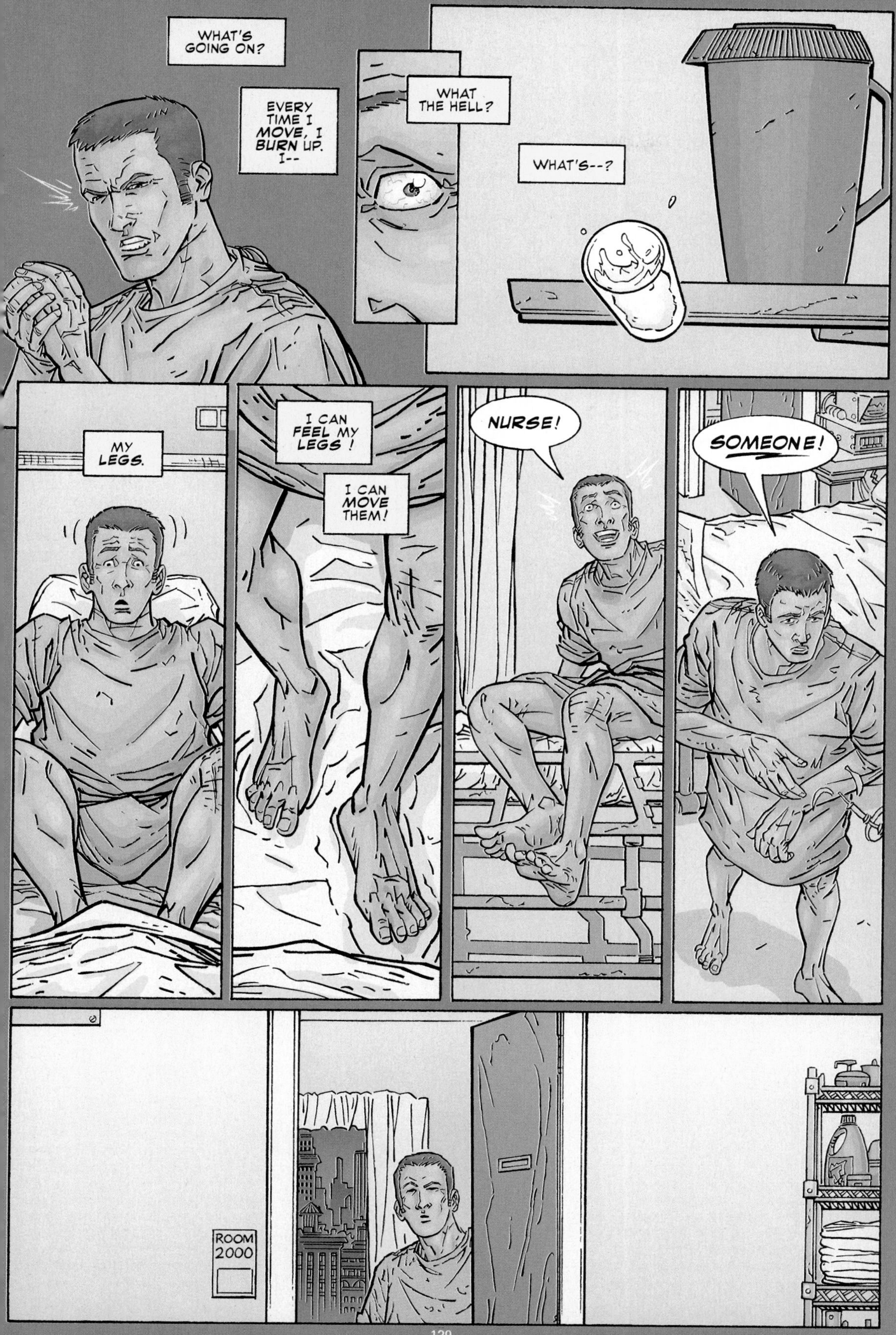

WHAT'S GOING ON?
EVERY TIME I MOVE, I BURN UP. I--
WHAT THE HELL?
WHAT'S--?
MY LEGS.
I CAN FEEL MY LEGS!
I CAN MOVE THEM!
NURSE!
SOMEONE!
ROOM 2000

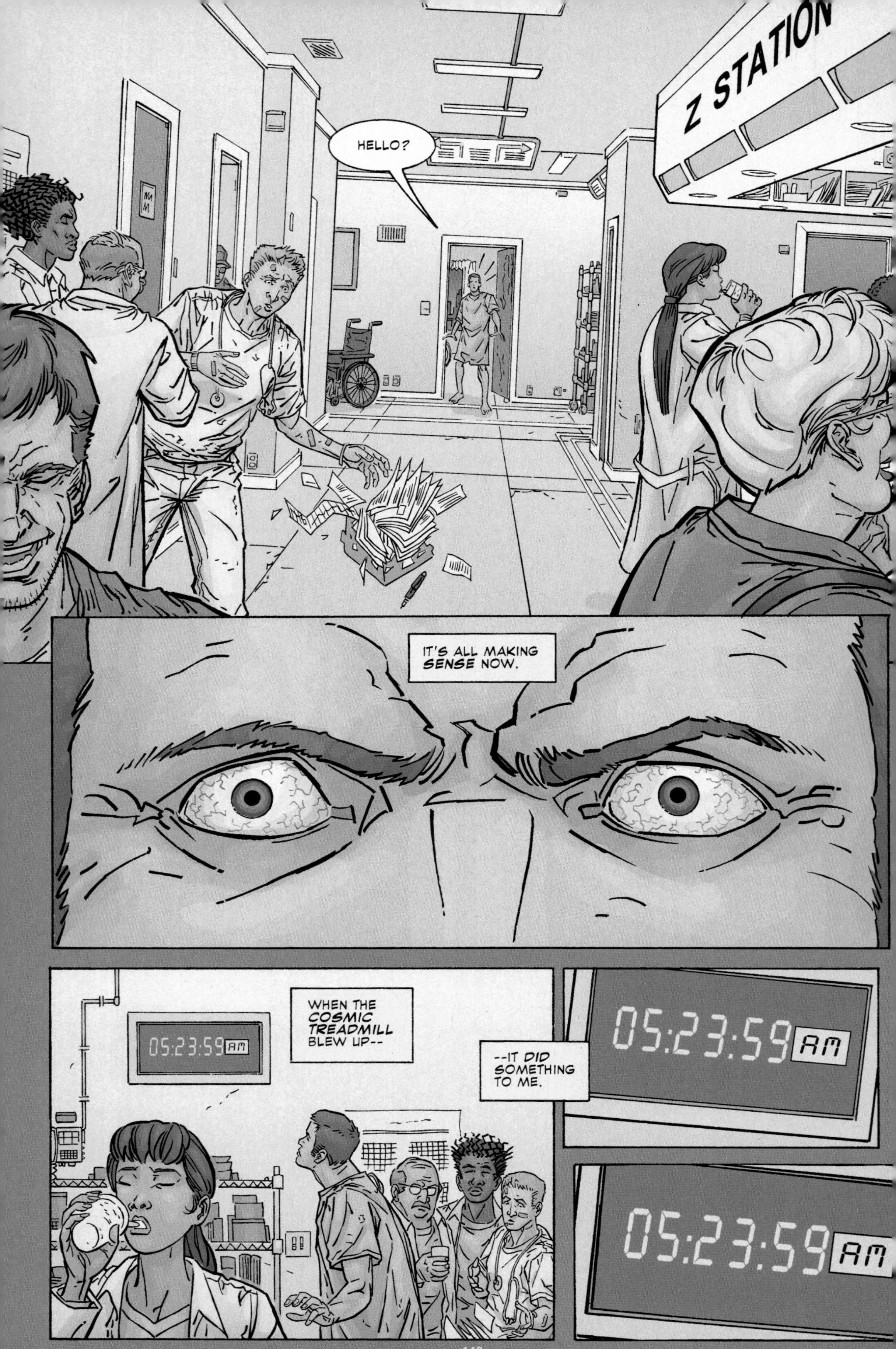
Z STATION
HELLO?
IT'S ALL MAKING SENSE NOW.
WHEN THE COSMIC TREADMILL BLEW UP--
05:23:59 AM
--IT DID SOMETHING TO ME.
05:23:59 AM
05:23:59 AM

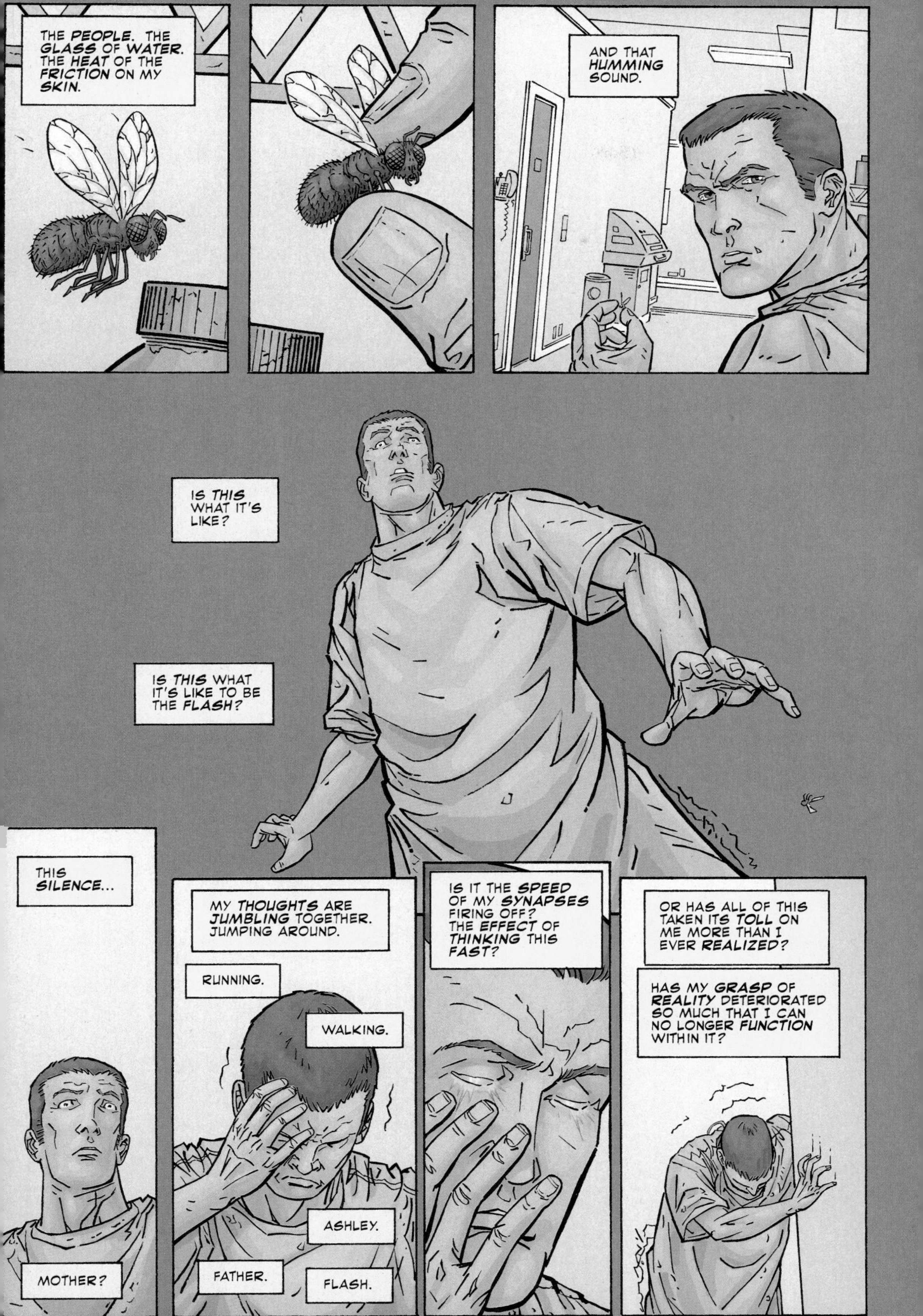
THE PEOPLE. THE GLASS OF WATER. THE HEAT OF THE FRICTION ON MY SKIN.
AND THAT HUMMING SOUND.
IS THIS WHAT IT'S LIKE?
IS THIS WHAT IT'S LIKE TO BE THE FLASH?
THIS SILENCE...
MOTHER?
MY THOUGHTS ARE JUMBLING TOGETHER. JUMPING AROUND.
RUNNING.
WALKING.
ASHLEY.
FATHER.
FLASH.
IS IT THE SPEED OF MY SYNAPSES FIRING OFF? THE EFFECT OF THINKING THIS FAST?
OR HAS ALL OF THIS TAKEN ITS TOLL ON ME MORE THAN I EVER REALIZED?
HAS MY GRASP OF REALITY DETERIORATED SO MUCH THAT I CAN NO LONGER FUNCTION WITHIN IT?

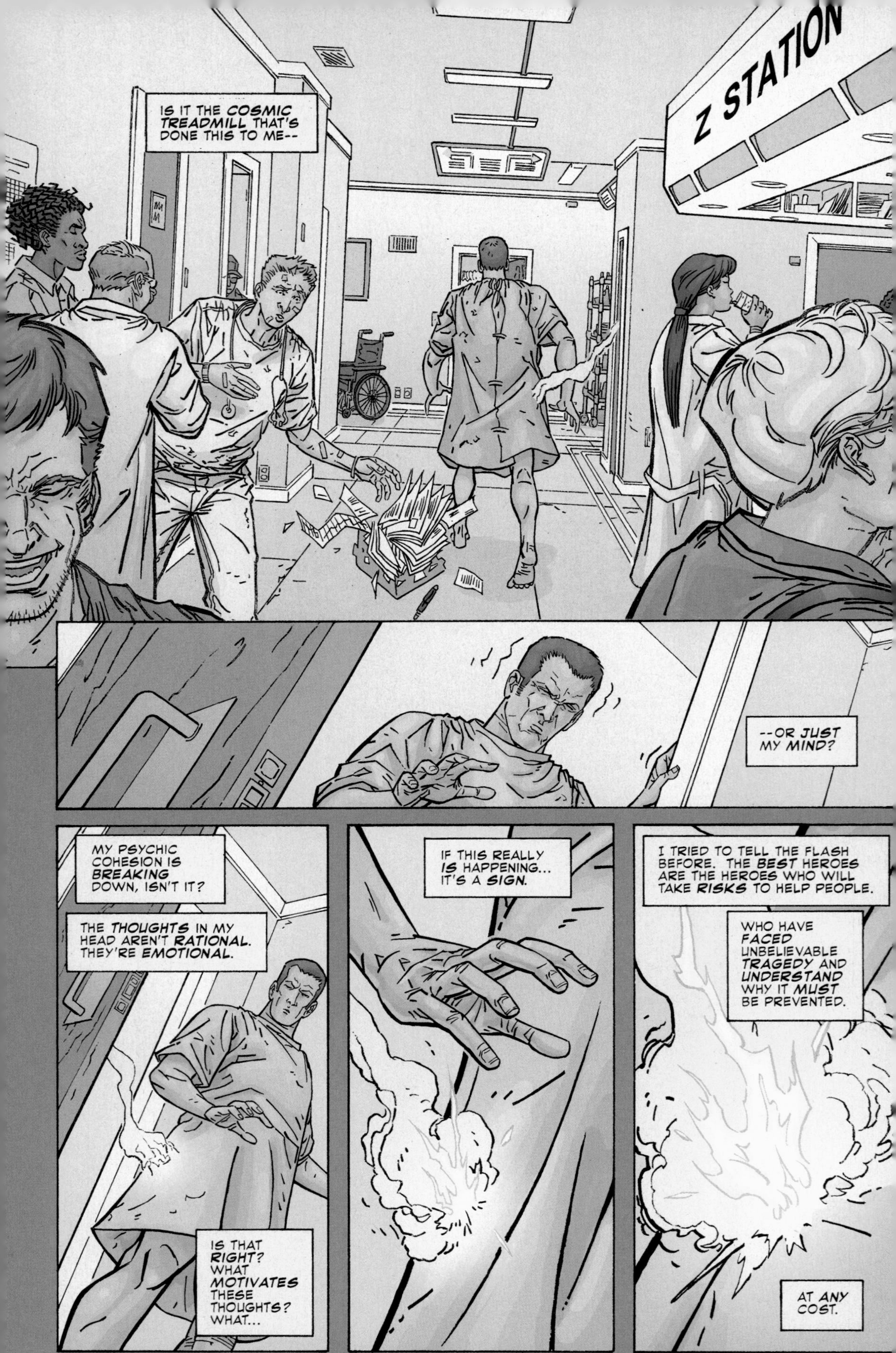
Z STATION
IS IT THE COSMIC TREADMILL THAT'S DONE THIS TO ME--
--OR JUST MY MIND?
MY PSYCHIC COHESION IS BREAKING DOWN, ISN'T IT?
THE THOUGHTS IN MY HEAD AREN'T RATIONAL. THEY'RE EMOTIONAL.
IS THAT RIGHT? WHAT MOTIVATES THESE THOUGHTS? WHAT...
IF THIS REALLY IS HAPPENING... IT'S A SIGN.
I TRIED TO TELL THE FLASH BEFORE. THE BEST HEROES ARE THE HEROES WHO WILL TAKE RISKS TO HELP PEOPLE.
WHO HAVE FACED UNBELIEVABLE TRAGEDY AND UNDERSTAND WHY IT MUST BE PREVENTED.
AT ANY COST.

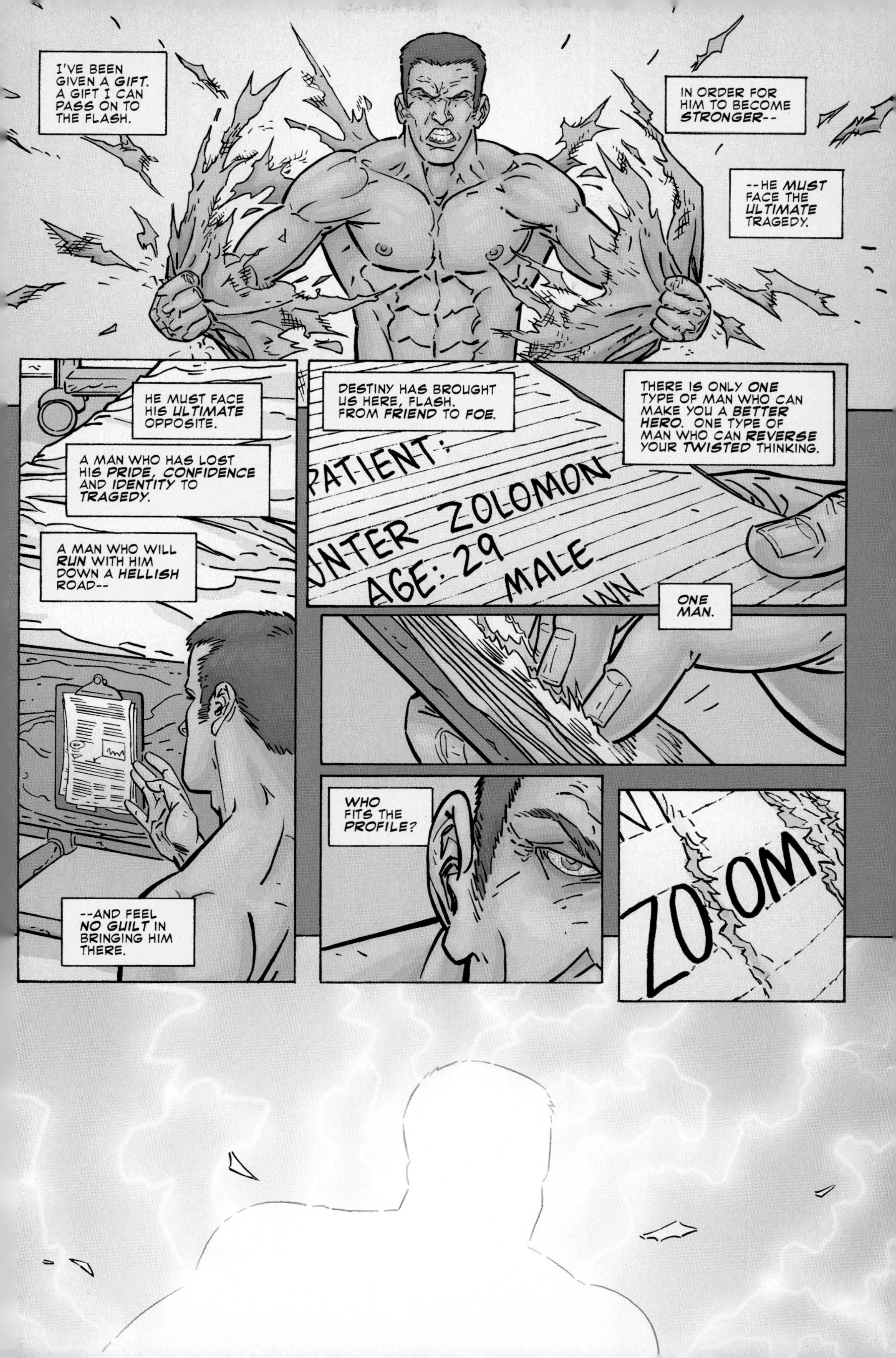
I'VE BEEN GIVEN A GIFT. A GIFT I CAN PASS ON TO THE FLASH.
IN ORDER FOR HIM TO BECOME STRONGER--
--HE MUST FACE THE ULTIMATE TRAGEDY.
HE MUST FACE HIS ULTIMATE OPPOSITE.
A MAN WHO HAS LOST HIS PRIDE, CONFIDENCE AND IDENTITY TO TRAGEDY.
A MAN WHO WILL RUN WITH HIM DOWN A HELLISH ROAD--
--AND FEEL NO GUILT IN BRINGING HIM THERE.
DESTINY HAS BROUGHT US HERE, FLASH. FROM FRIEND TO FOE.
THERE IS ONLY ONE TYPE OF MAN WHO CAN MAKE YOU A BETTER HERO. ONE TYPE OF MAN WHO CAN REVERSE YOUR TWISTED THINKING.
PATIENT:
UNTER ZOLOMON
AGE: 29
MALE
ONE MAN.
WHO FITS THE PROFILE?
ZOOM

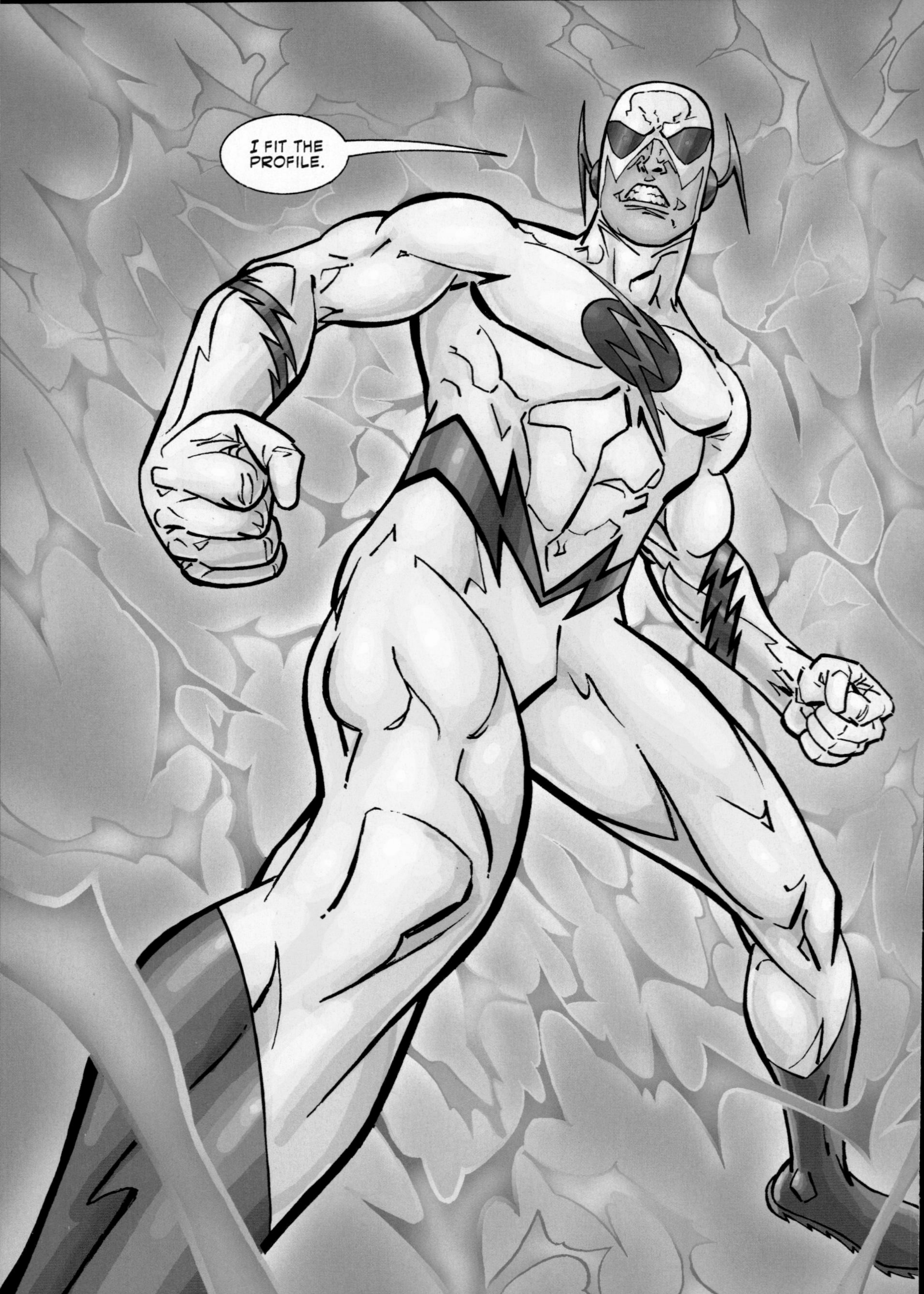
I FIT THE PROFILE.